Globalization

International Political Economy Yearbook
Volume 9

William P. Avery and David P. Rapkin,
Series Editors

Globalization:
Critical Reflections

edited by
James H. Mittelman

LYNNE
RIENNER
PUBLISHERS

BOULDER
LONDON

Published in the United States of America in 1997 by
Lynne Rienner Publishers, Inc.
1800 30th Street, Boulder, Colorado 80301

and in the United Kingdom by
Lynne Rienner Publishers, Inc.
3 Henrietta Street, Covent Garden, London WC2E 8LU

Library of Congress Cataloging-in-Publication Data
Globalization : critical reflections / James H. Mittelman, editor.
     p.   cm.   — (International political economy yearbook : v. 9)
     Includes bibliographical references and index.
     ISBN 1-55587-752-4 (alk. paper)
     1. International economic relations.   2. International relations.
I. Mittelman, James H. II. Series.
HF1410.1579 vol. 9
[HF1359]
375'.05 s–dc20
[337]
                                       96-1319
                                       CIP

British Cataloguing in Publication Data
A Cataloguing in Publication record for this book
is available from the British Library.

Printed and bound in the United States of America

The paper used in this publication meets the requirements
of the American National Standard for Permanence of
Paper for Printed Library Materials Z39.48-1984.

5 4 3 2 1

Contents

The Contributors

GLENN ADLER is senior lecturer in sociology and a staff associate in the Sociology of Work Unit at the University of the Witwatersrand in Johannesburg. He recently completed his Columbia University Ph.D. on the rise of trade unions in the South African motor industry and is the editor, along with Doris Suarez, of *Union Voices: Labor's Responses to Crisis* (1993). His current research projects are on labor and the transition to democracy and the impact of international institutions on domestic policy debates.

FANTU CHERU is associate professor of African and development studies at the School of International Service, American University, Washington, D.C. He is the author of *The Silent Revolution in Africa: Debt, Development and Democracy* (1989) and *Dependence, Underdevelopment and Unemployment in Kenya* (1987); coauthor of *From Debt to Development: Alternatives to the International Debt Crisis* (1985); and coeditor of *Ethiopia: Options for Rural Development* (1990).

ROBERT W. COX is professor emeritus of political science and social and political thought at York University, Toronto. He is the author of *Production, Power, and World Order: Social Forces in the Making of History* (1987) and, with Harold K. Jacobson et al., of *The Anatomy of Influence: Decision Making in International Organization* (1972). A collection of Cox's essays compiled with the help of Timothy Sinclair has been published under the title *Approaches to World Order* (1995).

GARY GEREFFI is professor of sociology at Duke University. He is the author of *The Pharmaceutical Industry and Dependency in the Third World* (1983); *Manufacturing Miracles: Paths of Industrialization in Latin America and East Asia* (1990), coedited with Donald Wyman; and *Commodity Chains and Global Capitalism* (1994), coedited with Miguel Korzeniewicz. His current research interests deal with global commodity chains, regional divisions of labor, and the social bases of international competitiveness, with a focus on the evolution of embedded networks in the apparel, footwear, automobile, and computer industries.

STEPHEN GILL is professor of political science at York University, Toronto. His publications include *The Global Political Economy: Perspectives, Problems and Policies* (1988), coauthored with David Law; *Atlantic Relations: Beyond the Reagan Era* (1989); *American Hegemony and the Trilateral Commission* (1990); *Gramsci, Historical Materialism and International Relations* (editor) (1993); and *Restructuring Global Politics* (1996), in Japanese.

CHRISTINE KOVIC is a graduate student at the City University of New York Graduate Center. She is currently working with the Center for Human Rights "Fray Bartolome de Las Casas" in Chiapas, Mexico. She is coauthor of *Con Un Pueblo Vivo, En Tierra Negada* (1994) with Patricia Jovita Gomez Cruz.

JAMES H. MITTELMAN is professor of international relations in the School of International Service at American University, Washington, D.C. He is the author of *Ideology and Politics in Uganda: From Obote to Amin* (1975); *Underdevelopment and the Transition to Socialism: Mozambique and Tanzania* (1981); and *Out from Underdevelopment Revisited* (1997), coauthored with Mustapha Kamal Pasha.

JUNE NASH is distinguished professor of anthropology at the City College of the City University of New York. She is the editor of *Crafts in the World Market: The Impact of Global Exchange on Middle American Artisans* (1993); *From Tank Town to High Tech: The Clash of Community and Industrial Cycles* (1989); *Women and Change in Latin America* (1986), with Helen Safa; and *We Eat the Mines and the Mines Eat Us: Dependency and Exploitation in Bolivian Tin Mining Industries* (2d ed., 1993).

LEO PANITCH is professor of political science at York University, Toronto. He is the editor of *The Socialist Register* (London and New York, annual) and one of the founders of the journal *Studies in Political Economy.* His books include *Social Democracy and Industrial Militancy* (1976); *Working Class Politics in Crisis* (1986); *The Assault on Trade Union Freedoms,* with Donald Swartz (2d ed., 1993); and the edited works *The Canadian State: Political Economy and Political Power* (1977) and *A Different Kind of State: Popular Power and Democratic Administration,* with Gregory Albo and David Langille (1993).

MUSTAPHA KAMAL PASHA is assistant professor of comparative and regional studies in the School of International Service, American University, Washington, D.C., specializing in political economy, Islamic studies, and South Asia. He is the author of several publications, including *Colonial*

Political Economy (1996) and, with James H. Mittelman, *Out from Underdevelopment Revisited* (1997).

AHMED I. SAMATAR is professor and dean of international studies and programming at Macalester College, specializing in international political economy and cultural studies with an emphasis on African development. His recent publications include, as editor, *The Somali Challenge: From Catastrophe to Renewal?* (1994) and, with Terrence Lyons, *Somalia: State Collapse and Multilateral Intervention* (1995).

SASKIA SASSEN is professor of urban planning and serves on the faculty of the School of International and Public Affairs at Columbia University. Her most recent books are *Cities in a World Economy* and *Immigrants and Refugees: A European Dilemma?* (forthcoming); she is currently writing a book about immigration policy in a world economy for The Twentieth Century Fund. She has begun a new five-year research project entitled "Governance and Accountability in a World Economy," the first phase of which are the 1995 Columbia University Schoff Memorial Lectures, to be published in 1996.

Preface

This book is organized around three themes: the thrust of globalization in the realms of production and the state, political and cultural responses to it, and the potential and limits of neoliberal globalization. The first two objects of study derive from Karl Polanyi's (1957b) important insight that a "double movement"—an expansion of market forces and a reaction to it in the form of demands for self-protection against capital's socially disruptive and polarizing effects—propels modern society. To extend Polanyi's concept, this book examines a third phase, which involves the opportunities and constraints presented by changing structured hierarchies at the turn of the millennium.

While there are several globalizing tendencies that need to be taken into account, we have sought to center attention on these key aspects of the process. We make no claim to providing a comprehensive study—an elusive goal in any event with a topic as broad as globalization. Our purpose is to deepen understanding of globalization and to stimulate other, more detailed, inquiries into the issues not investigated fully (or at all) here. If we accomplish that, our venture will have succeeded.

A debt of gratitude is due to the sponsors of the workshop that culminated in this volume: the International Studies Association (ISA), the International Political Economy Section of the ISA, and the Center for the Study of the Global South at American University.

In the School of International Service, American University, Joseph Clapper and Rana El-Khatib contributed importantly to the smooth running of the workshop and publication of this book.

Appreciation also goes to the graduate students who presented the authors' papers and offered critical comments: Leigh Engelhart and Abdul Latif Haji-Salleh (Duke University), Kiras Gharabaghi and Ann Griffiths (Dalhousie University), Enrique Pumar and Meliton Salazar (American University), and Magnus Ryner and Timothy Sinclair (York University, Toronto). Scholars who generously contributed their ideas were Philip Brenner, Samih Farsoun, Louis Goodman, Kenneth Kusterer, Clovis Maksoud, Şerif Mardin, Nicholas Onuf, Timothy Shaw, Diane Singerman, Ritu Vij, and Linda Yarr.

Special thanks are owed to the workshop organizing committee—

Enrique Pumar (coordinator), Meliton Salazar, and Rakhi Sehgal—whose unstinting efforts are reflected in this publication. Meliton Salazar and, later, Ashwini Tambe also helped with numerous editorial tasks.

Lynne Rienner, her staff, and an anonymous reviewer kindly insisted on high standards in the final preparation of the book. I am indebted to Gia Hamilton and Sally Jaskold for polishing the manuscript and making it more accessible to the reader.

—J.H.M.

James H. Mittelman 1
The Dynamics of Globalization

The dreams of modernization are coming true in many parts of the world, even in remote areas of underdeveloped countries, but, ironically, not as social scientists had envisaged and certainly not through the formal channels that some of them helped to build. In lieu of policy instruments or international agencies, globalizing structures interacting with individuals, households, and communities are delivering modernity to some—but not all—peoples formerly far removed from meaningful participation in cross-border flows of capital, knowledge, information, and consumer goods. A massive transformation is being compressed into a short time—a few years rather than many generations—and often despite officially managed processes.

The speed and direction of change in Pakistan's rural economy and social relations exemplify this transformation. Like many labor-exporting countries, Pakistan has in some years received more capital in migrants' remittances than the state has allocated for national development at the federal and local levels. From 1971 to 1988, Pakistani workers in the Middle East generated $20 billion in foreign exchange through official channels—a sum that exceeded the country's entire gross national product in a single year. In the peak year (1982), official remittances outstripped export earnings and represented more than half the foreign exchange costs of imports (Addleton 1992: 117, 120).

Reported remittances do not include remittances in kind (commodities purchased overseas and sold in the informal economy) or black market remittances, a category of funds that may be regarded as a form of resistance to the state's efforts to capture income flowing into rural areas. Unlike foreign aid, these flows come without strings attached and are not directed by the dominant classes. By strengthening the underground economy, remittances may undermine authoritative preferred modes of development and contribute to the state's loss of control within what had been portrayed as the national or domestic unit (Addleton 1992).

Individuals, households, and rural communities thereby become directly involved in global processes. For individual families drawn into transnational flows, there are vast changes in consumption patterns, exposure to a more diversified economy when sectors such as construction and retailing services expand, and new stresses on transformed social structures, especially marked in Pakistan by an overall decline in poverty and increased measures of inequality. This chain of far-reaching events is but one element in the whole pattern known as globalization.

Globalization is crucial to understanding international political economy, for it directs attention to fundamental changes under way in the post–Cold War era. The manifestations of globalization (some of them evident in the Pakistan example) include the spatial reorganization of production, the interpenetration of industries across borders, the spread of financial markets, the diffusion of identical consumer goods to distant countries, massive transfers of population within the South as well as from the South and the East to the West, resultant conflicts between immigrant and established communities in formerly tight-knit neighborhoods, and an emerging worldwide preference for democracy. A rubric for varied phenomena, the concept of globalization interrelates multiple levels of analysis: economics, politics, culture, and ideology.

But what explains globalization? What are its causes, mechanisms, and possibilities for transformation? Where can one focus an analysis? On the inner workings and logic of capital itself? On strategies and actors seeking to optimize their positions? On empirical indicators or trends said to constitute this process? On the complementary and contradictory interactions among localization, regionalization, and globalization? On the social and political consequences? These questions are central to the chapters that follow. The contributors to this volume—a diverse group of authors from seven countries (by origin if not current citizenship) who represent various academic disciplines—will present different hypotheses and interpretations as well as evidence. I have asked each of them to use my introductory series of questions and analytical propositions as a target to attack and a springboard for their own studies.

To open the conversation among the authors, I contend that world society is entering a new era in the relationship between power and the division of labor, which is globalized. What sets the context for conflict and cooperation in the post–Cold War period is an integrating yet disintegrating process known as globalization. Although any given world problem has many sources, globalization establishes novel challenges and opportunities for solutions.

In developing this argument, I will first explore varied meanings of the concept of division of labor and the multilayer character of the globalization process. Then I will anchor the discussion by examining one region—East Asia—within this framework; this section is obviously not a detailed account but a synopsis of the impact of globalization on a specific regional division of labor. Finally, I will turn to the seeds of future conflict sown by globalization and will discuss the implications for adaptation to a rapidly changing and highly competitive environment.

THE GLOBAL DIVISION OF LABOR

In *The Great Transformation,* Karl Polanyi analyzed the socially disruptive and polarizing tendencies in the world economy driven by what he called the self-regulating market, not a spontaneous phenomenon but the result of coercive power in the service of a utopian idea. He traced the tendencies in the global economy that generated the conjuncture of the 1930s and pro-duced—out of a breakdown in liberal-economic structures—the phenomena of depression, fascism, unemployment, and resurgent nationalism, collec-tively a negation of economic globalization, leading to World War II (Polanyi 1957b). The specific form of globalization providing the structural preconditions for world war included production focused primarily within territorially bounded spaces and linked to international finance; conver-gence between productive and statist forces; autarchic spheres of influence within economic blocs; and growing political rivalries. A Polanyian frame-work of "double movement" encapsulates unprecedented market expansion entailing massive social dislocation and a sharp political reaction in the form of society's demands on the state to counteract the deleterious effects of the market. Perhaps similar to the global economy of the 1930s, the contempo-rary globalization process appears to be approaching a conjuncture in which renewed liberal-economic structures will generate large-scale disruptions as well as sustained pressure for self-protection. The opportunities and chal-lenges arising from globalization are integral parts of this contradiction.

A worldwide phenomenon, globalization is a coalescence of varied transnational processes and domestic structures, allowing the economy, pol-itics, culture, and ideology of one country to penetrate another. The chain of causality runs from the spatial reorganization of production to international trade and to the integration of financial markets (on the impetus for global-ization, see Griffin and Khan 1992; Waters 1995). Driven by changing modes of competition, globalization compresses the time and space aspects of social relations.[1] In short, globalization is a market-induced, not a policy-led, process.

To examine this pattern, the choice of avenue of inquiry is crucial because it sets one's sights on research questions and provides a perspective on data. An appropriate starting point is the nature of the labor process and its products on a global level, for conflicts between capital and labor, and commerce and consumer tastes reflect what is produced and how it is pro-duced. Hence, attention must focus on how whole societies and their con-stituent groups try to influence and adjust to changes in the organization of production.

Although first studied by classical political economists and their fol-lowers, with implications for comparative advantages in trade, nowadays the global division of labor differs radically from the allocation of work and its reward in Adam Smith's time. In *An Inquiry into the Nature and Causes of the Wealth of Nations,* Smith contrasted the isolated producer and modern industry. He posited a subrational or nonutilitarian origin for specialization (but not its intensification) in a "propensity to truck and barter" innate in humankind. A novel form of specialization, modern industry separates the production process into compartments, each performing a different task, with implications for the rates of profit. To the extent that these separated producers and buyers and sellers are identified with nations, the international division of labor refers to the specialization of a country in a particular trade or product (e.g., Portugal in wine and England in textiles) (Smith 1970; Mittelman 1994b). Hence, the international division of labor highlights a set of relationships associated with an exchange of goods produced by individual units, namely, nation-states. As the old international division of labor evolved, a small number of industrial countries provided capital goods and consumer goods to exchange for the Third World's primary products.

However, a basic change in the international division of labor occurred in the 1960s: a restructuring involving the formation and expansion of a world market for both labor and industrial sites. Beginning in the 1960s, Asia's Four Dragons achieved spectacular economic growth by exporting not raw materials but manufactured goods. As an empirical study by Arrighi and Drangel shows, in the period from 1965 to 1980 the "core" deindustrialized in terms of the average percentage of the labor force employed by industry and the average portion of manufacturing in gross domestic product (GDP). By the late 1970s, the "semiperiphery"—an intermediate tier of countries—actually surpassed the core in share of GDP generated by industry (Arrighi and Drangel 1986: 55–56; Gereffi 1990a: 8–9). Manufactures relative to export volume in East Asia jumped 13.2 percent per year from 1980 to 1985, 19.3 percent in 1986, 23.8 percent in 1987, and 11.2 percent in 1988 (World Bank 1989b: 148–150). The core of course developed new technologies and began to convert to service industries, while growth in the semiperiphery occurred in the context of smaller economies.

With industrial upgrading, the newly industrializing countries (NICs) sought to transform their structures of production from an emphasis on labor-intensive to capital- and technology-intensive goods centering on high-value-added products. No longer was there a dichotomy between a small number of industrial countries and a Third World providing primary products. An emerging world market for labor and production entailed massive industrial relocation, the subdivision of manufacturing processes into multiple partial operations, major technological innovations, large-scale migratory flows, and the feminization of labor. From Asia's export processing zones to Mexico's maquiladora (assembly plants as subsidiaries or subcontracting firms for the manufacture of export-oriented goods) program, a barometer of the changing character of the labor force is the increasing number of women employed in manufacturing. Jobs take on characteristics identified with female employment: a minimum level of skills, low wages, and limited possibilities for promotion.

To explain this restructuring, scholars have devised the construct of "the new international division of labor." The title of a seminal study by Fröbel, Heinrichs, and Kreye, this thesis focuses on the "overriding pressure of competition" as the mainspring of a distinct set of conditions for global capital accumulation. These authors hold that observable changes in the international division of labor (the transfer of plants to the Third World, the fragmentation of production processes, etc.) are the result of "the conditions for the valorization and accumulation of capital" (Fröbel, Heinrichs, and Kreye 1980: 46; see also Lipietz 1985 and Amsden 1990).

> This new international division of labour is an institutional innovation of capital itself, necessitated by changed conditions, and not the result of changed development strategies by individual countries or options freely decided upon by so-called multinational companies. (Fröbel, Heinrichs, and Kreye 1980: 46)

For these authors, national strategies and the policies of multinational corporations are consequences, not causes, of new conditions, especially the need for additional industrial sites around the world.

This thesis centers on the expansion of capital and hence production as the force behind an international division of labor that is deemed new in that it restructures the classical division of labor between hewers of wood and drawers of water—Third World countries—and industrialized nations. Emphasis is placed on the spatial reorganization of production and increasing differentiation within the Third World. Clearly this mode of explanation advances understanding by providing a fruitful way to examine the relationships between developed and developing countries. However, some of the key tenets of the concept of the new international division of labor are flawed.

To begin with, exactly what is new about the new international division of labor? The claim that industrialization in the Third World is new overlooks the establishment of import-substituting industries in Argentina, Brazil, and Mexico in the 1930s and 1940s. In fact, industrial growth in some parts of Latin America stems from the interwar period (Gereffi 1990a: 3). Fröbelians give little attention to the role of the state during this period and underestimate the importance of international finance. Additionally, the new international division of labor has not replaced the old international division of labor. Properly understood, they coexist. In countries such as Mexico, jobs in export industries account for less than 10 percent of total employment. In many parts of the Third World, the share of primary goods in exports is more than half of all exports. The variance in job allocation among and within regions is sufficiently large to call into question the concept of the new international division of labor. What is more, to stress that cheap labor drives the movement of capital around the globe runs the risk of a mechanical and economistic explanation. It depoliticizes important aspects of production—namely, the specific forms of power relations and challenges to them in diverse industries and sectors.

By focusing so strongly on the logic of capital to the detriment of local social forces, the new international division of labor mode of inquiry is too abstract, too top-down. It is a useful starting point for investigation but neglects a fine-grained analysis of different spatial divisions of labor within various industries and sectors. Innovation and technological developments take place in certain industries and sectors but also transcend national boundaries. Within a globalizing division of labor, technological and managerial cores form specifically regional divisions and redivisions of labor and generate their own peripheries subject to both constraints and developmental opportunities (Cohen 1987; Henderson 1989: 22, 27). Distinct regional divisions of labor—a phenomenon ignored by new international division of labor theorists—provide diverse modes of coordinating capital flows but are ultimately subordinate to the globalization process. Macro regions—the European Union, the North American Free Trade Agreement [NAFTA] area, and Asia Pacific—may be regarded as loose spatial units larger than the state with some political and cultural bonds, however varied, tenuous, and sometimes conflictual. As we shall see, states—and indeed the interstate system—while diminished in scope in a global division of labor, may not be treated as mere epiphenomena.

PRODUCTION, THE STATE, AND NEW SOCIAL MOVEMENTS

The global division of labor may be conceived in a Braudelian manner as a system of interactions on a world scale. The French economic historian Fernand Braudel indicated that the world economy is not the ontology of world society but those entities, individual and corporate, that interact with and thus create patterns that may be called global structures (Braudel 1980b: 55; Helleiner 1990: 74; Cox 1986; Mittelman 1994a). Following Braudel's emphasis on interactions, but without invoking his whole method of different axes for analysis, one can conceptualize the implications of evolving divisions of labor as a series of relationships: economic globalization and the state; pressures on the state; globalization and democratization; and resistance to globalization.

Economic Globalization and the State

In recent decades, several states sought to protect their domestic economy against external forces and to limit the net outflow of surplus by adopting acts of economic nationalism: the nationalization of key industries, indigenization decrees, requirements for local incorporation of a portion of foreign capital, and so on. Some states (e.g., China under Mao; Burma; Tanzania) also professed a more radical course of self-reliance as a means of insulation from the world system. Today, however, there is little to commend strategies of economic nationalism or delinking, for transborder flows (migration, communications, knowledge, technology, etc.) have circumvented the globe and permeate the state.

The scope for state autonomy—a concept that drew considerable attention from scholars in the 1970s and 1980s—is reduced in the context of economic globalization. Additionally, the drive to bring the state back to the forefront of social theory requires fresh analysis in light of globalization (Evans et al. 1985). In a globalized division of labor, the state no longer primarily initiates action in, but rather reacts to, worldwide economic forces. To realize material gain from globalization, the state increasingly facilitates this process, acting as its agent (Cox 1987: 253–265). Surrounded by impersonal and unaccountable forces beyond leaders' control, their capacity to lead is diminished (Hughes 1990). Faced with the power of globalized production and international finance, including debt structures, leaders are constrained to concentrate on enhancing national conditions for competing forms of capitalism. Statecraft, tested as it is by nonstate actors, is reduced in efficacy relative to transnational forces. Among the public in different zones of the world economy, the politics of disillusionment is rife.

The state is at risk because of challenges to sovereignty in the aftermath of the Cold War. With the disintegration of socialist regimes came the eruption of subsurface tensions formerly stifled by the state. Now, state borders are subject to revision (Halliday 1990). East Germany has disappeared, the fifteen republics the former Soviet Union comprised have achieved independence, and Yugoslavia, now dismembered, is riven with ethnic conflict. Predating the end of the Cold War, separatist movements in Quebec, Northern Ireland, Basque country, and Corsica are challenging the status quo. While North Korea could be absorbed by South Korea, Balkanization is always a danger in Africa, where colonizers arbitrarily drew borders without regard to ethnic distribution and natural frontiers such as rivers and mountains. Ethiopia, for example, is a dubious proposition as a unified country.

Pressures on the State

This explosion of pluralism involves a renewal of historical forces—a maze of religious loyalties, ethnic identities, linguistic differences, and other forms of cultural expression. As noted, the state, especially in the former Soviet Union and Eastern Europe, had restrained these tensions. While globalization limits state power, there is a reassertion of historical forces. Just as globalization gives impetus to cultural homogenization (e.g., the diffusion of standard consumer goods throughout the world), so too does a global thrust undermine state power and unleash subterranean cultural pluralism. This contradictory process merges with a dialectic of subnationalism and supranationalism. Many polities are disrupted by substate actors and simultaneously seek advantage in global competition through regionalization. Despite the past failings of regional groupings, regional cooperation is widely regarded as a way to achieve mobility in the changing global division of labor. Thus, the state is being reformed from below by the tugs of subnationalism and from above by the pull of economic globalization.

Globalization and Democratization

Pressured by nonstate actors, the state seeks to fortify itself by adopting such measures as computerized surveillance in finance and establishing transnational police forces (e.g., Europol) to regulate migration. Nonetheless, the state must accommodate the new pluralism and allow for demands for political reforms. With the revolution in Eastern Europe, the release of Nelson Mandela from prison, and the assertiveness of the human rights movement, the drive toward democratization has won legitimacy. Equally important, pro-democracy forces have gained confidence. But what type of democracy is appropriate for the late twentieth century? While democracy is a universal concept, there are different versions of democratic theory.

From a liberal perspective, democracy centers on the principle of accountability: in some manner the right to rule should be based on the consent of the governed. Liberal democracy calls for public influence on government through such institutions as political parties, regular elections, and an alternation in power. However, critics point out that in practice, liberal democracies exclude some groups from both meaningful participation in politics and the distribution of economic benefits. In the Third World, it is often recognized that democracy is necessary for development, if democracy is understood to imply increasing social equality—an ingredient missing from ethnocentric and Western conceptions of democratization (Moreira Alves 1988: 9–13).

A restricted type of democracy has emerged in Latin America, most notably in Brazil and Argentina, which have experienced authoritarian and democratic phases of development. Authoritarian democracy (other qualifying adjectives, such as *limited, guided,* and *protected,* are sometimes attached to the term *democracy*) is an expression of the state's efforts to expand its links to civil society. In view of a regime's lack of legitimacy and weak economic performance, proponents of authoritarian democracy advocate a more flexible system of political representation and gradual liberalization. Class alliances are broadened, and the state makes concessions to pressure groups. However, such attempts to modernize the state leave unchanged the basic structures of power and domination. Programs for slow democratization typically include measures to restrain calls for social equality so that they can be accommodated by the political system. Armed with the power to enforce order, the state wields the means of coercion to safeguard the nation against "chaos." The transparency of this domination and its social ramifications engender mounting conflict: protests against abuses of human rights and demands for the pursuit of substantive justice (Mittelman 1990: 67; Moreira Alves 1988: 9–13).

A challenge to democracy as an ideology of domination emerges from the mobilization of social movements seeking to assert popular control. The self-aggrandizing individualism characteristic of liberal and authoritarian democracy, coincident to the lack of accountability to the governed integral to economic globalization, is rejected in favor of a belief that the individual depends on society for development. The liberal-economic conceptualization of globalization allows for tolerance of social inequality, a formulation that critics regard as inconsistent with democracy understood as the provision for all people to develop their potential (Macpherson 1977; Mittelman 1990: 67). In terms of actual performance, the ultimate test of democratization is whether a party, or in some cases the military, will relinquish its preeminent role in political life, disengage from the state, and permit real dissent. The alternative preferred by some critics, popular democracy, while noble in theory, has yet to be proven viable at the national level, surely because of a combination of internal and external pressures. These pressures coagulate into one seemingly supreme challenge: how both to manage the socially disruptive costs of economic reform and to democratize. Put differently, the major problem is how to make economic revitalization compatible with democratization.

At bottom, the question of democratization centers on contradictory forms of accountability. To whom are elected officials responsible? Whereas in theory democracy means accountability to the governed, in practice leaders are accountable to market forces, most notably debt structures and structural adjustment programs. Closely related, there is a marked contradiction between the emerging global preference for electoral democracy and the increasing economic polarization generated by world capitalism, which is not held accountable to elected officials.

Resistance to Globalization

In the drive for rapid economic growth, the East Asian NICs placed severe restraints on democratic rights. These states retained authoritarian controls to try to prevent the eruption of social tensions. Little dissent was tolerated, and the strong state is touted as a prerequisite for good government and modernization.

Citing the examples of Taiwan, Singapore, and South Korea, Deng

Xiaoping and his cohorts sought to justify their contention that restraining democratic rights is essential for successful economic development. In crushing the pro-democracy movement in 1989, the Dengists held that too much freedom promotes disruption and impedes economic reform. Silent on the matter of political reform, the leaders voiced concern that given the chaos and turmoil experienced by China in this century, disorder is the gravest threat to development. In the absence of effective links between the state and civil society, the regime could rely only on guns and terror. In fact, the economic reform program required more flexible political structures to deal with increasingly autonomous groups in civil society—families detached from cooperatives by decollectivization, private entrepreneurs and industrialists, international traders, and students and intellectuals attracted by novel ideas entering China's open door (MacFarquhar 1989: 8).

Just as autonomous groups are emerging in Chinese society, so too are new social movements bringing pressure to bear in global civil society. The globalization of civil society involves resistance from disadvantaged strata in a changing division of labor. The losers in global restructuring seek to redefine their role in the emerging order. In the face of the declining power of organized labor and revolutionary groups, the powerless must devise alternative strategies of social struggle. They aim to augment popular participation and assert local control over the seemingly remote forces of globalization. New social movements—women's groups, environmentalists, human rights organizations, etc.—are themselves global phenomena, a worldwide response to the deleterious effects of economic globalization.

With the globalization of social conflict, observers have been quick to celebrate the formation of autonomous movements within civil society. Relatively little attention has been given to the coalescence of these movements. Coordination is a crucial matter precisely because the proliferation of new social movements can splinter civil society, perhaps culminating in the Lebanonization of political life. The push for regional autonomy in areas such as Kurdistan has the potential to open a global Pandora's box. Another reason for caution is that new social movements can have a repressive side—e.g., the resurgence of Islamic fundamentalism in Africa and Asia and of anti-Semitism in the former Soviet Union and Eastern Europe. Before the disintegration of socialist regimes in 1989, the Soviet Union and its Eastern European allies adopted anti-Zionist and anti-Israeli policies. Although the state did not sanction popular expressions of anti-Semitism, Jews were subject to discrimination in the bureaucracy. With the demise of socialism, however, anti-Semitism is flagrantly exhibited at many levels, with little sign of restraint, the impetus coming from autonomous groups in civil society. In sum, not only production and the state but also civil society itself is being globalized.

REGIONALISM AND GLOBALIZATION: EAST ASIA

Paradoxically, regionalism both shields domestic society from and integrates it into the global division of labor, as evident in East Asia. Although each regional division of labor has its distinctive features, all regional experiences are fluid and tethered to the global division of labor. The linkages differ substantially from one region to another and provide an important comparative basis for better understanding globalization.

As noted, one common element among diverse regions is that the state is increasingly a mechanism in the globalization process and thus intervenes directly in the economy to promote capital accumulation. Outflanked by transnational flows partly beyond its control, the state adapts to a changing global division of labor by tightening the fit between the local economy and technological innovation, research and development (R&D), and natural resource exploitation. With a lessening of the state's ability to harness external forces, there has been a strengthening of regional groupings—largely a de facto process spearheaded by the private sector in the Pacific Rim, substantially a de jure process in Europe, and a mix of the two in North America, Mexico, and the Caribbean. The effects of regional cooperation as a means to enhance participation in globalization are not yet known. But it is clear that many Asian countries and firms look to improve regional cooperation for access to a burgeoning regional market and as a sound base for sharing in globalization (OECD 1989: 10–11, 26). The economic growth generated by the Japanese-led "flying geese" pattern of regional integration, involving countries at very different levels of development, suggests important distinctions among generations of countries to have penetrated global markets in diverse industries and sectors. In East Asia, there is a highly stratified division of labor among Japan, the Four Dragons, the countries constituting ASEAN (the Association of Southeast Asian Nations), southern China, and Indochina.

In the Japanese model of state capitalism, the government subsidizes favored industries and shields them from market forces, especially imports. The state acts more by guidance than by edict, giving capital a major role in setting directions. As is well known, the state helps coordinate industries, the financial system, and technological innovations. Remarkable economic gains by Japanese business have prompted corporations in other countries to experiment with switching from a *just-in-case* manufacturing system to a *just-in-time* method. This method requires precise synchronization and continual supply of materials to reduce storage and other overhead costs as well as to improve productivity. Just-in-time also implies tight discipline over labor—or else it might be *just-too-late* (Gill 1993c). Important in terms of the regional division of labor, the just-in-time method places a premium on spatial proximity between suppliers and producers. In other words, it is a system that seeks advantage through labor and spatial hierarchies. With this form of managerial and technological upgrading, Japanese industry has fanned out in East Asia in search of low-cost manual labor for such tasks as assembly operations.

Having negotiated financial and technological alliances between private capital and the state, other manufacturers in the region are attempting to follow in Japan's footsteps to establish protected domestic and expanding international markets. In light of the Japanese experience, the Hong Kong government initially sought to keep labor costs low, partly by its welfare provisions in such areas as public housing and also through its policies of taxation, a form of indirect subsidies. Moreover, there was little history of militancy in Hong Kong's trade union movement. Hong Kong also had the advantage of being able to deliver highly skilled technical engineering at a cost considerably below that of the advanced countries. In terms of sourcing, there emerged a cluster of components, materials, and skilled labor in Hong Kong (Henderson 1989: 102–117).

Another global city, Singapore, has similarly followed a path from low-cost, labor-intensive production to capital-intensive industries and is now attempting to convert its economy to a knowledge center. As Singapore climbed the value-added ladder, it invested increasingly large sums in R & D activities. The state, especially its Economic Development Board (EDB) arm, has created a propitious zone for direct foreign investment (DFI), a catchment for transnational corporations offering ready technologies. As one EDB official summarized Singapore's development strategy, "Inner globalization," or regionalization, "and outer globalization benefit each other. Outer globalization improves inner globalization" (Lee 1991). Too small to be anything but a regional power, Singapore lacks economies of scale to build large industrial parks and extensive facilities for a scientific culture. Unable to be on the cutting edge of R & D, Singapore emphasizes the D component, refining what others have invented. In other words, its technological capacity is borrowed, not indigenous. Singapore is a global power only to the extent that it has a DFI-driven economy. Optimizing its spatial advantages as a crossroads of major sea and air routes, Singapore has developed excellent infrastructure and state-of-the-art industrial services, making it a regional maintenance center that repairs equipment and provides aircraft services. With a large concentration of transnational corporations, numbering over three thousand in 1992, Singapore is an attractive location for banking, finance, distribution networks, and telecommunications operations. Today Singapore offers global technology and aspires to become an "information node" in the globalization process, but its own products are competitive primarily in regional markets (Economic Development Board 1992: 1; Wong 1991).

To gain advantage, Singapore promotes subregional integration. Within

ASEAN, there is a move to link three nodes—the city-state of Singapore, Johor state in peninsular Malaysia, and Indonesia's Riau Islands—in a "Growth Triangle." This strategy of subregional integration seeks to combine Singapore's highly skilled human capital and well-developed infrastructure, Johor's land and semiskilled labor, and Riau's land and low-cost labor. The Singapore-Johor-Riau growth triangle is derived partly from the experience of the twinning of Hong Kong and Shenzen, reputedly China's fastest growing city. Also to pull subregional entities into a tighter web are the plans for twinning the city-states of Hong Kong and Singapore. Thus, while Singapore upgrades its industrial and technological capacities, low-value-added activities are shifted to neighboring countries, not unlike the strategy pursued by Hong Kong and Taiwan.

In addition to triangular ties among Hong Kong, Taiwan, and China's provinces of Guangdong and Fujian, the Greater South China Economic Zone includes the participation of the ASEAN countries, with their powerful Chinese business communities, as investors in South China. An emerging Chinese transnational division of labor builds on Hong Kong's and Taiwan's extensive kinship networks with Guangdong and Fujian. The fusion of these networks and subregional culture forms strong economic linkages among Hong Kong, Taiwan, the ASEAN countries, and South China. The frequent movement of population, industry, and capital across borders is establishing a "transfrontier metropolis." China's economic integration with the region is furthered by its coast-oriented development strategy, most notably granting special favorable policies to select provinces and designating fourteen coastal "open cities" to further attract DFI (Xianming citing Herzog 1990).

In a changing regional division of labor, China faces competition from other low-wage countries such as the Philippines and Indonesia, and some of the Four Dragons' neighbors, particularly Malaysia and Thailand, are experiencing remarkable economic growth. While the latter countries increasingly serve as magnets for DFI, questions are nevertheless raised about the NICs' future viability as industrial societies. Until recently viewed as the next Japan, South Korea is losing competitiveness in some key industries. Industries that fueled South Korea's economic dynamism—such as shoes, clothing, and simple consumer products—are now relocating in countries with lower wages. The shift from low-tech, labor-intensive industries is being hastened by democratic reforms demanded by formerly suppressed workers. Strikes in the 1980s led to a tripling of wages in some industries, causing Nike, Reebok, and other big firms to seek alternative production sites. Similarly, exports of personal computers from South Korea plummeted more than 57 percent in the first half of 1992 from the comparable period in 1991 ("After Stall . . . " 1992). The policy debate now rife in South Korea, just as in Singapore and other NICs, concerns how to jump the elusive last hurdle in the race toward developed-nation status. The challenge is to move up in the technological division of labor, which requires indigenous, not merely imported, capacity for innovation.

Meanwhile, resistance to restructuring is mounting, not least in South Korea from critics who challenge government assistance to a few huge conglomerates, known as *chaebol*. There are complaints about state subsidies favoring the *chaebol* and protecting them from imports, especially short of any reform of the financial system. In Hong Kong, worker mobility, most apparent among women in factories, is a sign of discontent. Notwithstanding economic growth for the country as a whole, Singapore faces disquiet among various ethnic groups and social movements. With English as the national language, and given a highly Westernized culture, many Chinese-educated members of Singapore's Chinese community feel that they have been left behind in economic development. Clearly the Singaporeans who are the chief beneficiaries of the system are English-educated Chinese. The share of wealth accruing to Singapore's Indian community, relative to that of the country's other ethnic groups, has declined in recent years. Singapore's Malays have found it hard to break into Chinese businesses, the upper echelons of the civil service, and the military. Flanked by two predominantly Islamic countries, Malaysia and Indonesia, Singapore has established barriers for its Malays who seek to join the air force. Some Singaporean Malays claim to be caught in a spiral: poverty lessens the opportunity for education, and a low level of education begets poverty. It is not surprising that Singapore's ethnic and Christian fundamentalist movements are gaining a following (Correspondents 1991).

The developmental routes mapped here are unlikely to be replicated elsewhere, because global trends articulate with regional conditions in very different ways. The Four Dragons integrated into a "new international division of labor" when the world economy was robust and when the Cold War generated not only extraordinary superpower conflict but also material assistance for allies in a strategically key region. On the fringes of the Third World, meanwhile, a strategy of subsidizing nonexistent infant industries and protecting small markets within the ambit of heavy debt structures is of little use (Mittelman 1991). Although the external and domestic obstacles encountered by parvenus are now greater than in the past, the nature of the interactions between the contemporary globalization trend, which has superseded the "new international division of labor" of bygone decades, and social conflict offers important lessons for the future.

FUTURE DIRECTIONS

I began this chapter by suggesting that the nation-state and social strata are embedded in a world society propelled by the unparalleled productive capacities of economic globalization. Formulating the problematic of globalization in this way directs attention to a Polanyian method of focusing on an expansion of the market and responses from regional and local entities that directly encounter its disruptive and socially polarizing effects. This chapter has tried to extend Polanyi's conceptualization to a world scale, showing interactions and the implications of globalization for conflict and cooperation.

Further, I have argued that the evolution of the theory of division of labor provides a key to comprehending globalization, its opportunities, and its challenges. The discussion of this theory has concentrated on two theses, while taking the opportunity to propose a third and alternative conceptualization. First, classical political economy focused on efficiencies stemming from specialization of functions, with implications for developing particular products for trade and thus deriving comparative advantages on the international level. Although Adam Smith adumbrated a notion of interest-based politics centering on the division of labor, as did David Ricardo and Karl Marx, the concept of division of labor remained largely dormant and, notwithstanding Max Weber's and Émile Durkheim's contributions to sociological theory, did not advance significantly until the second half of the twentieth century.

A conversation about "the wealth of nations" began anew in the 1960s. The emergence of the NICs sparked interest in the prospects for mobility in the international division of labor. Setting forth a structural analysis, the new international division of labor theorists sought to explain the shift of manufacturing from advanced capitalist to developing countries. In their view, the process is driven by declining profits in industrial centers, causing firms to seek new investment opportunities where labor costs are cheap. Hence, manufacturing operations are fragmented, with low-skilled tasks being transferred while the bulk of R & D activities is retained in the heartlands of capitalism. To this day, technological development, especially basic research, continues to be far less globalized than are manufacturing and sales.[2] Also, the control centers of international finance are confined to Tokyo, London, and New York, with a second tier in Frankfurt and Paris, followed by offshore facilities in such escape hatches as the Cayman Islands.

As we have seen, the new international division of labor thesis underlines the supposed logic of capital itself but does not examine the interactions between global trends and varied local circumstances. In fact, during the 1980s global restructuring entailed an unprecedented correlation of economic forces, political power, and social structure. Along with a change in emphasis from a Fordist model of mass production and mass consumption to a post-Fordist (or perhaps one might say "Toyotaist") system of flexible production for niche markets came important technological innovations in certain industries, enabling NICs to move into higher-value-added and upgraded operations, deepening the production structure in select countries, partly as a result of their own initiatives, and opening the way for integrated industries. The decomposition of the production process was accompanied by technological devolution to the NICs in crucial sectors linked to transport and communications: major strides in containerized shipping making the spread of production facilities more profitable, improved engineering techniques speeding operations, and pervasive computer applications providing instantaneous data processing to augment the efficiency of global business (Hoogvelt 1987). Important in this transformation is the relatively "borderless" nature of technology and of a region, where complementary operations can easily be mounted and, if need be, transferred from country to country.

Beyond a "new" international division of labor, there have been remarkable changes in the global political economy in the past decade. In the emerging global division of labor, there are regional coordinating centers in specific industries in such hubs as Hong Kong and Singapore, with offshore assembly and natural resources situated in neighboring countries. The regional centers have upgraded and moved into even higher-value-added operations. They have sought to gain a technological edge by investing in R & D capacity. Although there is no technological quick fix for adjusting to an extremely competitive global environment, raising spending on R & D promotes access to qualified scientists and engineers with advanced training, enhanced facilities for the reproduction of this form of labor, as well as other sources of investment in local universities and research institutes (Chalmers 1991; Henderson 1989: 45). A handful of countries has used the impetus of the market and tried to cushion its full impact. Nonetheless, upward mobility in the global division of labor remains relatively limited. It still takes place at the margins of the global political economy and is only partially determined by policy initiatives.

Globalization encompasses contradictory trends. On the one hand, the unaccountable forces of globalization—such as cross-border flows of undocumented workers and modern communications with instantaneous speed—are partially beyond the control of effective state regulation. To adjust, the state responds to the globalization process by more fully integrating the domestic economy into world markets. On the other hand, the state pulls in the opposite direction by using a variety of government interventions to create a competitive edge. All countries industrializing late rely on large-scale interventions—most important, direct involvement in the production process, establishment of social and economic infrastructure, generous terms of credit, and material support for shifting from imitative to indigenous technological capacity. The options are clearly restricted, and the question is not whether the state should intervene in the economy but what type of state and what interventions are most appropriate in a specific context? And policy initiatives in whose interest? Will state intervention be subject to popular control? Given the limits on state policies and the promise of unprecedented productive capacity, new small states such as Georgia, the Baltic countries, Slovenia, or Croatia can do no better than negotiate the channels of globalization, recognizing that freer markets entail greater social costs and hence must be popularly controlled. For these new states, as for all others, globalization limits the range of choice. Only within its ambit may actual possibilities and specific limitations be gauged.

As countries maneuver for position within the global division of labor, conflicts erupt anew because the opportunity for ascent is quite constrained. It is constrained precisely because in a post–Cold War world there is one, and only one, metastructure—capitalism—establishing the rules for mobility, whether upward or downward. Intraregional inequality is spearheaded by increased levels of interaction with the global economy. Hence, contradictions and conflicts have emerged among the Asia Pacific countries, with heightened regional disparities, new competitors, and changing spatial orientations. Within China itself, the uneven distribution of DFI, interacting with state policies of encouraging some areas and localities to be more integrated in the global division of labor, have either exacerbated economic differences or reconfigured them. Empirical research shows that the overwhelming proportion of DFI in China is directed to coastal provinces and municipalities, with the vast interior beset by underdevelopment (Xianming 1993).

The global division of labor is also marked by interregional differences centered on three axes: Asia Pacific, Europe with the impending participation of erstwhile socialist countries, and North America joined by Mexico and the Caribbean. The emergence of competing regional blocs could lead to increased global conflict, probably originating with instability in the Third World. Poverty and nondemocratic rule are the main sources of this instability. A host of proximate issues could ignite regional and global conflict—among others, a resurgence of ethnic or religious rivalries, a crisis of legitimacy, and the proliferation of advanced weaponry. In the absence of superpower restraints that were meant to head off a confrontation between the United States and the Soviet Union, regional powers now have greater leeway to pursue their own agendas. (Hence, Iraq marched into Kuwait partly because Saddam Hussein sought to fill what he regarded as a power vacuum.) Paradoxically, globalization engenders the regionalization of conflict.

With globalization, power is dispersed among more actors and interregional competition is heightened. Given the instability characteristic of triads, an alliance between two of the three macroregions is a likely outcome. With the vast size of the European single market, the United States and Japan represent counterbalancing economic power. Currently first and second in size in GNP, the United States and Japan have mutual interests in a new world order. However, a new world order based on military superpower cannot be sustained by outside financing. The world's largest debtor nation, the United States derives jobs and investment capital from Japan, which in turn relies on its North American ally for innovation in industry and military power to guarantee the supply of vital resources, especially oil from the Middle East.

Yet for large numbers of people there is no hint of a new world order or upward mobility in a changing division of labor. Rather, life is marked by a deepening divide between rich and poor. The mosaic of globalization reflects a transformation of poverty in which three continents were most adversely affected by globalization to the marginalization primarily of a single world region and of enclaves in other regions. According to projections by the World Bank, in Asia the number in poverty will fall from 805 million in 1985 to 435 million by the end of this century; and in Latin America and the Caribbean, from 75 million to 60 million in the same period. In sub-Saharan Africa, the number of poor will rise by 85 million, to 265 million in the year 2000. Thus, Asia's share of the world's poor will decline to 53 percent from 72 percent in 1985; Latin America's and the Caribbean's will drop to 11.4 percent from 19.1 percent; and sub-Saharan Africa's will double from 16 percent to 32 percent (World Bank 1990: 139). In other words, there are holes in the global mosaic. Although the data point to a net reduction of poverty-stricken people, polarization is evident among regions—truncated globalization debars the bulk of Africa from gaining access to world society's productive processes. For the countries of Africa, the greatest challenge is to demarginalize when national options are severely constrained by the forces of globalization.

Against a backdrop of transformation from a hegemonic and state-centered structure to a multipolar and politically decentered world system, globalization is both an agent and a product of social conflict. Globalization sets in train conflicts among competing capitalisms, generates deeper or reconfigured intraregional disparities, engenders interregional rivalries among neomercantilist coalitions, and has combined with local forces to consign, at the end of this millennium, 265 million people on one continent to poverty, with little hope for escape in sight. The foremost contradiction of our time is the conflict between the zones of humanity integrated in the global division of labor and those excluded from it.

Embedded in the foregoing overview are various analytical propositions that require scrutiny. Subsequent chapters will deepen the discussion by confronting my interpretations and reformulating the discourse over globalization. For the contributing authors, the ultimate challenges are to reconceptualize globalization and delimit alternative globalization projects. Going one step further, the task is to anticipate postglobalization by identifying the bearers of change and their strategies in a new double movement: the integration wrought by market forces and a transnational protectionist reaction against the disintegration of extant forms of social and political organization.

NOTES

Some of the ideas in this chapter were first presented at the Dalhousie University International Symposium "Surviving at the Margins: Political Economy and Foreign Policy in the South in the 1990s," 26–28 September 1991, Halifax, Nova Scotia, organized by Timothy Shaw and Larry Swatuk. The chapter draws on my article "The Globalization of Social Conflict," in Volker Bornschier and Peter Lengyel, eds., *World Society Studies,* vol. 3: *Conflict and Its Solution in World Society* (New Brunswick: Transaction Publishers, 1994). I owe a debt of gratitude to Robert W. Cox for sharing ideas, as well as to Stephen Gill and Linda Yarr for valuable comments on a draft of this chapter. Finally, the research reported here (part of an ongoing project) was funded by grants from the World Society Foundation and the Professional Staff Congress of the City University of New York. I gratefully acknowledge these sources of support.

1. The definition of *globalization* as a compression of time and space builds on the theoretical lineage of D. Harvey (1989), Giddens (1990), Robertson (1992), and others. Following Polanyi, I have attached a notion of social embeddedness.

2. Comparing present-day trends with those of "the decades of American technological hegemony," the *New York Times* ("Technology without Borders Raises Big Questions for the U.S.," 1 January 1992) reports that despite various transnational flows, only 10 percent of U.S. corporate research and development funds is spent overseas. Motorola, for instance, derives half its revenue from international sales and stations 40 percent of its workforce abroad, but only 20–25 percent of product development and 5 percent of basic research are conducted outside the United States.

Robert W. Cox 2

A Perspective on Globalization

Globalization compresses the time and space aspects of social relations. —James H. Mittelman (Chapter 1)

The world at the end of the Short Twentieth Century is in a state of social breakdown rather than revolutionary crisis.
—Eric Hobsbawm (1994)

It is particularly important to take some distance from a term that has become fashionable in both academia and mass media in order to place it in historical perspective. The word *globalization* invokes this challenge. James Mittelman, in setting forth the guidelines for the symposium that resulted in this book, did well to stress the time and space dimensions within which the term is to be understood.[1]

For world-systems theorists, capitalism has always been global, whether its origins are traced to the seventeenth-century Eurocentric world or to more ancient civilizations—global in vocation if not in geographic extent. In this perspective, there is nothing essentially different about the last three decades of the twentieth century.

During what Eric Hobsbawm calls the *Short Twentieth Century* (1914–1991), capitalism was challenged by another potentially global force: "real socialism," in its own terms, or "world communism," in the perception of its capitalist opponents. (For world-systems theory, consistent with its own premises, this was merely a deviant face of capitalism.) By the end of the Short Twentieth Century, *real socialism* was a spent force, leaving capitalism as the only apparent claimant to global reach. World-systems theory seemed vindicated. Real socialism had been just a blip on the screen.

THE CRISIS OF THE MID-1970s

Nevertheless, in a closer perspective than that of megahistorical world-systems theory, there was a significant breaking point in the mid-1970s when the specific form of economic and social relations that are now referred to as "global" began to be apparent. My first recollection of it was in reading an article by Bernadette Madeuf and Charles-Albert Michalet entitled "A New Approach to International Economics" (1978). The authors argued that it had become necessary to make a distinction between international economy and world economy. The international economy was what classical economic theory had concerned itself with: movements in trade, investments, and payments crossing national frontiers that were regulated by states and by international organizations created by states. The world economy, in contrast, was the sphere in which production and finance were being organized in cross-border networks that could very largely escape national and international regulatory powers.

The perception of this distinction coincided with a number of changes in world political economy accentuated by the recession that hit the developed capitalist economies from 1973 and affected by extension the less developed countries. There was also a growing sclerosis of the economies of real socialism. The late 1970s was an era of generalized economic crisis.

The crisis put an end to the hopes of what was still called the Third World for a new international economic order. Indeed, First World financing of Third World development was substantially reversed. Third World countries abandoned import substitution in favor of export promotion, which also meant sacrificing production for domestic consumption and satisfaction of basic needs in favor of earning foreign exchange. The conditions for rolling over foreign debt also required these countries to cut state expenditures, devalue their currencies, and remove restrictions on the movement of capital, all of which made the burden of adjustment fall most heavily on the poor and on national and local enterprises. It accentuated the separation between those small, privileged groups integrated with the world economy and the larger part of the population that remained outside.

The more developed capitalist societies also felt financial and market discipline. Perhaps its major effect was to accelerate a restructuring of production away from mass production of standardized goods toward less energy- and labor-intensive methods and more capital- and knowledge-intensive ones. The Fordist mode of production—which had been based on a well-paid labor force able to buy its own products and protected by institutionalized collective bargaining and by redistributive state policies acting as an economic stabilizer—came under attack. The new strategies emphasized a weakening of trade union power, cutting of state budgets (especially for social policy), deregulation, privatization, and priority to international competitiveness. Advances in technology in production and communications, always the servant of dominant capital, enhanced all of these tendencies.

The impact of these tendencies in different parts of the world accelerated migratory movements of populations, the direct causes of which were the destruction of previous means of existence (e.g., peasant agriculture in poor countries displaced by export-oriented capitalist farming, job loss in the mass production industries of richer countries from "restructuring") and political repression associated with regimes prepared to enforce the new economic rules by sacrificing the welfare of most of their people.

All of these interacting and mutually reinforcing tendencies constitute one meaning of *globalization*—the complex of forces, born of the crisis of the mid-1970s, that reversed the different complex of forces that had become consolidated during the three decades following World War II. These were decades of economic growth, buttressed in the advanced capitalist countries by a corporatist social consensus, which also recognized the desirability of some minimal transfer of resources to aid development in the Third World.

GLOBALIZATION AS IDEOLOGY

The relationship between international and world economies has been dialectical. The world economy grew by taking advantage of the territorial fragmentation of the international economy. This allowed capital to choose the most propitious sites in which to locate diverse phases of a geographically disseminated production process, taking account of differences in labor costs, environmental regulations, fiscal incentives, political stability, and so on. It also allowed capital to manage its accounts so that profits would accrue where the lowest taxes prevailed.

The multinational corporations and banks, principal agents of globalization, henceforth represented themselves (and after a time were perceived by many governments and academic theorists) as primary agents of economic development. They were also a growing force for national and international deregulation in trade and finance. Globalization began to be represented as a finality, as the logical and inevitable culmination of the powerful tendencies of the market at work. The dominance of economic forces was regarded as both necessary and beneficial. States and the interstate system would serve mainly to ensure the working of market logic.

Thus, in a second meaning, *globalization* became an ideology. The forces and policies that sustained the complex of tendencies just mentioned came to be regarded as inevitable ("there is no alternative") and in the long run beneficent, at least for some people. For others, different policies would be required (it must be recognized that many people, not just in poor countries but also in those that had been relatively rich, would remain outside the integrated sphere of the world economy). The ideology of globalization left understood but unstated the need for repressive police and military force to prevent destabilization of the world economy by outbursts of protest from the disadvantaged outsiders.

GLOBALISM AND THE BIOSPHERE

Another concern emerged also in the mid-1970s with a distinct and to some extent competing implication for the role of states: an ecological concern that the planet was reaching the limits of its capacity to sustain human settlement under prevailing conditions of production, resource depletion, and attendant pollution. This concern also had global implications in both senses of that term—it involved the entire planet and it raised questions about the total organization of human life and work within the larger realm of nature. This concern is sometimes referred to as "globalism" ("think globally, act locally"). Globalism and globalization arose together as orientations for thought and action.

Globalization and globalism were thus the product of specific historical conditions in the last three decades of the twentieth century. They emerged first in the advanced capitalist societies, and with the knowledge, prestige, and resources present in these societies they were disseminated as objective truth among these societies' subordinate classes and to peoples in the rest of the world.

Among these subordinate classes and other peoples the contradictions of both globalization and globalism became apparent. Globalization widened the gap in living conditions between most of the world's population and the relatively small segment integrated into global production and financial networks. Globalism raised the ethical question of what the rich, who were already consuming the lion's share of the world's resources and had done most of the polluting, could offer to meet the aspirations of the poor for development and higher living standards.

SPACE AND TIME

In 1889 the French philosopher Henri Bergson published his *Essai sur les données immédiates de la conscience* (which has been translated into English as *Time and Free Will*). Bergson broke with both Cartesian and Kantian traditions on the question of time; for him, there were two meanings of *time*. There was what we could call "clock time," which was a uniform, homogeneous, medium measuring from outside whatever was happening. This, in effect, was time reduced to space. The sequence of events is spread out over this homogeneous medium. Time in this sense is nature's way of making sure that everything that is going to happen does not happen all at once.

The other kind of time Bergson rendered by the French word *durée*, of which "duration" is perhaps a misleading translation. If it is taken to mean just the period elapsing between the beginning and end of a series of events, we fall back into the spatial view of time. By *durée* Bergson meant lived time, experienced time—the subjective feeling of acting and choosing and of pressures limiting action and choice—time from within, the time in which we experience both freedom and constraints.

This distinction is important when it comes to thinking about social and political change. The historian who tries to explain an event, a revolution, or the inertia of a society attempts an imaginative reconstruction from the evidence of individual actions, of the meanings of collective actions for participants in social movements, and of the mental and physical constraints on action. All this is *durée*. This is the time through which we may understand historical structural change. It is time reexperienced by the historian and social analyst from within the process of change itself.

Bergson's thoughts about time referred to individual psychology. More than half a century later, Fernand Braudel (1980a) spelled out categories of time as an aid to thought in historiography and the social sciences. He identified different flows of time in different fields of human activity—politics, economy, culture, technology, the structuring of society, and the development of language. Time in these different fields moved at different speeds—sometimes slowly, then accelerating, and then again more slowly. These fields interacted but did not move in concert. The momentum of culture, for instance, might continue after politics had ceased to be creative. Such was the case, for instance, with seventeenth-century Spanish high culture and possibly for U.S. pop culture today.

Moreover, Braudel saw three levels of time. Events time is the immediately perceptible level—instantaneous time, or cybernetic "real time." But events do not explain themselves. They have to be placed within the context of what Braudel called *conjonctures,* or the set of forces that prepare the ground for events and account for their consequences. Conjunctural time is medium term, the span of an economic cycle, of a certain configuration of social forces, or of a certain paradigm of scientific knowledge. The shift from the complex of forces that characterized the postwar decades to those that characterized the emergence of globalization discussed earlier was such a change in conjunctural time.

At the deepest level is what Braudel called the *longue durée,* which involves structures of thought (*mentalités*) that are very slow to change: economic organization, social practices, political institutions, language, and values. These structures are all cohesive and interdependent, yet each moves at a different pace. Conjunctural changes that become consolidated and stabilized could signal a change in the *longue durée.*

Structural change, for Braudel, results from a "dialectic of duration." Events are conditioned and shaped by the structures of the *longue durée,* but events may also cumulatively challenge, undermine, and transform these structures. The explanation of historical structural change involves the interaction of all three levels of time. Well-grounded strategies for making a better future—for a realistic application of collective free will—involve as a starting point an understanding of the limits of the possible through an awareness of the *longue durée*.

Time in the Braudelian sense is the medium in which the collective creative powers of human society continually invent the future within the limits of the possible. Space (and spatially conceived time) orients the mind toward the present complex of relationships. The present seems fixed, determined. Within the spatial orientation of mind, the future is imaginable only as the further development of tendencies apparent in the present. The ideology of globalization is sustained by space-oriented thinking. The possibility of transcending this ideology will depend on recovering the time dimension in thought that will enable human action to use the contradictions of globalization to envisage a possible alternative future. The time dimension is the remaining medium of freedom.

THE CONTRADICTIONS OF GLOBALIZATION

One contradiction of globalization is that social polarization exists both among and within countries. The social structure of the world shaped by globalization takes the form of a three-part hierarchy. At the top are people who are integrated into the global economy, including everyone from the global economy managers down to the relatively privileged workers who serve global production and finance in reasonably stable jobs. The second level in the hierarchy includes those who serve the global economy in more precarious employment—an expanding category segmented by race, religion, and sex as a result of the "restructuring" of production by post-Fordism. The bottom level consists of superfluous labor—those excluded from the global economy and who serve it only as a potentially destabilizing force; at this level are the objects of global poverty relief and riot control.

Whole regions of Africa belong to the bottom level. Most of the former Soviet sphere is joining this category as well, with excessive polarization of new rich and new poor. The success stories of the former Third World (the newly industrializing countries [NICs]) constitute a very small population. Most significant, perhaps, is that polarization is increasing within so-called rich countries with high levels of unemployment, a decrease in high-paying (integrated) jobs and an increase in low-paying precarious work, erosion of social services (health and education), and fiscal attack on redistributive policies. Tiny segments of poor-country populations are integrated into the world economy network, while rich countries are generating their own internal Third Worlds (UNRISD 1995; Galbraith 1992).

Another contradiction concerns the loss of autonomous regulatory power by states. States and intergovernmental organizations play a role in enforcing the rules of the global economy and in enhancing national competitiveness, but their powers of shielding domestic economies from negative effects of globalization have diminished. The cure for these negative effects is generally regarded as more globalization. Is there any regulatory power at the level of the global economy itself? There appears to be a mechanism for arriving at general policy consensus among rich-country political managers (through various unofficial and official bodies, from the Trilateral Commission and regular Davos meetings to the OECD and G7 summits). I have referred to this partially visible, or transparent, complex as a *nébuleuse* (see Chapter 5). The visible form is a photo opportunity accompanied by an anodyne press communiqué. Far from being a sinister occult power, the *nébuleuse* may turn out to be a Wizard of Oz. Perhaps no one, or no coherent structure, is really in control.

A third contradiction of globalization is that there is a widespread but uneven tendency toward decomposition of civil society. This takes the form both of a fragmentation of social forces and of a growing gap between the base of society and political leadership. References to the "political class" imply an alienation of people from their political institutions. The politicians are thought of as a distinct category of beings, serving their own interests, probably both corrupt and incompetent. This is markedly evident by recent events in Italy and Japan and in varying degrees in other advanced capitalist countries. People have lost confidence in politicians because of widespread corruption and, more specifically linked to the globalization effect, because of a conviction that politicians do not understand and cannot resolve the major problems confronting their societies. Where a break appears in this skepticism, it may be populist illusion propagated by a rich and powerful controller of mass media promising salvation—a Ross Perot or Silvio Berlusconi. In the poorest countries, there is evidence that people are turning their backs on the state and international organizations, which they see as their enemies rather than as possible supports.

This tendency toward decomposition is accompanied by a resurgent affirmation of identities (defined by, for example, religion, ethnicity, or gender) and an emphasis on locality rather than wider political authorities. Locality here can be seen as a product of "globality" insofar as globalization has undermined the authority of conventional political structures and accentuated the fragmentation of societies. There is an open challenge as to whether new bases of political authority can be constructed from these fragments.

POTENTIAL FOR TRANSFORMATION

Thought in the time dimension is dialectical. It begins with an understanding of the contradictions and proceeds to identify the potential for transformation based on concerted action by self-conscious social forces. It seems fairly evident that transformation is not going to come from the summits of power in the state system and global economy. The *nébuleuse* will at best succeed in ad hoc confrontation of crises to sustain the status quo. For transformative potential we have to look both at latent tendencies within the summits of power and especially at the possibility of a recomposition of civil society at the base. We must also examine the long-term relationship of society with nature.

I would signal three elements worthy of attention in a time-oriented perspective. The first is a tendency toward a differentiation of what Karl Polanyi (1957a) called substantive economies within the overarching concept of globalization. Both liberal and Marxist economics represent capitalism in formal terms as a single system with its own laws of motion. But we can see several distinct substantive capitalisms, all of which have significant differences for people living within them: a hyperliberal Anglo-American form (Cox 1987), a social market central and northern European form (Albert 1991), and an East Asian form with several variants (Johnson 1982; Fallows 1994). Large geographic zones may be organized very differently from the standpoint of the social and ethical content of the economy. The issues today in the European Union focus on the choice between the hyperliberal and the social market forms for future European society.

Second, the process of decomposition and recomposition of civil society in all parts of the world, which will underpin any new forms of political authority and world order, will not follow a uniform pattern. This is where civilizations become an important object for study. We can think of civilizations as distinct realms of intersubjectivity rather than as geographic zones or religious or ethnic communities. By intersubjectivity, I mean the basic unarticulated assumptions shared by people concerning the nature of the real world; they are unarticulated because they are so naturally taken for granted.

These visions of reality are represented through different mental structures, but these structures in turn have to be understood as distinct ways social practices have responded to material conditions of existence. Civilizations constitute the mental frameworks through which peoples understand and interpret their world and contrive their responses to the challenges that confront them.

A new consensual world order could arise from an encounter of civilizations in a spirit of mutual respect. On this basis it should be possible to work toward a supraintersubjectivity that, while being aware of and respecting the intersubjectivities of different civilizations, would be capable of defining some common principles of consensual coexistence.

The third object of concern is how to reconcile the complex mutation of human organization and the coexistence of different intersubjectivities with the biosphere (i.e., the interaction of humanity with other forms of life and life-sustaining substances within that thin envelope encompassing the planet from the upper atmosphere to the seabeds). Only recently have we begun to understand the ways the biosphere has become an actor in the human drama. To the difficulty of mutual understanding among differently constituted human minds, expressed through different civilizations, is added the difficulty of achieving some mutual understanding of the role the biosphere plays in world politics. This will involve revision of our own mental frameworks. In formal economics, nature, represented by land, has been subordinated to market logic. Nature, however, has its own logic, based on the interdependencies of different forms of human and nonhuman life. So long as economic logic did not lead to a destabilization of nature, so long as there was enough slack in nature for the consequences of economic logic to be tolerated, this subordination of nature to the market went unnoticed.

Now, however, the limits to nature's tolerance are being tested. The hole in the ozone layer, global warming, deforestation, soil erosion, the depletion of fish stocks, the loss of biodiversity—all these phenomena articulate nature's protest and imply that we need to rethink economics as being subordinate to a science of nature. This is more than an intellectual task. It implies a revision of our ways of producing and our model of consumption—our ways of life and work.

This endeavor raises the ultimate challenge to the ideology of globalization. Consumption is the motor of capitalism, and the motivation of consumer demand is indispensable to capitalism's continuing development. There are significant cultural variations—for instance, Japanese people seem to have a greater propensity to save and North Americans a greater propensity for debt and consumption—but on the world scale, aspiration toward the U.S. and Western European consumption model has been the dynamic behind market liberalization in the Third World, China, and the former Soviet empire, and the driving force of economic globalization.

It would seem that a fairly radical change in patterns of consumption will become essential to maintenance of the biosphere. Preparing for the 1992 Rio de Janeiro Earth Summit, U.S. president George Bush said, "Our lifestyle is not open to negotiation." He was implicitly acknowledging that a change of lifestyle is necessary to biospheric survival and at the same time that political survival in modern democracies makes it highly dangerous for politicians to advocate such change.

All this leads to some pessimistic conclusions. As Eric Hobsbawm (1994) reasoned, the late twentieth century is in a state of social breakdown rather than revolutionary crisis. The forces that polarize society and fragment opposition among the disadvantaged and dispossessed remain dominant. They are sustained by the hegemonic ideology of globalization. Instances of revolt, such as has occurred in Chiapas in the south of Mexico, can be dealt with in isolation by dominant power so long as concerted transnational opposition remains weak. Furthermore, the seduction of consumerism turns people away from opposition and makes them accomplices of the globalizing forces.

I end this chapter with a measure of hope. Perhaps awareness of the consequences of globalization, advanced by work such as is embodied in this book, may shift thinking away from a passive, space-oriented present-mindedness toward a time-oriented strategy for action. If revolution is but a dim prospect, social breakdown is a dangerous and depressing condition. Only realistically based action can ensure that globalization has not brought us to the "end of history."

NOTE

1. Etymologically, the word *global* has two meanings that tend to become merged in the neologism *globalization*. One meaning refers to the planet earth (the French term *mondialisation,* used as an equivalent to *globalization,* is confined to this meaning). The other refers to a whole, or a set of factors conceived as a whole, giving *globalization* a totalizing connotation. The latter meaning is evoked by the consequences often perceived as those of the globalization process: a world increasingly homogenized—economically, socially, and culturally. The dialectical response to homogenization has been the affirmation of difference, equally present if lacking the material force of the apparently dominant homogenizing tendency. *Globalization,* in current usage, is to be understood in this dialectical manner.

Part 1

The Thrust of Globalization: Production and the State

Saskia Sassen 3

The Spatial Organization of Information Industries: Implications for the Role of the State

Today's global economy is commonly conceptualized in terms of the new technical capacities for instantaneous transmission of information output over any distance. A more critical account of globalization focuses on the power of transnational firms to operate globally. Different as they are, both accounts feed into propositions about the shrinking role of the national state in an increasingly global economy. On the one hand, the ascendance of information technologies has contributed to a sharp increase in the mobility and liquidity of capital. This is particularly, though not exclusively, evident in today's leading information industries—international finance and advanced corporate services—which operate globally and partly in electronic spaces that escape conventional jurisdictions. On the other hand, the key to globalization is found in the power of multinational corporations and their capacity to avoid the state's regulatory umbrella on significant components of its operation.

Both accounts contain important elements integral to economic globalization—technology, hypermobility, and power. But they leave out or minimize (1) the importance of infrastructure and work processes necessary for the operation of global economic systems and (2) the role of the state in implementing the new global economic systems and in producing the new legal forms within which such systems operate. Introducing place and the law into analyses of economic globalization leads to a more qualified examination of the shrinking role of the state in the global economy. Many of the strategic places where global processes materialize are embedded in national territories and hence fall, at least partly, under various state-centered regulatory umbrellas. And producing and legitimating new forms of legality remain tasks mainly in the hands of states. To a large extent, in the current phase of the global economy these issues of space and the law are confined to the highly developed countries.

This chapter uses the case of the leading information industries in the global economy and international finance and advanced corporate services to examine these issues. These industries are among the most intensive users of telecommunications and computer networks, the indispensable technology of today's global economy. Precisely because they are the most advanced and hypermobile industries, they push the matter of the role of the state to its limits. My argument is that we need to go beyond the immateriality of information outputs and the hypermobility this entails to better understand questions of governance in the global economy.

A central proposition here is that we cannot take the existence of a global economic system as a given, but rather we need to examine the particular ways the conditions for economic globalization are produced. This requires examining not only communication capacities and the power of multinationals but also the infrastructure of facilities and work processes necessary for the implementation of global economic systems, including the production of those inputs that constitute the capability for global control and the infrastructure of jobs involved in this production. The emphasis shifts to the practice of global control—the work of producing and reproducing the organization and management of a global production system and a global marketplace for finance, both under conditions of economic concentration. Power is essential in the organization of the world economy, but so is production. The recovery of place and production also implies that global processes can be studied in great empirical detail.[1]

The first part of this chapter examines how global processes, and in particular advanced information industries, materialize in particular places. We can see that in the case of these industries globalization is constituted through a global grid of strategic sites, which emerges as a new geography of centrality. The existence of such a grid may carry significant regulatory implications but it would require transnational legal/regulatory regimes and hence considerable innovation around current regimes. The second part of the chapter discusses what we could think of as elements for an analysis of the role of the state in the implementation of the various systems and regimes necessary for the forms of globalization evident in the current phase.[2]

SPATIAL CONCENTRATION IN
A GLOBAL INFORMATION ECONOMY

Telematics and globalization have emerged as fundamental forces in the reorganization of economic space. This reorganization ranges from the spatial virtualization of a growing number of economic activities to the reconfiguration of the geography of the built environment *for* economic activity. Whether in electronic space or in the geography of the built environment, this reorganization involves institutional and structural changes. One outcome of these transformations has been captured in images of geographic dispersal at the global scale and the neutralization of place and distance through telematics in a growing number of economic activities.

But is a space economy lacking points of physical concentration possible in an economic system characterized by significant concentration in ownership, control, and the appropriation of profits? In other words, can such an economic system operate without centers? Further, how far can forms of centrality constituted in electronic space go in replacing some of the functions commonly associated with geographic/organizational forms of centrality?

I explore here the ways centrality remains a key property of the economic system. The transformation in the spatial correlates of centrality through new technologies and globalization engenders a whole new problematic around the definition of *centrality* in our economic system, where i) a share of transactions occurs through technologies that neutralize distance and place, and do so on a global scale; and ii) where centrality has historically been embodied in certain types of built environment and urban form, e.g., the central business district. Further, the fact of a new geography of centrality, even if transnational, would contain possibilities for regulatory enforcement that are absent in an economic geography lacking strategic points of agglomeration.

New Forms of Centrality

Simplifying an analysis made elsewhere (Sassen 1994), one can identify four forms assumed by centrality today. (See also generally Friedmann 1995; Knox and Taylor 1995; Castells 1989; Brotchie et al. 1995; Hall 1995; Fainstein 1993; Frost and Spence 1992; Abu-Lughod 1995.)

First, while there is no longer a simple, straightforward relation between centrality and such geographic entities as the downtown or the central business district, the CBD remains a key form of centrality. But the CBD in major international business centers is one profoundly reconfigured by technological and economic change.

Second, the center can extend into a metropolitan area in the form of a grid of nodes of intense business activity. One might ask whether a spatial organization characterized by dense strategic nodes spread over a broader region constitutes a new form of organizing the territory of the center rather than, as in the more conventional view, an instance of suburbanization or geographic dispersal. Insofar as these various nodes are articulated through cyber-routes or digital highways, they represent a new geographic correlate of the most advanced type of center. The places that fall outside this new grid of digital highways, however, are peripheralized. This regional grid represents a reconstitution of the concept of region. Far from neutralizing geography, the regional grid is likely to be embedded in conventional forms of communications infrastructure—notably, rapid rail and highways connecting to airports. Ironically perhaps, conventional infrastructure is likely to maximize the economic benefits derived from telematics. I think this is an important issue that has been lost somewhat in discussions about the neutralization of geography through telematics.

Third, we are seeing the formation of a transterritorial center constituted via telematics and intense economic transactions (Sassen 1991). The most powerful of these new geographies of centrality at the interurban level binds the major international financial and business centers: New York, London, Tokyo, Paris, Frankfurt, Zurich, Amsterdam, Los Angeles, Sydney, and Hong Kong.[3] But this geography now also includes cities such as São Paulo and Mexico City. The intensity of transactions among these cities, particularly through the financial markets, trade in services, and investment has increased sharply, as have the orders of magnitude involved.[4] At the same time, there has been a sharpening inequality in the concentration of strategic resources and activities between each of these cities and others in the same country.[5] For instance, Paris now concentrates a larger share of leading economic sectors and wealth in France than it did fifteen years ago, whereas Marseilles, once a major economic hub, has lost share and is suffering severe decline.

Fourth, new forms of centrality are being constituted in electronically generated spaces. Electronic space is often considered purely technological and in that sense a space of innocence. But if we consider, for instance, that strategic components of the financial industry operate there we can see that it is a space where profits are produced and power is thereby constituted. Insofar as these technologies strengthen the profit-making capability of finance and make possible the hypermobility of finance capital, they also contribute to the often devastating impacts of the ascendance of finance on other industries, on particular sectors of the population, and on whole economies. Cyberspace, like any other space, can be inscribed in a multiplicity of ways—some benevolent or enlightening but others not (see Sassen 1994). I argue that structures for economic power are being built in electronic space and that their highly complex configurations contain points of coordination and centralization.

These four forms of centrality are not necessarily mutually exclusive. On the contrary, a good share of the agglomeration of specialized service functions in cities represents the nodes in larger transnational networks that correspond to the second, third, and/or fourth forms of centrality. This global grid of linkages and nodes constitutes a new geography of centrality upon which states can act, but only as international actors in an interstate effort.

Spatial Concentration: Some Empirical Referents

One of the clearest forms of centrality is represented by the unexpected continued concentration of financial and corporate service functions in major cities in highly developed countries and the growing specialization of those centers in financial functions (Drennan 1992; Amin and Thrift 1992; Sassen 1991; *Le Débat* 1994). It represents in many ways a paradox at a time when the development of telematics maximizes the potential for geographic dispersal, leading experts to predict the demise of cities as economic units.[6]

The case of Toronto, a city whose financial district was built up only in recent years, allows us to see to what extent the pressure toward physical concentration is embedded in an economic dynamic rather than simply being the consequence of having inherited a built infrastructure from the past, as was perhaps the case in older centers such as London or New York. It also shows that certain industries are subject to the pressure toward spatial concentration—notably, finance and its sister industries (Gad 1991; Todd 1995). We see similar growth in the financial concentration and specialization of the downtowns of such cities as Frankfurt and Zurich (Hitz et al. 1995).

The case of Sydney illuminates the interaction of a vast, continental economic scale and pressures toward spatial concentration. Rather than strengthening the multipolarity of the Australian urban system, the developments of the 1980s—increased internationalization of the Australian economy; sharp increases in foreign investment; and a strong shift toward finance, real estate, and producer services— contributed to a greater concentration of major economic activities and actors in Sydney. Melbourne, long the center of commercial activity and wealth in Australia, lost a share of such activities and actors (Daly and Stimson 1992; O'Connor 1995).

Finally, one might have expected that the growing number of financial centers now integrated into the global markets would have reduced the extent of concentration of financial activity in the top centers. One would further expect this given the immense increases in the global volume of transactions.[7] Yet the levels of concentration remain unchanged in the face of massive transformations in the financial industry and in the technological infrastructure this industry depends on.[8] Included in this trend toward ongoing concentration is the major move by large German banks to acquire and set up operations in London, now sometimes referred to as London am Main.

Service Production and Service Intensity:
Their Impact on Centrality

What contributes to the importance of centrality in economic systems with immense technological capacities for global dispersal to the most advantageous sites? It is precisely the combination of the spatial dispersal of numerous economic activities and telematic global integration that has influenced a strategic role for major cities in the current phase of the world economy (Sassen 1991). Economic globalization has raised the scale and complexity of transactions, thereby feeding the growth of central functions (e.g., top-level management, planning, coordination). Some of these central functions are embedded in corporate headquarters, but others are "produced" by specialized corporate service firms.

A second process, one that intersects only partly with globalization, has given cities a strategic economic function. This process is the growth of service intensity in the organization of all industries (Sassen 1991: chap. 5; 1994: chap. 4).[9] It has contributed to massive growth in the demand for services by firms in all industries, from mining and manufacturing to finance and consumer services.[10] Cities are key sites for the production of services for firms. Hence, the increase in service intensity in the organization of all industries has had a significant growth effect on cities since the 1980s.[11]

Both processes—the growth of central functions and of service intensity in economic organization—are also evident at smaller geographic scales and lower orders of complexity than the global economy. Firms that operate regionally need not negotiate the complexities of international borders and the regulations of different countries. Yet they are still faced with a regionally dispersed network of operations that requires centralized control and servicing. Many of these central functions, or components of them, are not produced in-house but are bought from specialized corporate service firms. Similarly, the growing service intensity in the organization of all industries has contributed to services growth in cities at different levels of a nation's urban system. Some of these cities cater to regional or subnational markets, others cater to national markets, and yet others cater to global markets. There is a large literature in the United States on the spatial distribution of top-level corporate functions and corporate services across the urban system; though there are theoretical and empirical disagreements, most studies show considerable growth of these activities in the 1980s at various levels of the urban system (Noyelle and Stanback 1984; Wheeler 1986; Holloway and Wheeler 1991; Lyons and Salmon 1995; Ward 1994). In the case of cities that are major international business centers, the scale, power, and profit levels of this new core of economic activities are vast.[12] In this context, globalization becomes a question of scale and added complexity in a process that is also taking place at lower levels of the urban hierarchy and with a national or regional orientation rather than a global one.

The production process in advanced corporate services benefits from proximity to other specialized services. This is especially the case in the leading and most innovative sectors of these industries. Complexity and innovation often require multiple highly specialized inputs from several industries. The production of a financial instrument, for example, requires inputs from accounting, advertising, legal expertise, economic consulting, public relations, designers, and printers. The particular characteristics of production of these services, especially those involved in complex and innovative operations, explain their pronounced concentration in major cities. Producer services, unlike other types of services, are not necessarily dependent on spatial proximity to the consumers (i.e., firms) served. Rather, economies occur in such specialized firms when they locate close to others that produce key inputs or whose proximity makes possible joint production of certain service offerings. The accounting firm can service its clients at a distance, but the nature of its service depends on proximity to specialists such as lawyers and programmers. Face-to-face communication is often part of a production process that requires multiple simultaneous inputs and feedbacks. At the current stage of technical development, immediate and simultaneous access to the pertinent experts is still the most effective way, especially when dealing with a highly complex product. The concentration of the most advanced telecommunications and computer network facilities in major cities is a key factor in what I refer to as the production process of these industries.[13] The acceleration of economic transactions and the premium put on time have also created new forces for agglomeration. Routine operations can easily be dispersed, but where time is of the essence, as it is today in many of the leading sectors of these industries, the benefits of agglomeration are still extremely high.

There is a strong suggestion in all of this that the agglomeration of the leading sectors of producer services in major cities actually constitutes a production complex. This producer services complex is intimately connected to the world of corporate headquarters, often thought of as forming a joint headquarters–corporate services complex. But we need to distinguish the two. Although headquarters still tend to be disproportionately concentrated in cities, many have moved out over the last two decades. Headquarters can indeed locate outside cities, but they need a producer services complex somewhere to buy or contract for the needed specialized services and financing. Further, headquarters of firms with very high overseas activity or in highly innovative and complex lines of business tend to locate in major cities. In brief, firms in more routinized lines of activity, with predominantly regional or national markets, appear to be increasingly free to move or install their headquarters outside cities. Firms in highly competitive and innovative lines of activity and/or with a strong world market orientation appear to benefit from being located at the center of major international business centers, no matter how high the costs.

Both types of firms, however, need a corporate services complex to be located somewhere. Where this complex is located is probably increasingly unimportant from the perspective of many, though not all, headquarters. From the perspective of producer services firms, such a specialized complex is most likely to be in a city rather than, for example, a suburban office park. The latter will be the site for producer services firms but not for a services complex. And only such a complex is capable of handling the most advanced and complicated corporate demands.

In brief, the combination of spatial dispersal and global integration has contributed to a strategic role for certain types of places in the current phase of the world economy. This is most evident with major cities. Beyond their sometimes long history as centers for world trade and banking, such cities now function as command points in the organization of the world economy; as key locations and marketplaces for the leading industries of this period — finance and corporate services; and as sites for the production of these services.[14] Both growing service intensity and globalization rely on and are shaped by the new information technologies. The growing service intensity in economic organization generally and the specific conditions under which information technologies are available combine to make cities once again a strategic "production" site, a role they had lost when large-scale mass manufacturing became the dominant economic sector.

It is through these information-based production processes that centrality is constituted. But centrality emerges as significant precisely because it is a function of the vast global network of operations of the leading industries in the current phase of globalization. And the transnational character of this network has rendered national states less capable of regulating key sectors of their economies.

THE STATE AND THE NEW SPACE ECONOMY

The analysis just presented points to a space economy for major new transnational economic processes that diverges in significant ways from the global/national duality presupposed in much analysis of the global economy.[15] The shrinking capacity of the state to regulate these industries cannot be explained simply by the fact that they operate in the global economy rather than in the national economy. The spatial organization of the leading information industries makes it clear that these are not mutually exclusive spaces. Rather, the globalization of finance and corporate services is embedded in a grid of strategic sites that are partly embedded in national territories. Further, firms that operate globally still require the guarantees of rights of property and contract they expect within their national territories.

The analysis of these industries also makes it clear that insofar as transnationalization and deregulation have been a key to their growth and distinct contemporary character they have reduced the regulatory role held by the national state until quite recently. This is illustrated by the worldwide pressure experienced by national states to deregulate their financial markets to allow integration into the global markets. London saw its "big bang" of 1984 and Paris saw "le petit bang" a few years later under governments as diverse as the Tories in England and the Socialists in France.[16] The declining regulatory role of national states can be quite different between highly developed countries and less developed countries. This is illustrated by the case of the December 1994 Mexican crisis and the different roles played by the U.S. and Mexican governments. Perhaps the most telling aspect of this crisis was the extent to which the solution was conceived in financial terms and engineered by the U.S. secretary of the treasury rather than the secretary of state, as would have been the case twenty years ago.[17] It signals the extent to which the state itself has been transformed by its participation in the implementation of globalization and by the pressures of the globalization agenda. (See Chapters 1, 5, and 10.)

Finally, advanced information industries make it clear that unlike in the prior eras of the world economy, the current forms of globalization do not necessarily contribute to reproduce or strengthen the interstate system. International finance especially reveals the extent to which the forms of internationalization evident in the last two decades have produced regulatory voids that lie beyond not only states but also the interstate system. This can be illustrated with the case of the foreign currency markets, which have reached orders of magnitude that have weakened the regulatory role of central bankers (notably, the impact of concerted international action on foreign exchange rates).

I will examine these issues in greater detail to provide a more qualified understanding of the role played by the state in the current era of globalization than that contained in the widespread proposition about the declining significance of the state in a global economy.

The Role of the State in New Transnational Regimes

Some of the features of economic globalization associated with the declining regulatory role of the state are by now well known. Globalization has contributed to a massive push toward deregulation across the board in many of the highly developed countries. Aman Jr. (1995) notes that though not all industries in a nation are equally subject to intense global competition, the existence of such competition in general contributes to an overall political context that encourages domestic regulatory reform in all industries: "Political movements and regulatory trends do not tend to discriminate among industries once the momentum for certain reforms is under way" (Aman Jr. 1995: 433).[18] The impact of global competition on the domestic politics of regulation goes well beyond the industries in which this competition is most intense. Economic globalization pushes local jurisdictions into competition for industries that operate nationally and/or transnationally. The possibility of moving from one jurisdiction to another with lower regulatory demands puts downward pressures on regulations across all jurisdictions—the quintessential race to the bottom. Whole countries are now engaged in this competition. (For some recent formulations in what is a vast literature, see Chapter 4; Sklair 1991; Bonacich et al. 1994; *Social Justice* 1993; Bose and Acosta-Belen 1995; *Competition and Change* 1995.)

Globalization was a key feature of the expansion of finance and the advanced corporate services, not simply a matter of raising profits and lowering costs, as with many manufacturing industries. Reducing the existing regulatory role of states was the necessary mechanism. We have seen country after country in Latin America and Asia deregulate stock and other financial markets to become integrated into the global financial market. The competing jurisdictions in this case have typically been the capital cities, as these concentrate the existing banking, financial, and top-level services sectors. (There are exceptions, such as São Paulo, which is Brazil's leading financial center but not the country's capital.) There clearly are also non-geographic jurisdictions, such as markets. However, as we examined in the first section, key aspects of many of the global financial markets are embedded in places through the material infrastructure and the work processes they require. These places are, again, mostly leading business centers of a country. For instance, the International Banking Facilities in the United States (sort of free zones for finance) are almost all located in New York City, though they don't necessarily have to be because such facilities are not a geographic concept.

One key property of the current era is that the more that national states implement deregulation to raise the competitiveness of their nations and localities within them, the more they contribute to strengthen transnational networks and actors. Current regulatory frameworks in probably most of the highly developed countries were not designed to handle this. One result is that while states may still be extremely (if not the most) powerful actors in the world scene, their role and power are no longer as clear as in earlier eras. This is especially true today, when deregulation and transnationalization are key characteristics of the space economy of the leading information industries and globalization seems to be driven by multinational companies without strong national attachment or identification.

The globalization and deregulation of finance show that it is not simply a matter of a space economy extending beyond a national realm. What deregulation in finance makes clear is that it has had the effect of partly denationalizing national territory precisely because of the pronounced globalization of this industry (Sassen 1991: pt. 1; 1996). This can be illustrated with the example of the International Banking Facilities in the United States.

Yet, firms operating transnationally need to ensure the functions traditionally exercised by the state in the national realm of the economy—notably, guaranteeing property rights and contracts (cf. Chapters 1, 5, and 10). Insofar as economic globalization extends the economy beyond the boundaries of the nation-state and hence its sovereignty, this guarantee would appear to be threatened.

In fact, globalization has been accompanied by the creation of new legal regimes and practices and the expansion and renovation of some older forms that bypass national legal systems. We are seeing the formation of transnational legal regimes and their penetration into national fields hitherto closed (see e.g., Trubek et al. 1993; Dezalay and Garth 1995). Further, national legal fields are becoming more internationalized in some of the major developed economies. Some of the old divisions between the national and the global are becoming weaker and, to some extent, neutralized.

But these transnational regimes are assuming a specific form, one wherein the states of the highly developed countries play a strategic geopolitical role. The hegemony of neoliberal concepts of economic relations, with its strong emphasis on markets, deregulation, and free international trade, influenced policy in the 1980s in the United States and the UK and now increasingly also in continental Europe. This has contributed to the formation of transnational legal regimes that are centered in Western economic concepts.[19] Dezalay and Garth (1995) note that the "international" is itself constituted largely from competition among national approaches. Thus the international emerges as a site for regulatory competition among essentially national approaches, whatever the issue—environmental protection, constitutionalism, human rights, and so on (Charny 1991; Trachtman 1993). From this perspective, the "international" or the "transnational" has recently become a form of Americanization. The most widely recognized instance of this is of course the notion of a global culture that is profoundly influenced by U.S. popular culture. Though less widely recognized and more difficult to specify, this has also become very clear in international finance and in the advanced corporate services, a subject we return to later. Through the International Monetary Fund (IMF) and the International Bank for Reconstruction and Development (IBRD), as well as the General Agreement on Tariffs and Trade (GATT), this vision has spread to the developing world.

The competition among national legal systems or approaches is particularly evident in business law, where the Anglo-American model of the business enterprise and merchant competition is beginning to replace the Continental model of legal artisans and corporatist control over the profession (Dezalay 1992; see also Carrez 1991; Sinclair 1994). This holds even for international commercial arbitration, a system of private justice with deep roots in the Continental tradition, especially the French and Swiss traditions, which nonetheless is becoming increasingly Americanized.

Globalization and government deregulation have not meant the absence of regulatory regimes and institutions for the governance of international economic relations. Among the most important such elements in the private sector today are international commercial arbitration and the variety of institutions that fulfill rating and advisory functions essential for the operation of the global economy. Over the past twenty years, international commercial arbitration has been transformed and institutionalized as the leading contractual method for the resolution of transnational commercial disputes (Dezalay and Garth 1995; Aksen 1990). In a major study on international commercial arbitration (summarized in Dezalay and Garth 1995). Dezalay and Garth conclude that it is a delocalized and decentralized market for the administration of international commercial disputes, connected by more or less powerful institutions and individuals who are both competitive and complementary.[20] It is in this regard far from a unitary system of justice "organized perhaps around one great *lex mercatoria*— that might have been envisioned by some of the pioneering idealists of law" (Dezalay and Garth 1995; see also Carbonneau 1990).[21]

The enormous growth of arbitration over the last decade arising out of the globalization of economic activity has produced sharp competition for the arbitration business. Indeed, it has become big legal business (Salacuse 1991). Dezalay and Garth (1995) found that multinational legal firms further sharpen the competition since they have the capacity to forum shop among institutions, sets of rules, laws, and arbitrators. The large English and U.S. law firms have used their power in the international business world to impose their conception of arbitration and more largely of the practice of law.[22]

This is well illustrated by the case of France. French firms rank among the top providers of information services and industrial engineering services in Europe and have a strong though not outstanding position in financial and insurance services. But France has found itself at an increasing disadvantage in legal and accounting services. French law firms are at a particular disadvantage given the difference between their legal system (the Napoleonic Code) and Anglo-American law in a context where the latter dominates in international transactions. Foreign firms with offices in Paris dominate the servicing of the legal needs of firms operating internationally, both French and foreign firms operating out of France (Carrez 1991).

Another instance of a private regulatory system is represented by debt security or bond rating agencies, which have come to play an increasingly important role in the global economy. In his study of credit rating processes, Sinclair (1994) found that these agencies function as mechanisms of "governance without government." He found that they have leverage because of their distinct gatekeeping functions with regard to investment funds sought by corporations and governments. He posits that they can be seen as a significant force in the operation and expansion of the global economy. As with business law, the U.S. agencies have expanded their influence overseas (see generally Salacuse 1991; Aksen 1990). Sinclair (1994: 150) notes that ten years ago Moody's and Standard & Poor's had no analysts outside the United States; by 1993 they each had about one hundred, in Europe, Japan, and Australia.

These and other such transnational institutions and regimes raise questions about the relation between state sovereignty and the governance of global economic processes. International commercial arbitration is basically a private justice system, and credit rating agencies are private gatekeeping systems. Along with other such institutions they have emerged as important governance mechanisms whose authority is not centered in the state. Yet they contribute to maintaining order at the top, one could say. Does the ascendance of such institutions and regimes entail a decline in state sovereignty?

The State Reconfigured

In many ways the state is involved in this emerging transnational governance system. But it has itself undergone transformation and has participated in legitimating a new doctrine about its own role in the economy (see Chapters 2 and 5). Central to this new doctrine is a growing consensus among states to further the growth and strength of the global economy. This is illustrated by some of the aspects of the December 1994 crisis in Mexico discussed earlier (see n. 17).

Many governments now see their responsibilities going beyond foreign policy as traditionally conceptualized and extending into world trade, the global environment, and global economic stability (Aman Jr. 1995: 437). This participation of the state in the international arena is an extremely multifaceted and complex matter, which cannot be adequately addressed here. Some of these roles in the international arena can be seen as benevolent (e.g., in matters concerning the global environment); others, hardly so (e.g., the role of the governments of the highly developed countries, particularly the United States, in pushing for worldwide market reform and privatization).

Confining the analysis here to the economic arena, the international role of the state has been read in rather diverse manners, not necessarily mutually exclusive. For instance, according to some (see Chapter 5), much of this new role of states in the global economy is dominated by a furthering of a broad neoliberal conception to the point that it represents a constitutionalizing of this neoliberal project. Others emphasize that effective international participation by national governments can contribute to the strengthening of the rule of law at the global level (Aman Jr. 1995; Young 1989; Rosenau 1992). Yet others see participation of the state in international systems (e.g., multilateral agreements like GATT) as a loss of sovereignty because national governments have to adjust some of their policies to international standards.[23]

An important question running through these different interpretations is whether the new transnational regimes and institutions are creating systems that strengthen the claims of certain actors (e.g., corporations, the large multinational legal firms) and correspondingly weaken the position of smaller players and states. Ruggie (1993: 143) has pointed out that the issue is not whether such new institutions and major economic actors will substitute national states but rather that there may be the possibility of major changes: "Global markets and transnationalized corporate structures . . . are not in the business of replacing states," yet they can have the potential for producing fundamental change in the system of states.

What matters for the purposes of this chapter is that global capital has made claims on national states and these have responded through the production of new forms of legality. The new geography of centrality had to be produced, both in terms of the practices of corporate actors and the requisite infrastructure and in terms of the work of the state in producing new legal regimes. Representations that characterize the national state as simply losing significance fail to capture this very important dimension, reducing what is happening to a function of the global/national duality—what one wins, the other loses. I view deregulation not simply as a loss of control by the state but as a crucial mechanism to negotiate the juxtaposition of the global and the national.

There are two distinct issues here. One is the formation of new legal regimes that negotiate between national sovereignty and the transnational practices of corporate economic actors. The other is the particular content of this new regime, one that contributes to strengthening the advantages of certain types of economic actors and to weakening those of others. That is to say, one could posit two distinct issues regarding governance. One is centered on the effort to create viable systems of coordination/order among the powerful economic actors now operating globally, such as international commercial arbitration and credit rating agencies discussed in the previous section. A second issue focuses on equity and distributive questions in the context of a globally integrated economic system with immense inequalities in the profit-making capacities of firms and in the earnings capacities of households. Furthermore, this is a global economic system increasingly dominated by finance to the point where the global financial markets can now pressure national governments to follow certain policies and not others. Even as supportive an organ as *The Economist* recently complained that perhaps the international financial markets are getting too much power to discipline national governments. To whom are the major economic actors and the global financial markets accountable? (See Sassen 1996 for a fuller discussion.)

The international role of the state in the global economic arena has involved to a large extent furthering deregulation, strengthening markets, and pushing for privatization. By their very nature these measures easily lead to the position that such international participation does indeed entail a shrinking role of the state and a loss of sovereignty. But does it have to be this way? The participation of national states in the global environmental arena has led frequently to the signing of multilateral agreements aimed at supporting measures that protect the environment. This is not to say that they are effective, but they create a framework that legitimates both the international pursuit of a common good and the role of national states in that pursuit (Rosenau 1992; Young 1989). The role of the state in the international economic arena, on the other hand, seems to have been largely confined to pursuing the goal of maximizing the profitability of certain (but not all) economic sectors and actors.[24]

Can national states pursue a broader international economic agenda, one that addresses questions of equity and mechanisms for accountability vis-à-vis the major global economic actors? International cooperation and multinational agreements are on the rise: about one hundred major treaties and agreements on the environment have gone into effect since 1972, though not all remain in force (Birnie and Boyle 1992; Young 1989). Aman Jr. (1995) notes that it is in the interest of the state to play an increasingly active role at the global level (see also Ruggie 1993; Jessop 1989). In the longer term it is more likely that stronger legal regimes will develop on a global basis if the global issues involved have a national regulatory counterpart. Even when such regulatory approaches use the market as a tool for compliance, they can strengthen accountability and the rule of law (nationally and globally). The participation of national states in new international legal regimes of this sort may contribute to the development of transnational frameworks aimed at promoting equity.

A larger theoretical/political question underlying some of these issues has to do with which actors gain legitimacy for governing the global economy and taking over rules and authorities hitherto encased in the national state (see Sassen 1996 for a fuller discussion). There is also a question about the condition of international public law. Do the new emerging systems for governance and the confinement of the role of national states in the global economy to furthering deregulation, markets, and privatization, indicate a decline of international public law (cf. Kennedy 1988; Negri 1995)?

CONCLUSION

The issues discussed in this chapter provide insight into the dynamics of contemporary globalization processes as they materialize in specific places and in new regulatory regimes. A focus on the production process in information industries illuminates the question of place (particularly the kind of place represented by cities) in processes of economic globalization. Specialized services are usually understood in terms of outputs rather than the production process involved. Their characteristics of production allow us to understand the locational concentration of leading sectors in urban centers in the face of globalization, massive increases in the volume of international transactions, and revolutionary changes in technology that neutralize distance. Concentration, then, remains a critical dimension particularly in the leading sectors such as international finance. There is, however, a multiplicity of spatial correlates for this concentration. In this sense we see emerging a new geography of the center, one that can include transterritorial spaces connecting major cities worldwide through specific markets and transactions.

The examination of international finance and its operation in a global grid of strategic places seeks to contribute to an elaboration of a different conception of government regulation and of the sites for regulatory enforcement. The fact that the major economic actors on the global scene have sought to frame their new identities and practices in legal forms, many of them innovations, indicates that there is room for national states to innovate as well. Here I have sought to emphasize the possibility of a new regulatory context illustrated by some of the characteristics of the leading information industries. The components of this new regulatory context are a new transnational economic geography of strategic sites with high concentrations of resources, and a growing internationalization of both national states and the interstate system.

NOTES

The author thanks the Russell Sage Foundation for general support while a visiting scholar there in 1992–1993 and Ms. Vivian Kaufman for her invaluable assistance in preparing this paper.
1. There is a set of issues around the question of method that cannot be addressed here. See, for instance, the work of Smith and Timberlake (1995) on using network analysis (particularly the concept of centrality) to study cities in the global economy. (See also Sassen 1994: chap. 5, on empirical applications of some of the theorization about global cities.)
2. The second part of the chapter is from a larger project currently under way (see Sassen 1996).
3. In the case of a complex landscape such as Europe's, we see in fact several geographies of centrality—one global and others continental and regional (see Kunzmann and Wegener 1991). A central urban hierarchy connects major cities, many of which in turn play central roles in the wider global system of cities: Paris, London, Frankfurt, Amsterdam, Zurich. These cities are also part of a wider network of European financial/cultural/service capitals (some with only one function and others with several of these functions) that articulate the European region and are somewhat less oriented to the global economy than Paris, Frankfurt, or London. And then there are several geographies of marginality: the east-west divide and the north-south divide across Europe as well as newer divisions. In Eastern Europe, certain cities and regions (notably, Budapest) are rather attractive for purposes of investment, both European and non-European, whereas others will increasingly fall behind (notably, Romania, Yugoslavia, and Albania). We see a similar differentiation in the south of Europe: Madrid, Barcelona, and Milan are gaining in the new European hierarchy; Naples, Rome, and Marseilles are not.
4. The pronounced orientation to the world markets evident in such cities raises questions about the articulation with their nation-states, their regions, and the larg-

er economic and social structure in such cities. Cities have typically been deeply embedded in the economies of their region, indeed often reflecting the characteristics of the latter. But cities that are strategic sites in the global economy tend, in part, to disconnect from their region. This conflicts with a key proposition in traditional scholarship about urban systems—namely, that these systems promote the territorial integration of regional and national economies.

5. Though at a different order of magnitude, these trends also became evident during the late 1980s in a number of major cities in the developing world that have become integrated into various world markets. São Paulo, Buenos Aires, Bangkok, Taipei, and Mexico City are only a few examples (see generally Sassen 1994; Armstrong and McGee 1985; Simon 1995; Friedman 1995; Kowarick and Campanario 1986; Grosfoguel 1995). Many of the major cities in the developing world also have seen a new urban core fed by the deregulation of financial markets, an ascendance of finance and specialized services, and integration into the world markets. The opening of stock markets to foreign investors and the privatization of what were once public sector firms have been crucial institutional arenas for this articulation. Given the vast size of some of these cities, the impact of this new core on the broader city is not always as evident as in central London or Frankfurt, but the transformation is still very real.

6. Globalization, deregulation (an essential ingredient for globalization), and securitization have been key to this mobility—in the context of massive advances in telecommunications and electronic networks. One result is growing competition among centers for hypermobile financial activity. In my view there has been an overemphasis on competition in general and in specialized accounts on this subject. As I have argued elsewhere (Sassen 1991: chap. 7), there is also a functional division of labor among various major financial centers. In that sense we can think of a transnational system with multiple locations.

7. For example, international bank lending grew from U.S. $1.89 trillion in 1980 to U.S. $6.24 trillion in 1991—a fivefold increase in a mere ten years. New York, London, and Tokyo accounted for 42 percent of all such international lending in 1980 and for 41 percent in 1991, according to data from the Bank of International Settlements, the leading institution worldwide in charge of overseeing banking activity. There were compositional changes: Japan's share rose from 6.2 percent to 15.1 percent, and the UK's share fell from 26.2 percent to 16.3 percent; the U.S. share remained constant. All increased in absolute terms. Beyond these three countries, Switzerland, France, Germany, and Luxembourg bring the total share of the top centers to 64 percent in 1991, which is just about the same share these countries had in 1980. One city, Chicago, dominates the world's trading in futures, accounting for 60 percent of worldwide contracts in options and futures in 1991.

8. Along these lines, it is worth noting that much of the discussion around the formation of a single European market and financial system has raised the possibility, and even the need if it is to be competitive, of centralizing financial functions and capital in a limited number of cities rather than maintaining the current structure in which each country has a financial center.

9. Using input-output tables from 1972 to 1987, Sassen and Orlow (1995) examined the use of service-based commodities in eleven four-digit Standard Industrial Classification (SIC) industries (ranging from wholesale trade to mining). The service-based industries examined as the intermediate commodity input, down to the four-digit SIC code, included, among others, finance and insurance and business services. For the sake of simplicity, the following figures cover the 1972–1982 period only because after this date the comparison becomes too complicated to describe in a footnote. Of all the industry combinations studied, the level of service inputs from the finance industry was most prominent (tripling from 1972 to 1982) in

banking, wholesale trade, and insurance. The use of business services increased sharpest in the following industry groups: motor vehicles and equipment, insurance carriers, wholesale trade, and banking. The use of business services in banking more than tripled from 1972 to 1982. (See Sassen and Orlow 1995 for a full description; also see Sassen 1996.)

10. The expansion of producer services is a central feature of current growth in developed countries. In country after country we see a decline or slowdown in manufacturing alongside sharp growth in producer services. Whether in manufacturing or in warehousing, firms use more legal, financial, advertising, consulting, and accounting services. These services can be seen as part of the supply capacity of an economy because they facilitate adjustments to changing economic circumstances; they are part of a broader intermediary space of economic activity. (See Delaunay and Gadrey 1987; Castells 1989; UN 1991b; UNCTAD 1993; Daniels 1991.)

11. Though disproportionately concentrated in the largest cities, producer services are actually growing at faster rates at the national level in most developed economies. The crucial process feeding the growth of producer services is the increasing use of service inputs by firms in all industries. Households have also raised their consumption of services, either directly (e.g., the growing use of accountants for preparation of tax returns) or indirectly via the reorganization of consumer industries (e.g., buying flowers or dinner from franchises or chains rather than from self-standing and privately owned mom-and-pop shops). Services directly bought by consumers tend to be located wherever population is concentrated. In that regard they are far less concentrated than producer services, especially those catering to top firms. The demand by households for specialized services, from accounting to architectural services, may be a key factor contributing to the growth of these services at the national level.

12. This suggests that we are seeing the formation of a new urban economy in these major cities. This is so in at least two regards. First, even though these cities have long been centers for business and finance, since the late 1970s there have been dramatic changes in the structure of the business and financial sectors, as well as sharp increases in the overall magnitude of these sectors and their weight in the urban economy. Second, the ascendance of the new finance and services complex, particularly international finance, engenders what may be regarded as a new economic regime; that is, although this sector may account for only a fraction of the economy of a city, it imposes itself on that larger economy. Most notably, the possibility for superprofits in finance has the effect of devalorizing manufacturing insofar as the latter cannot generate the superprofits typical in much financial activity. This is not to say that everything in the economy of these cities has changed.

13. The telecommunications infrastructure also contributes to concentration of leading sectors in major cities. Long-distance communications systems increasingly use fiber-optic wires. These have several advantages over traditional copper wire: large carrying capacity, high speed, more security, and higher signal strength. Fiber systems tend to connect major communications hubs because they are not easily spliced and hence are not desirable for connecting multiple lateral sites. Fiber systems tend to be installed along existing rights of way, whether rail, water, or highway (Moss 1986, 1991). The growing use of fiber-optic systems thus tends to strengthen the major existing telecommunication concentrations and therefore the existing hierarchies.

14. The implantation of global processes and markets has meant that the internationalized sector of the economy has expanded sharply and has imposed a new valorization dynamic—that is, a new set of criteria for valuing or pricing various economic activities and outcomes. This has had devastating effects on large sectors of the urban economy (Sassen 1991). High prices and profit levels in the international-

ized sector and its ancillary activities, such as top-of-the-line restaurants and hotels, have made it increasingly difficult for other sectors to compete for space and investments. Many of these other sectors have experienced considerable downgrading and/or displacement, as, for example, neighborhood shops tailored to local needs are replaced by upscale boutiques and restaurants catering to new high-income urban elites.

15. Various scholars are working along these lines in a variety of fields. See, for example, Mazlish and Buultjens (1993); Gereffi and Korzeniewicz 1990; Castells (1989); Smith and Timberlake (1995); Beneria (1989); *Competition and Change* (1995).

16. Globalization restricts the range of regulatory options of national governments, as these and many other cases (notably, the Mexican crisis) illustrate. Aman Jr. (1995) shows how a global perspective on domestic regulatory politics helps explain the absence of radical differences in the regulatory outcomes of different U.S. administrations over the last fifteen years. The pressures of global competition, the nature of corporate entities involved, and domestic political pressures to minimize costs and maximize flexibility militate in favor of new, more market-oriented forms of regulatory reform.

17. Mexico's crisis was defined rather generally in international political and business circles, as well as in much of the press, as the loss of confidence by the global financial markets in the Mexican economy and government leadership of that economy. The U.S. government defined it as a global economic security issue, one with direct impact on the U.S. economy, and it pushed hard to get the U.S. legislature and other governments in the highly developed countries to come to Mexico's aid. It opted for a financial solution, an aid package that would allow the Mexican government to pay its obligations to foreign investors and thereby restore confidence in the Mexican economy by foreign (and national) investors. A financial response to this crisis was but one of several potential choices. For instance, there could have been an emphasis on promoting manufacturing growth and protecting small businesses and small homeowners from the bankruptcies now faced by many. The U.S. government could also have exhorted the Mexican government to give up on restoring confidence in the global financial markets and to focus on the production of real value added in the Mexican economy. Furthermore, as mentioned in the text, this matter was handled not by the secretary of state but by the secretary of the treasury, who had been the so-called dean of Wall Street. There are two rather important novel elements here: that Treasury should have handled this international crisis and that the secretary of that agency was a former top partner at Goldman Sachs, one of the leading global financial firms. The point here involves not the potential for corruption but rather a question of what is seen as desirable economically.

18. This spread effect can also work in the opposite regulatory direction, as was the case with reform in the New Deal era (see Hawley 1969).

19. This hegemony has not passed unnoticed and is engendering considerable debate. For instance, a well-known issue that is emerging as significant in view of the spread of Western legal concepts is the critical examination of the philosophical premises about authorship and property that define the legal arena in the West (see, e.g., Coombe 1993).

20. International commercial arbitration represents one mechanism for business disputing. The larger system includes arbitration controlled by courts, arbitration that is parallel to courts, and various court and out-of-court possibilities such as mediation.

21. Anglo-American practitioners tend not to support the Continental, highly academic notion of a *lex mercatoria* (see Carbonneau 1990). The so-called *lex mercatoria* was conceived by many as a return to an international law of business inde-

pendent of national laws (Carbonneau 1990). Insofar as these practitioners are Americanizing the field, they are moving it further away from academic law and the *lex mercatoria*.

22. There was a time when the International Chamber of Commerce (ICC), located in Paris, was the definitive center of the field of international commercial arbitration, and it was dominated by Continental jurists of great academic reputations. This has changed over the last ten years with the ascendance of the Anglo-American law firms. But Dezalay and Garth (1995) note that although the ICC has lost its quasi-monopoly position, it remains the central institution for international commercial arbitration. It is a sort of UN of commerce and international arbitration, with members from about one hundred countries, national committees in sixty countries, and a powerful image worldwide of neutrality and legitimacy. It has double sponsorship in the form of a major business group and a group of learned jurists who were the founding fathers. ICC also has a close relation to the state in the form of support from the French government, the public/private careers of key figures in the arbitration community, and other such features. Thus the ICC is one of the key places where the politics of arbitration gets elaborated and expressed.

23. Agreements such as GATT and institutions such as the World Trade Organization (WTO) are seen by some sectors in the United States as a restriction on national sovereignty. For instance, there is concern that the WTO will be used to enforce GATT trade regulations to the point of overturning federal, state, and local laws since the WTO places the principle of free trade above all other considerations. This is then seen as jeopardizing a nation's right to enact its own consumer, labor, and environmental laws.

24. Many who supported GATT did not like the WTO because they did not like the idea of binding the United States to an international dispute resolution tribunal not fully controlled by the United States; they objected to the regulatory aspects of the WTO.

Gary Gereffi 4

The Elusive Last Lap in the Quest for Developed-Country Status

In the 1950s and 1960s, the world economy was an aggregation of reasonably distinct domestic economies. The production process tended to be organized within national boundaries. International trade consisted, to a large degree, of raw materials flowing from the periphery to the industrialized core of the world economy, while manufactured exports were sent by U.S., European, and Japanese firms from their home bases to all corners of the globe. Direct foreign investment in manufacturing emerged as a response to the protectionist policies implemented by core and peripheral nations alike that wished to diminish the foreign exchange drain of an excessive reliance on imports and to augment the employment benefits from locally based production.

Since the 1960s, however, the world economy has undergone a fundamental shift toward an integrated and coordinated global division of labor in production and trade. Today the most dynamic industries are organized in transnational production systems. There are new patterns of specialization between countries involving the fragmentation and geographic relocation of many manufacturing processes on a global scale in ways that slice through national boundaries. As almost every factor of production—money, technology, information, and goods—moves effortlessly across borders, the very idea of distinct U.S., Japanese, or German economies is virtually meaningless. In an era where products consisting of many components are made in a wide variety of countries, what is an "American" car, a "Japanese" computer, a "Korean" microwave oven, or a "German" camera? Corporations, capital, products, and technology are becoming increasingly disconnected from their home nations as investors, manufacturers, traders, and buyers simultaneously scour the globe for profitable opportunities.

This chapter focuses on the main features of economic globalization, as well as its consequences for Third World development. The central argument is that Third World progress is uneven across as well as within regions; further success will require the adoption of new development strategies that emphasize the creation of a local institutional environment conducive to

53

technological upgrading and integrated industrial production. Given the emphasis on export-oriented development in the 1980s and 1990s, it is especially important to understand the nature of the global production systems that shape the Third World's insertion into the international economy. While transnational corporations have been a prominent feature of the Third World's industrial landscape since the 1950s, many of today's dynamic export industries are controlled by large retailers and brand-named designers in core countries, which in the past couple of decades have given the lion's share of their orders to overseas suppliers concentrated in East and Southeast Asia. Other areas of the Third World have been less successful, however, in exploiting the backward and forward linkages inherent in this type of export activity. The development options for Third World countries thus depend to a significant degree on the kinds of export roles they assume in the global economy and their ability to advance to more sophisticated, high-value industrial niches.

The structure of the chapter is as follows. First, the current global manufacturing system is described with reference to recent production and trade trends in principal regions of the Third World. Second, the debate over Third World development strategies is assessed, with an emphasis on the need to exploit the synergies between inward- and outward-oriented development. Third, a global-commodity-chains perspective is introduced to reconceptualize the linkages across industrial sectors in the world economy. A distinction is drawn between producer-driven and buyer-driven chains, which represent alternative modes of organizing international industries. Triangle manufacturing is highlighted, along with several other mechanisms used to sustain Third World exports in the face of growing economic competition and political uncertainty. Fourth, several Third World strategies for "moving up" in the global economy are identified: government policies to increase productivity; new relations with foreign and domestic capital; and linkages with regional economic blocs. These options are evaluated in terms of their implications for integrated development and improved welfare in the Third World.

THE CONTEMPORARY ERA OF ECONOMIC GLOBALIZATION

Modern industrialization is the result of an integrated system of global trade and production. Open international trade has encouraged nations to specialize in different branches of manufacturing and even in different stages of production within a specific industry. This process, fueled by the explosion of new products and technologies since World War II, has led to the emergence of a global manufacturing system in which production capacity is dispersed to an unprecedented number of developing as well as industrialized countries (Harris 1987). What is novel about this system is not that economic activities are spread across national boundaries per se but rather that international production and trade are globally organized by core corporations that represent both industrial and commercial capital.

Various factors have shaped the globalization of economic activities in recent decades. Innovative technologies in the transportation and communication fields have shrunk both space and time, thus permitting managers to run complex global organizations in an integrated fashion. Major breakthroughs in transport systems include the introduction of commercial jet aircraft, the development of vastly larger oceangoing vessels (superfreighters), and the shift to containerization, which simplifies transshipment from one mode of transport to another (e.g., from sea to land) and increases the speed and security of shipments. Together with global communications systems utilizing satellites, cables, and faxes, these improvements radically reduce the time as well as the cost required to send goods, messages, and people from one part of the world to another. Finally, state-of-the-art information technologies, based primarily on microelectronics (such as CAD/CAM and CNC machinery), give "flexible" automation the potential to manufacture high-quality, diversified goods cheaply and efficiently in small batches as well as large volumes (see Hoffman 1985; Hoffman and Kaplinsky 1988).

The heightened production capability of Third World countries, stimulated not only by low labor costs but also by the improved skill levels and growing productivity of workers, means that the global sourcing of production is becoming a virtual necessity for every corporation that seeks to enhance its competitive position worldwide. The old international division of labor, defined by capital's global search for raw materials and growing markets, has been supplemented by a new international division of labor in which capital chases cheap labor all over the globe. However, low wages are a relative condition. In the last decade, the East Asian newly industrializing countries (NICs) have experienced rapid increases in their domestic wage rates, along with significant exchange rate hikes vis-à-vis the U.S. dollar, which has made their exports more expensive in overseas markets. This has led to a search by manufacturers in these nations for new low-wage export platforms in various parts of Asia, Africa, and Latin America.

A favorable international trading and investment regime was indispensable to the globalization of production in the postwar era. The relatively liberal international trading environment embodied in the provisions of the General Agreement on Tariffs and Trade (GATT) since World War II gave many Third World exporters extensive access to developed-country markets, especially the United States. Throughout the history of the GATT regime, however, a variety of exceptions has been made to the nondiscrimination norm.[1] In particular, protectionist policies in the core countries played a major role in fostering the globalization of economic activity. Tariffs, import quotas, and other restrictive measures were used by the European Community, the United States, and Canada for over thirty years to regulate trade in industries like textiles and apparel, footwear, automobiles, color televisions, and appliances (Yoffie 1983). Attention initially was focused on manufactured exports from Japan and the East Asian NICs. Although the intent of these policies was to protect developed-country firms from a flood of low-cost imports that threatened to disrupt major domestic industries, the result was exactly the opposite: protectionism sharpened the competitive capabilities of Third World manufacturers. Governments in both core and peripheral economies alike thus used state policies to try to improve the position of their countries in global production and trading networks with an emphasis on moving from high-volume to high-value economic activities.

These broad determinants of economic globalization facilitated the interdependence of nations at all levels of development. Three specific trends in the international economy serve to illustrate the nature of the contemporary global manufacturing system in greater detail: the spread of diversified industrialization to large segments of the Third World; the shift toward export-oriented development strategies in peripheral nations, with an emphasis on manufactured exports; and high levels of product specialization in the export profiles of most Third World countries, along with continual industrial upgrading by established exporters among the NICs. These processes of change had an uneven impact across Third World regions.

Worldwide Industrialization

A new global division of labor has changed the pattern of geographic specialization between countries. The classic core–periphery relationship in which the developing nations supplied primary commodities to the industrialized countries in exchange for manufactured goods is outdated. Since the 1950s, the gap between developed and developing countries has been narrowing in terms of industrialization. By the late 1970s, the NICs as a whole not only caught up with but overtook the core countries in their degree of industrialization (Arrighi and Drangel 1986: 54–55). As developed economies shift overwhelmingly toward services, vigorous industrialization has become the hallmark of the periphery. This can be seen by taking a closer look at production and trade patterns within the Third World.

Industry outstripped agriculture as a source of economic growth in all regions of the Third World. From 1965 to 1990, industry's share of gross domestic product (GDP) grew by 13 percentage points in East and Southeast Asia, 10 percent in sub-Saharan Africa, 5 percent in South Asia, and 3 percent in Latin America. Agriculture's share of regional GDP, on the other hand, fell by 16 percentage points in East and Southeast Asia, 11 percent in South Asia, 8 percent in sub-Saharan Africa, and 6 percent in Latin America.[2]

Manufacturing has been the cornerstone of development in East and Southeast Asia, as well as in Latin America. In 1990, 34 percent of the GDP of East and Southeast Asia was in the manufacturing sector, compared with 26 percent for Latin America, 17 percent for South Asia, and only 11 percent for sub-Saharan Africa. The manufacturing sector's share of GDP in some developing nations, such as China (38 percent), Taiwan (34 percent), and South Korea (31 percent), was even higher than Japan's manufacturing/GDP ratio of 29 percent. These differences in performance are corroborated over time as well. The manufacturing sector exhibited much greater dynamism in East and Southeast Asia than anywhere else in the Third World. Between 1965 and 1990, manufacturing increased its share of GDP in these two regions by 10 percentage points, compared with net sectoral growth rates of 4 percent in sub-Saharan Africa and 2 percent in South Asia and Latin America.

Diversified, Export-Oriented Industrialization

World trade expanded nearly thirtyfold in the three decades since 1960. Manufactured goods as a percentage of total world exports increased from 55 percent in 1980 to 75 percent in 1990. Furthermore, the share of the NICs' manufactured exports that can be classified as high tech soared from 2 percent in 1964 to 25 percent in 1985, and those embodying medium levels of technological sophistication rose from 16 percent to 22 percent during this same period (OECD 1988: 24).

Hong Kong and China topped the list of developing country exporters in 1993 with $135 billion and $92 billion in overseas sales, respectively, followed by Taiwan ($85 billion), South Korea ($82 billion), and Singapore ($74 billion). In the next tier, several of the Southeast Asian nations (Malaysia, Thailand, and Indonesia), along with Brazil and Mexico, generated substantial exports, ranging from $30 billion to $47 billion. Exports accounted for 24 percent of GDP in East and Southeast Asia, in contrast to an export/GDP ratio of 23 percent for sub-Saharan Africa, 16 percent for the advanced industrial nations, 11 percent for South Asia, and 10 percent for Latin America and the Caribbean. Saudi Arabia illustrates the declining fortunes of the world's major oil-exporting states. Its 1993 export total of $41 billion, while double that of its nearest Middle East competitor, United Arab Emirates, is less than 40 percent of Saudi Arabia's 1980 exports (Table 4.1).

In exports as in production, manufactures are the chief source of the Third World's dynamism. In 1993, manufactured items constituted well over 90 percent of total exports in three of the four East Asian NICs, and they were approximately three-quarters of all exports for the entirety of Asia. In Brazil and Mexico, the share of manufactures in total exports is over one-half, while in sub-Saharan Africa the manufacturing figure is nearly one-quarter of all exports (Table 4.1). There is a strong "South Africa effect" on sub-Saharan Africa's regional total, however. If we exclude South Africa, which accounts for just 7 percent of sub-Saharan Africa's population but 38

Table 4.1   Growth of Exports in Major World Regions, 1980–1993

Region/Country	Exports (U.S.$ billions)		Exports/GDP (%)		Manufactured Exports/ Total Exports (%)	
	1980	1993	1980	1993	1980	1993
Advanced Industrial Countries	NA	2,896.8	NA	16	NA	82[a]
United States	216.7	464.8	8	7	68	82
Germany	192.9	380.2	24	20	86	90
Japan	129.2	362.2	12	9	96	97
East and Southeast Asia	NA	308.1	NA	24	NA	74[a]
Hong Kong	19.7	135.2	97	150	93	93
Taiwan	19.8	84.7	48	39	91	93
South Korea	17.5	82.2	30	25	90	93
Singapore	19.4	74.0	185	134	54	80
Malaysia	13.8	47.1	58	73	19	65
Thailand	6.5	36.8	19	29	29	72
Indonesia	21.9	33.6	31	23	2	53
Philippines	6.0	11.1	17	21	37	76
China	18.3	91.7	8	22	47	81
South Asia	NA	34.0	NA	11	NA	73[a]
India	6.7	21.6	5	10	59	75
Pakistan	2.6	6.6	12	14	50	85
Bangladesh	0.8	2.3	7	9	66	82
Latin America and Caribbean	NA	135.0	NA	10	NA	38[a]
Brazil	20.1	38.6	10	9	39	60
Mexico	15.3	30.2	9	9	39	53
Argentina	8.0	13.1	6	5	23	32
Sub-Saharan Africa	NA	61.7	NA	23	NA	24[a]
South Africa	26.1	22.9	35	22	54	73
Nigeria	26.0	11.9[a]	29	40[a]	1	2
Kenya	1.3	1.4	22	29	16	29[a]
Tanzania	0.5	0.4	12	20	16	15[a]
Middle East	NA	NA	NA	NA	NA	NA
Saudia Arabia	109.1	40.9	95	34	0	9
United Arab Emirates	20.6	20.5	69	59	NA	4[a]
Iran	13.5	16.7	NA	16	1	4

Sources: World Bank, *World Development Report 1982*, pp. 114–115, 124–125; *World Development Report 1983*, pp. 166–167; *World Development Report 1995*, pp. 166–167, 186–187. The 1980 data for Taiwan are from Republic of China, Council for Economic Planning and Development, *Taiwan Statistical Data Book 1991*, pp. 23, 199, 208, while the 1993 calculation for exports/GDP is from the *Taiwan Statistical Data Book 1994*, pp. 27, 190.
Notes: a. 1992.
GDP=gross domestic product. NA=not available.

percent of its overall exports and 74 percent of its manufactured exports, the manufacturing share in the region's total exports falls from 24 percent to 10 percent.

In every region of the world, the relative importance of primary commodities in exports as well as GDP has decreased, usually quite sharply, since 1970. Asian nations have moved fastest and furthest toward manufactured exports during this period. Sub-Saharan Africa and Latin America are still mostly primary commodity exporters, although to a lesser degree than in the past and with substantial subregional variation (Table 4.2).

The maturity or sophistication of a country's industrial structure can be measured by the complexity of the products it exports. Here again, the East Asian NICs are the most advanced. In Singapore and South Korea, overseas sales of machinery and transport equipment, which utilize capital- and skill-intensive technology, grew as a share of total merchandise exports by 44 percent and 36 percent, respectively, from 1970 to 1993. Taiwan's exports in this category increased by 23 percent and Hong Kong's by 12 percent. In Southeast Asia, Malaysia (39 percent) and Thailand (28 percent) have been strong performers in this sector, while in Latin America, Mexico (20 percent) and Brazil (17 percent) also made machinery and transport equipment a dynamic export base (Table 4.2).

Textiles and clothing, the preeminent export sector in the East Asian NICs in the 1960s and 1970s, actually shrank as a proportion of total exports in these nations between 1970 and 1993. This fact highlights the workings of the product life cycle and industrial upgrading in the Asian region. While the NICs in East Asia were shifting into higher-value-added production in the 1980s and 1990s, clothing exports became a growth pole for countries at lower levels of development, such as Bangladesh, Pakistan, Sri Lanka, Indonesia, and Thailand. Furthermore, a more detailed look at this sector indicates that Taiwan, South Korea, and Hong Kong have increased their shipments of textile fibers, yarn, and fabrics to the same Asian nations that now are displacing the East Asian NICs as exporters of finished apparel.[3] The textiles and apparel complex, despite its status as a declining sector in developed countries, still represents the leading edge of economic globalization for many Third World nations.

Geographic Specialization and Export Niches

While the diversification of the NICs' exports toward nontraditional manufactured items is a clear trend, less well recognized is the tendency of the NICs to develop sharply focused export niches. In the footwear industry, for example, South Korea has specialized in athletic footwear, Taiwan in vinyl and plastic shoes, Brazil in low-priced women's leather shoes, Spain in medium-priced women's leather shoes, and Italy in high-priced fashion shoes. Mainland China traditionally was a major player in the low-priced end of the world footwear market, especially in canvas and rubber shoes.

Table 4.2   Structure of Merchandise Exports by Type of Industry, 1970–1993

| | Percentage Share of Merchandise Exports | | | | | | | |
| | Primary Commodities | | Textile Fibers, Textiles, and Clothing | | Machinery and Transport Equipment | | Other Manufactures | |
Region/Country	1993	Δ1970–1993	1993	Δ1970–1993	1993	Δ1970–1993	1993	Δ1970–1993
Advanced Industrial Countries[a]	18	−9	5	−1	43	+8	34	+2
United States	18	−12	3	0	49	+7	30	+5
Germany	10	−1	5	−1	48	+1	37	0
Japan	3	−4	2	−11	68	+27	27	−13
East and Southeast Asia[a]	26	−41	20	+7	25	+19	30	+16
Hong Kong[a]	5	+1	40	−4	24	+12	31	−9
Taiwan	7	−17	15	−14	40	+23	38	+8
South Korea	7	−17	19	−22	43	+36	32	+4
Singapore	20	−50	4	−2	55	+44	21	+7
Malaysia	35	−58	6	+5	41	+39	18	+13
Thailand	28	−64	15	+7	28	+28	30	+30
Indonesia	47	−51	17	+17	5	+5	31	+30
Philippines	24	−69	9	+7	19	+19	49	+43
China[b]	19	−9	31	+1	16	0	34	+8
South Asia[a]	27	−26	41	+13	5	+2	28	+11
India	25	−23	30	+3	7	+2	38	+18
Pakistan[b]	15	−22	78	+22	0	0	7	0
Bangladesh[a]	18	−18	72	+23	0	−1	9	−6
Latin America and Caribbean[a]	62	−26	3	+2	14	+12	21	+13
Brazil	40	−46	4	−5	21	+17	35	+33
Mexico	47	−21	3	−8	31	+20	18	+7
Argentina	68	−18	3	−5	11	+7	18	+16
Sub-Saharan Africa[a]	76	−7	2	+1	3	+1	19	+5
South Africa	27	−32	3	−3	8	+1	63	+35
Nigeria	98	0	0	−2	0	0	2	+1
Kenya[a]	71	−16	3	+2	10	+10	16	+5
Tanzania[a]	85	−2	7	+5	1	+1	8	−3
Middle East	NA	NA	NA	NA	NA	NA	NA	NA
Saudi Arabia	91	−9	0	0	2	+2	7	+7
United Arab Emirates[a]	96	0	0	0	1	0	2	0
Iran	96	0	4	0	0	0	0	0

Sources: World Bank, *World Development Report 1994*, pp. 190–191; *World Development Report 1995*, pp. 190–191.
Notes: a. The data are for 1992 and Δ1970–1992. b.The data are for Δ1970–1992.
NA=not available. Δ1970–1993=increase or decrease in percentage share of total exports from 1970 to 1993.

Because of its low wages and vast production capacity, however, China now has displaced Taiwan and South Korea from many of their midlevel niches, and it is challenging Brazil, Spain, and even Italy in the fashionable leather footwear market (Gereffi and Korzeniewicz 1990). Today China is the world's foremost volume exporter of inexpensive consumer goods, such as clothing, footwear, toys, and bicycles.

Similar trends are apparent for many consumer items and even intermediate goods, such as semiconductors. South Korea, for instance, has focused on the mass production of powerful memory chips; Taiwan, by contrast, makes high-value designer chips that carry out special functions in toys, videogames, and electronic equipment. Singapore has upgraded its activities from the assembly and testing of semiconductors to the design and fabrication of silicon wafers, while Singapore and Malaysia produce the majority of hard disk drives for the world's booming personal computer market. Although the location of hard disk drive production in Singapore and Malaysia reflects efforts by transnational corporations (TNCs) to reduce manufacturing costs, these nations were chosen as export sites primarily because of their skilled labor, well-developed transportation and communication infrastructures, and appropriate supporting industries (such as precision tooling).

The global production systems discussed in this chapter raise a host of questions for Third World development. How can countries assure that they enter the most attractive export niches in which they have the greatest relative advantages? To what extent is a country's position in the global manufacturing system structurally determined by the availability of local capital, domestic infrastructure, and a skilled workforce? What is the range of development options available to Third World countries? While these queries cannot be answered fully here, various implications of current global changes for Third World development will be suggested.

THIRD WORLD DEVELOPMENT STRATEGIES

National development strategies in the periphery have played an important role in forging new production relationships in the global manufacturing system.[4] Third World nations usually are claimed to have followed one of two alternative development strategies. The relatively large, resource-rich economies in Latin America (e.g., Brazil, Mexico, and Argentina), South Asia (e.g., India and Bangladesh), and Eastern Europe have pursued import-substituting industrialization (ISI) in which industrial production was geared to the needs of sizable domestic markets. The smaller, resource-poor nations like the East Asian NICs adopted the export-oriented industrialization (EOI) approach that depends on global markets to stimulate the rapid growth of manufactured exports. Although the historical analysis of these transitions often is oversimplified, today it seems clear that many economies are opting for an expansion of manufactured or nontraditional exports to earn needed foreign exchange and raise local standards of living. The East Asian NICs best exemplify the gains from this path of development.

In several important respects, however, the development-strategies literature challenges the conventional wisdom of those who believe that Latin America and other inward-oriented Third World regions can simply follow the East Asian model of development. First, the contrast between the outward-oriented and inward-oriented development strategies is frequently overdrawn. Each of the leading economies in East Asia and Latin America, for example, has pursued a combination of both ISI and EOI approaches. Export promotion always starts from a base in ISI; thus many Latin American nations with an ISI background now are pursuing EOI quite aggressively. This mix of development strategies helps us understand how industrial diversification (secondary ISI) has led to enhanced export flexibility and competitiveness (secondary EOI) in the East Asian and Latin American NICs in the 1980s and 1990s, signaling notable areas of convergence in the two regions.[5]

Second, both inward and outward approaches have inherent vulnerabilities that prevent either from being a long-term solution to development problems. For example, the benefits of ISI are limited by the following conditions: the size of the domestic market (which in Latin America and South Asia is skewed by severe income inequalities), ISI's import-intensive nature (consumer goods ISI pushes imports toward intermediate and capital goods industries, instead of eliminating imports in an absolute sense), its tendency to aggravate sectoral imbalances in an economy (industry is preferred over agriculture), and its foreign exchange vulnerability (the overvalued exchange rates associated with ISI discourage exports). Similarly, EOI has its own drawbacks: it is constrained by the technical impossibility of serving certain domestic needs through traded goods industries; EOI employment in labor-intensive industries is unstable because of competition from low-wage nations; and EOI is threatened by protectionism and slow growth in key overseas markets.[6] In addition, Fishlow cautions against what he calls a "fallacy of composition"—namely, if all developing countries tried to pursue EOI at the same time, the ensuing competition would drive down the gains for all (Fishlow 1985: 138).

Third, export-oriented development strategies may well lead to the fragmentation rather than the integration of national economies. Whereas ISI policies of the past established a pattern of national segmentation in which parallel national industries were set up to supply highly protected domestic markets with finished goods, the turn to EOI has fostered a logic of transnational integration based on geographic specialization and global sourcing. As a result, national economies confront very different development challenges in the era of global capitalism than they have in the past.

Fourth, unique cultural and historical factors make it difficult to generalize from the East Asian experience. Various writers have argued that Confucianism confers certain advantages in the quest for economic development over other traditions, such as the Ibero-Catholic or Hispanic heritage in Latin America, Hinduism in South Asia, and Islam in the Middle East and much of Africa. Because Confucian beliefs place a high value on hard work, loyalty, respect for authority, and education, these characteristics are thought to have facilitated the national consensus around high-speed economic growth evident in Japan and the East Asian NICs since the 1950s and 1960s (see Hofheinz and Calder 1982; Pye 1985; Berger and Hsiao 1988). Simplistic cultural arguments, however, run into a variety of problems (see Ellison and Gereffi 1990: 394–397). First, regions are not culturally homogeneous. Taoism, Buddhism, and Christianity, along with Confucianism, all have large followings in East Asia. Second, timing is a problem. The Confucian, Hindu, Islamic, and Ibero-Catholic civilizations have existed for centuries, whereas the dynamic shifts in economic performance that gave rise to the NICs have occurred only in recent decades.[7] Third, discussions of culture have been inconsistent. The same Confucian beliefs that now are claimed to facilitate rapid industrialization in East Asia were criticized by several generations of Western scholars for inhibiting economic development (Hamilton and Kao 1987). More sophisticated cultural representations are needed that see culture as historically situated and mediated through institutions.

Many scholars thus remain skeptical that development strategies are the predominant reason for the divergent patterns of growth in East Asia and much of the rest of the Third World. Two major alternatives to development strategies as an explanation of East Asia's success in recent decades are (1) its linkages to the world system (the East Asian NICs benefited disproportionately from U.S. hegemony and the politics of the Cold War era, while economic growth in other regions was hampered by their heavy reliance on transnational corporations, external debt, and/or foreign aid) (see Cumings 1984; Deyo 1987b), and (2) the institutional configuration of societies (the developmental state, the longevity of authoritarian regimes, the spread of education, industrial structures where local rather than foreign capital is in a privileged position, dynamic export-oriented subcontracting networks, and entrepreneurial familism have all been cited as giving an edge to East Asia over other regions) (see Berger and Hsiao 1988; Gereffi and Wyman 1990; Haggard 1990). In general, the transferability of the East Asian development model is viewed as increasingly difficult to the extent that one's assessment of its key features shifts from economic policies to local institutions to world-system linkages to culture.

In summary, the development-strategies literature is not primarily concerned with accounting for the fact of economic growth in the NICs. Both inward-oriented and outward-oriented development strategies have proven capable of spawning high-growth economies in distinct regions of the world. Rather, its main emphasis has been twofold: to explain the determinants of policy choice that have led the NICs in different regions of the world to adopt diverse sequences of ISI and EOI development paths, and to highlight the fact that similar development strategies have diverse institutional bases across societies, which shape the implementation, sustainability, and local consequences of these policies. This cross-regional agenda has diverted our attention, however, from a universal phenomenon—the globalization of production—which has redefined the roles of all nations in the world economy. The theoretical suppositions and comparative methods of this approach are fundamentally different from those used in studies of development strategies, as we will see later in the chapter.

GLOBAL COMMODITY CHAINS
AND REGIONAL DEVELOPMENT

Global commodity chains (GCCs) are rooted in transnational production systems that link the economic activities of firms to technological and organizational networks that enable companies to develop, manufacture, and market specific commodities. In the transnational production systems that characterize global capitalism, economic activity is not only international in scope; it also is global in its organization. While internationalization refers simply to the geographic spread of economic activities across national boundaries, globalization implies a degree of functional integration among these internationally dispersed activities. This administrative coordination is carried out by diverse corporate actors in centralized as well as decentralized economic structures.

The commodity-chains perspective entails a fundamental departure from the development-strategies approach in terms of its main units and levels of analysis, its chief substantive concerns, and its principal research methods (see Gereffi and Korzeniewicz 1994).[8] Economic globalization has reduced the theoretical centrality of the nation-state, which was the key unit of analysis in the development-strategies literature. The global integration of goods, services, capital, and labor markets is eroding the power of states to set economic rules within their borders. Although protectionist policies still shape the international flow of investment and trade, national regulatory regimes are giving way to international agreements that cede sovereignty to broad regional trading blocs and transnational economic actors. As a result, crucial concepts in our social science lexicon, such as national development and domestic industries, are now rendered problematic.

The commodity-chains framework targets the study of global capitalism, not national development. Industries and firms, not nation-states, constitute its primary analytical units. Different patterns of national development are an outcome, not the starting point, of this research. From a GCC perspective, diverse global industries, where the dynamics of capitalist competition are played out, are taken as microcosms of the world economy. Firms and the economic networks that connect them are the essential building blocks of transnational production systems in which countries play a variety of specialized and shifting roles. Firms do not exist in a vacuum, of course. Their behavior is conditioned by factors operating at various levels of analysis: global economic and geopolitical conditions; regional integration schemes (de jure and de facto); the economic policies of national governments; the impact of domestic institutions and cultural norms on economic activity; and the wage rates, skills, productivity, and degree of organization of local labor forces. But nation-states are not free-floating actors either. The GCC approach argues that the development prospects of countries are conditioned, in large part, by how they are incorporated into global industries.

There are similarities as well as differences between the GCC perspective and world-systems theory.[9] Both approaches are global and encompass nations at all levels of development within their overarching conceptual frameworks (i.e., the tripartite world system and GCCs). Both assert that the world economy is organized in an international division of labor made up of vertical as well as horizontal linkages, whose geographic scope and modes of integration vary over time. Finally, both argue that global capitalism generates an unequal division of wealth between and within societies, and they try to identify the mechanisms through which this occurs and its developmental consequences.

Notwithstanding these affinities, there also are significant contrasts between the GCC and world-systems perspectives. First, the starting point for GCC analysis is represented by products and industries, rather than broad zones of development (core, semiperiphery, and periphery) in the world economy. While firms are the main units of analysis in studying GCCs, world-systems theory is predominantly state-centric. Empirical explorations of world-systems theory often rely on measures of national wealth to define a state's position in the world economy. Almost no attention is given to the structure of global industries, corporate strategies and rivalries, and economic and social networks. Second, world-systems theory favors a long view of history in which change usually is measured in centuries. The GCC framework, on the other hand, employs the tools of industry studies to focus on patterns of international competition that are contemporary and of much shorter duration. Third, GCC studies try to bridge the macro–micro gap in comparative research by highlighting the local social context of global production. Commodity chains "touch down" in communities and industrial districts where one can examine households, their connections to enterprises and states, and related issues of gender segmentation and racial/ethnic conflict in the workforce. From a GCC perspective, economic globalization actually strengthens the forces of localization in the world economy.

What does GCC analysis explain? How does it handle regions? Commodity-chains research, first and foremost, is concerned with explaining the governance structures of coordination and control in global industries. Two distinct types of GCCs have emerged in recent decades, which for the sake of simplicity can be called producer-driven and buyer-driven commodity chains (see Figure 4.1).[10] Producer-driven commodity chains are those in which large, usually transnational, manufacturers play the central roles in coordinating production networks (including their backward and forward linkages). This is characteristic of capital- and technology-intensive industries such as automobiles, aircraft, computers, semiconductors, and heavy machinery. Buyer-driven commodity chains, on the other hand, are those in which large retailers, brand-name designers, and trading companies play the pivotal role in setting up decentralized production networks in a variety of exporting countries, frequently located in the Third World. This pattern of trade-led industrialization is common in labor-intensive consumer goods industries such as garments, footwear, toys, housewares, and consumer electronics. While producer-driven commodity chains controlled by giant industrial firms have a long history in the world economy, buyer-driven commodity chains dominated by commercial capital are newer and less well understood.

Second, instead of seeing regions as the sum of geographically proximate nation-states, the GCC perspective allows us to empirically document the emergence and transformation of regional divisions of labor that vary by industry.[11] The linkages between countries within a region are the flows of investment capital, technology, goods, services, and people that make up commodity chains. Regional divisions of labor tend to be internally structured in similar ways: core countries supply much of the technology, capital, and high-end services (communications, transportation, and banking); semiperipheral nations do relatively advanced manufacturing and low-end services (e.g., quality control, component sourcing); and the periphery carries out low-wage, routinized production. In East Asia's division of labor, Japan is the core, the East Asian NICs are the semiperiphery, while Southeast Asia and the People's Republic of China constitute the periphery.[12] An analogous regional division of labor exists in North America, with the United States as the core, Canada and parts of northern Mexico as a semiperiphery (making a range of capital-intensive and high-technology products like automobiles and their engines, computers, and electrical machinery), and the rest of Mexico plus a number of Central American and Caribbean nations forming the periphery (Gereffi 1993). A key conclusion that emerges from GCC research is that economic growth is not blocked by these regional divisions of labor; under appropriate local conditions,

Figure 4.1
Organization of Producer-Driven and Buyer-Driven Global Commodity Chains

Producer-Driven Commodity Chains

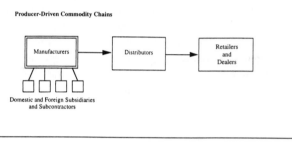

Domestic and Foreign Subsidiaries
and Subcontractors

Buyer-driven Commodity Chains

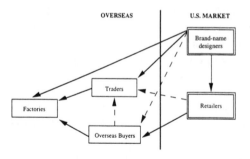

Note: Solid arrows are primary relationships; dashed arrows are secondary relationships.

development can be fostered even within peripheral areas of the world economy.

Third, the GCC perspective explores many of the institutional mechanisms by which countries learn how to compete in world markets. Nations progress through fairly predictable industry development cycles in which organizational learning is continuous. At an early stage of an industry's development, people learn how to make and export products according to the price, quality, and delivery specifications of domestic and foreign buyers. Later, when initial exports are threatened by low-wage competitors, or by protected or saturated overseas markets, local producers typically pursue several options to maintain a significant role in these industries. One is industrial upgrading to improve the kinds of products a firm makes. Another option is direct foreign investment in low-wage countries to duplicate the products that no longer are competitive at home. A third mechanism is triangle manufacturing, whereby the erstwhile exporters become intermediaries between established foreign buyers and new production sites in less developed countries. These patterns of adjustment to industrial decline reveal surprising regularities in the kinds of institutions and information that must be generated if economic learning is to take place. This melding of development and organizational insights is facilitated by the GCC perspective.

Mapping Global Commodity Chains

Global commodity chains have three main dimensions: an input-output structure (i.e., a set of products and services linked together in a sequence of value-adding economic activities), a territoriality (i.e., spatial dispersion or concentration of production and marketing networks, comprising enterprises of different sizes and types), and a governance structure (i.e., authority and power relationships that determine how financial, material, and human resources are allocated and flow within a chain). The construction of GCCs thus involves mapping three types of economic networks, whose units are products, countries, and organizations.

At the product level, commodity chains encompass the full production-consumption cycle: raw material supply, the design and manufacture of components and finished goods, export, wholesale distribution, and retail. These products and services are connected in a sequence of value-adding economic activities. A distinctive feature of this product mapping is that it includes both backward and forward linkages from the production stage rather than focusing on manufacturing alone, as standard industrialization studies do. This allows one to show the relationship between industries ordinarily thought to be discrete (such as agriculture, petrochemicals, textiles, garments, shipping, wholesaling, and retailing for the apparel commodity chain).

At the country level, the geography of the GCC is superimposed on this production system. One needs to identify where each of the products in the commodity chain is made. An interesting finding here is that virtually all GCCs include countries at every level of economic development. For example, although the apparel, automobile, and aircraft commodity chains represent vastly disparate levels of industrial sophistication, each chain involves core, semiperipheral, and peripheral nations in the world system. Thus, international divisions of labor are built into the very structure of GCCs.

Finally, at the organizational level, the focus shifts to the kinds of firms that make, distribute, and market the products in GCCs. Among the issues to be addressed is the degree to which these companies are specialized or vertically integrated, large or small, and transnational or domestic, and whether they participate in interfirm networks across industry and country boundaries. The organizations that populate GCCs mold the chain's governance structure.

Triangle Manufacturing

One of the most important adjustment mechanisms for maturing export industries in East Asia is the process of "triangle manufacturing," which came into being in the 1970s and 1980s. The essence of triangle manufacturing is that U.S. (or other overseas) buyers place their orders with the NIC manufacturers they have sourced from in the past (e.g., Hong Kong or Taiwanese apparel firms), who in turn shift some or all of the requested production to affiliated offshore factories in one or more low-wage countries (e.g., China, Indonesia, or Vietnam). These offshore factories may or may not have equity investments by the East Asian NIC manufacturers: they can be wholly owned subsidiaries, joint-venture partners, or simply independent overseas contractors. The triangle is completed when the finished goods are shipped directly to the overseas buyer, under the U.S. import quotas issued to the exporting nation. Payments to the non-NIC factory usually flow through the NIC intermediary firm.

Triangle manufacturing thus changes the status of the NIC manufacturer from a primary production contractor for the U.S. buyers to a middleman in the buyer-driven commodity chain. The key asset of the East Asian NIC manufacturers is their relationship with the foreign buyers, which is based on the trust developed through numerous successful export transactions. Since the buyer has no direct production experience, the buyer prefers to rely on the East Asian NIC manufacturers he or she has done business with in the past to assure that the buyer's standards in terms of price, quality, and delivery schedules will be met by untested contractors in other Third World locales. As the volume of orders in new production sites like China, Indonesia, or Sri Lanka increases, the pressure grows for the U.S. buyers to eventually bypass their East Asian NIC intermediaries and deal directly with the factories that fill their large orders.

The process of third-party production began in the late 1960s when Japan relocated numerous plants and foreign orders to the East Asian NICs (often through Japanese trading companies, or *sogo shosha*) for both economic and environmental reasons. When U.S. import quotas were imposed on Hong Kong, Taiwan, South Korea, and Singapore in the 1970s, this led to the search for new quota-free production sites elsewhere in Asia.[13] In the 1980s, the shift toward triangle manufacturing accelerated because of domestic changes—increased labor costs, labor scarcity, and currency appreciations—in the East Asian NICs. Today, the East Asian NICs are extending their factory networks to far-flung production frontiers in Asia, Latin America, and Africa.[14]

Triangle manufacturing has several important implications for Third World development. First, the increased pace of economic specialization in the world economy due to such manufacturing appears to be shortening the product cycles for countries pursuing export-oriented development. As industries have become globalized and producers in different parts of the world are more tightly linked, the pace of change has quickened and exporters in particular have shorter periods of time in which to exploit their competitive advantages.[15] These changes are due to a variety of causes, including rapid technological innovation, the growing number of buying seasons for fashion goods, the proliferation of new models of popular consumer products,[16] the spread of Third World manufacturing capabilities, and the speed with which the United States and other developed countries are imposing tariffs, quotas, and other import restrictions on successful exporting countries. As export windows for Third World manufacturers narrow more quickly, countries face the problems of boom-and-bust cycles of economic growth tied to fluctuating external demand and intense regional competition. One solution has been for Third World exporters to decrease their reliance on their traditional overseas markets, especially the United States, whose consumer demand has fueled East Asia's export growth for nearly three decades. By 1989, the four East Asian NICs had cut their dependence on the U.S. market to between one-quarter and two-fifths of their total exports.[17]

The second implication of triangle manufacturing is for social embeddedness. Each of the East Asian NICs has a different set of preferred countries where they set up their new factories. Hong Kong and Taiwan have been the main investors in China (Hong Kong has taken a leading role in Chinese production of quota items like apparel made from cotton and synthetic fibers, while Taiwan is a leader for nonquota items like footwear,[18] as well as leather and silk apparel); South Korea has been especially prominent in Indonesia, Guatemala, the Dominican Republic, and now North Korea; and Singapore is a major player in Southeast Asian sites like Malaysia and

Indonesia. These production networks are explained in part by social and cultural networks (e.g., ethnic or familial ties, common language), as well as by unique features of a country's historical legacy (e.g., Hong Kong's British colonial ties gave it an inside track on investments in Jamaica and Mauritius).

Finally, the difficulties involved in coordinating triangle manufacturing networks have led a number of East Asian entrepreneurs to move beyond contract manufacturing by setting up their own retail outlets, with an eye toward large Asian markets such as China and Japan, and by exporting their own branded products to a wide variety of European and North American locations. If there is a strong move toward consolidated regional trading blocs, as many now predict, the territorial boundaries of transnational production systems may become more clearly delineated within global regions.

THIRD WORLD STRATEGIES FOR "MOVING UP" IN THE GLOBAL ECONOMY

Both technological advance and organizational learning are required to climb the ladder of industrial development. Progress requires a dynamic enterprise base, supportive state policies, and improvement in skills and higher wages in the workforce. For most nations in the Third World, reaching the status of core countries is an ever receding frontier, complicated by a growing technology gap and a constantly changing international environment. Third World nations have utilized several strategies in recent decades to try to improve their global positions. These include government policies and organizational initiatives to increase productivity, new relations with foreign and local capital, and participation in regional economic blocs.[19]

Narrowing the Productivity Gap

Third World regions confront a significant productivity gap with regard to the developed nations. This gap, which is a rough indicator of the effect of disembodied technological progress on long-term economic growth, is about 2.5 to 1 between Latin America and the OECD countries, and it has grown wider over time. East Asia, by contrast, appears to have made major strides in closing this gap, while less advanced regions like sub-Saharan Africa and South Asia presumably lag the furthest behind the global pacesetters. In the period 1950–1989, Latin America's increase in joint factor productivity was one-seventh that of the East Asian NICs and one-fifth that of the developed nations (ECLAC 1994a: 141). A major problem is that most Third World countries fail to use internationally available "hard" and "soft" technologies. This is apparent in outdated equipment, obsolete production methods, a deficient organization of labor, rigidly vertical industrial relations, inadequate product quality, poor after-sales services, and so on.

In their efforts to narrow the productivity gap, Third World states have pursued a variety of policy and institutional reforms. A coherent macroeconomic program that emphasizes stable exchange rates, low inflation, and moderate to high interest rates is widely assumed to be the necessary starting point for improved economic performance. This frequently is coupled with related mesoeconomic changes that shore up the institutional environment within which firms operate (e.g., improved infrastructure, linkages with the scientific and technological system, training, finance, and the promotion of new exports or overseas markets). There is much less agreement, however, on the role to be played by microeconomic policies that directly affect the operations of firms in specific industrial sectors. In general, industrial policy has been discredited in neoclassical versions of the EOI development model, despite the significant role of industrial policy in East Asia's high-growth "miracle" economies, such as Japan, South Korea, and Taiwan (see Johnson 1982; Amsden 1989; Wade 1990; Gereffi and Wyman 1990).

Institutional support has been forthcoming from Third World governments to attract the foreign capital needed for export processing zones (EPZs). Serious questions have been raised, however, about the contributions made by these low-wage export industries to broader development objectives in the Third World, such as upgraded skills, technology transfer, backward linkages to local suppliers, and improved living conditions. The experience of Mexico typifies these dilemmas. Until the last decade, Mexico's maquiladora plants were relegated to a low-wage, export-processing role in the world economy. A major concern for Mexico was how to push beyond the enclave model of EOI represented by its traditional, labor-intensive maquiladora plants to adopt a more dynamic, industrially upgraded development strategy. This would generate higher incomes and better skills for Mexico's workers and at the same time allow Mexican exports to be internationally competitive in technologically advanced sectors.

In the 1980s, a new wave of maquiladora plants began to push beyond this enclave model to a more sophisticated type of component-supplier production, making parts for capital- and technology-intensive consumer durable items like automobiles and computers (Gereffi 1996). To successfully carry out this shift, however, Mexico must move from its wage-depressing export strategy to more productivity-enhancing strategies. So far, it has taken the easy road to export expansion, since the sharp devaluations of the Mexican peso in the 1980s depressed real wages in the manufacturing sector by over 50 percent. The East Asian NICs, meanwhile, are moving in the opposite direction. They have diversified their exports in the face of a substantial appreciation (rather than devaluation) of their currencies, rising (not declining) real wages, and labor scarcity (rather than labor surpluses).

Although policy reforms have been central concerns of the political economy literature on Third World development, scant attention has been given to the role of local innovations in stimulating economic growth and productivity increases in developing nations. Several kinds of innovation should be distinguished in the process of economic development. First, there are breakthrough innovations—new products and processes that allow leading firms to fundamentally redefine the cost structure of modern industries so that old products and technologies become obsolete. Examples include the restructuring of the telecommunications industry around fiber optics and satellite systems (instead of copper cables) and the information science revolution that replaced the mechanical and electrical business machines of several decades ago with a dazzling array of handheld and desktop computers, plugged into global information networks. Pathbreaking innovations of this sort tend to be introduced in the most advanced nations, which helps them to retain their competitive edge in the world economy by initiating new product cycles.

A second form of progress stems from less dramatic adaptive innovations, which are increasingly found in the NICs, especially in East Asia. These innovations involve the use of modern technologies by small and medium-size firms in traditional as well as advanced sectors. In the export-oriented garment industries of South Korea, Taiwan, and Hong Kong, for example, new synthetic materials, laser cutting machines, and computer-aided designs are routinely employed to enhance the upgrading of exports destined for developed-country markets. Adaptive innovations are commonplace in the NICs' other major export industries as well, such as footwear, toys, semiconductors, and computers.

A third form of productivity-enhancing innovation that is often overlooked in developing nations is organizational in nature. Numerous organizational innovations have been critical to East Asia's economic superiority in recent decades. Japan is widely attributed with pioneering "lean production" as an alternative to mass production in the automobile industry (Womack, Jones, and Roos 1991), a form of manufacturing that is now being widely emulated in other industries and by TNCs of all nationalities. East Asian production and export networks in producer-driven and buyer-driven commodity chains rely on a wide range of regionally adaptive vertical and horizontal organizational forms (e.g., trading companies, dense subcontracting networks, specification contracting, and triangle manufacturing), with strong bases in ethnicity, kinship, and local communities. Finally, the original equipment manufacturing (OEM) and original brandname manufacturing (OBM) export roles contain many innovative elements that are dynamic sources of competitive advantage in the world economy. Improvements in the organization of production represent one of the social foundations of East Asia's export success, and it is an area where there is considerable scope for local innovations.

New Relations with Foreign and Local Capital

Economic liberalization has forced Third World states to renegotiate their relationship with private capital, both foreign and local. Liberalization trends alone, however, are not sufficient to attract increased foreign direct investment (FDI). A country's stance toward foreign capital is only one element in a coherent and well-balanced national development policy package that typically includes both macroeconomic and political stability, good infrastructure, modern economic institutions, and a clear sense of the ground rules by which enterprises must operate. One of the most important lessons learned during the 1970s and 1980s is that FDI policy should involve explicit commitments with respect to key national priorities such as export promotion and technological innovation and that successful local firms represent an important element in national development strategies. In the past decade, FDI has grown dramatically in most of the Third World regions. By 1992, the global stock of FDI reached approximately $2 trillion, with worldwide outflows of FDI recording steady gains from 1982 until 1991 and 1992, when there were declines. Whereas developing countries account for only 5 percent of the global stock of FDI, they received about 25 percent of all inflows in 1991 (UNCTAD 1993: 1).

The resurgence of FDI in the 1980s and 1990s was fostered by a variety of new economic conditions, such as advances in information technology, the growth of developing country markets, a convergence in national patterns of consumer demand, intense global competition, and the rise of FDI by East Asian and other Third World investors. There were facilitating factors at the policy level as well, including the liberalization of trade and investment regimes; the spread of privatization programs and debt-for-equity swaps; swings in exchange rates that boosted outward FDI from countries with strong currencies, particularly Japan; and regional integration schemes (such as the European Union and the North American Free Trade Agreement [NAFTA]) that are expanding trade and investment flows within as well as between regions.

The trend toward a liberalization of FDI policies, which accelerated during the 1980s, is continuing. In 1992, seventy-nine new legislative measures were adopted in forty-three countries and all liberalized the rules on FDI; in 1991, eighty of eighty-two measures were more liberal. These regulatory reforms to attract FDI have been complemented by privatization programs. In 1990, more than seventy nations had active privatization initiatives and their sales of state enterprises totaled over $185 billion (UNCTAD 1993: 2; 1992: 86). Many countries in Latin America and South Asia, which had adopted highly regulatory environments and policies of assertive industrialization in the 1970s, have reopened sectors like mining and agriculture that previously were off limits to foreign capital, and they have lowered joint-venture requirements and other entry barriers in manufacturing and services.

The recent wave of liberalization has had a particularly strong impact on services FDI. The transnationalization of services usually lags behind primary (natural resource) activities and manufacturing, despite the rapid growth of the service sector's share of GDP in many countries. This disparity is due largely to national restrictions on inward investments in services for strategic, political, or cultural reasons, which now appear to be lessening. Financial TNCs (banks and insurance firms) and trading companies (e.g., Japanese *sogo shosha*) account for two-thirds of the services FDI stock in developed countries and the majority of foreign service investments in many Third World nations. Old restrictions are starting to change in capital-intensive service industries as well—telecommunications, various forms of transportation, and public utilities—which could rival finance and trading as sources of services FDI. As the growth of services has been increasingly propelled by "soft" technologies (especially information science), the process of technology transfer has shifted from harder to softer technologies, where the contribution of TNCs is crucial (UNCTAD 1993: chap. 3).

Regional and global strategies by TNCs are replacing those geared to maximizing profits in individual countries. There has been an affinity among the ISI development strategies followed in most Third World regions in the 1960s and 1970s, the predominance of TNCs at the manufacturing stage, and the emergence of producer-driven commodity chains. Conversely, the move toward EOI in the 1970s and 1980s in East Asia coincided with the rise of networks and other nonequity ties with foreign buyers in the Third World and the prominence of buyer-driven commodity chains. Today, integrated international production allows foreign industrial and commercial capital to reap the benefits of economies of scale and scope as TNC strategies evolve toward greater functional and geographic integration, both within and across firms. The challenge for Third World governments is to harness the productive potential of TNCs while learning how to benefit from multiple ways of linking up with the global economy.

The economic restructuring of the 1980s and 1990s has changed the incentives for leading NIC manufacturers. East Asian firms have responded to rising wage rates and labor shortages at home and protectionism abroad in three ways, which are not mutually exclusive: industrial upgrading to higher-value-added export products that take full advantage of East Asia's manufacturing expertise, skilled labor, and well-developed local supplier base; offshore sourcing to low-cost export platforms in the Third World for labor-intensive products in which the NIC manufacturers are no longer directly competitive but can assume middleman roles in triangle manufacturing networks; and diversification out of export sectors and into more profitable economic activities, such as services and real estate. These changes, together with the relaxing of government controls on the outflow of foreign exchange from the East Asian NICs, are consolidating a two-tier pattern of cross-border FDI in manufacturing in Asia: from Japan into the regional NICs and from the NICs to China, Indonesia, Malaysia, the Philippines, and Thailand.

Shifting Patterns of Regional Integration

A great deal of attention has been given to the growth of regional economic blocs in the past decade. These blocs take two quite different forms. On the one hand, the United States has joined the European countries in promoting formal regional agreements. Both the European Union and NAFTA are trade-based regional blocs, created and sustained by government policies. The Asia Pacific Economic Cooperation (APEC) forum, by contrast, is a fledgling agreement that advocates free trade by the year 2020 within a framework of "open regionalism." One of the issues at stake here is whether regional economic blocs are a stepping-stone to strengthening of multilateral institutions like the World Trade Organization (WTO) or whether regional integration is merely a defensive maneuver used to exclude certain groups of countries from global markets. If Europe, North America, and Asia do indeed set up full-fledged trade blocs, closed to outsiders and open to insiders, regionally integrated TNCs are likely to capitalize on this trend by pursuing corporate strategies of globalization through regionalization.

While trade tends to promote regional integration, FDI appears to be better at spanning different regional blocs and moving toward global economic integration. Trade-based forms of cross-border linkage, including EPZs, outsourcing, and free-trade areas, are "shallow" forms of economic integration. "Deep" integration, on the other hand, involves the production of goods and services as a result of transnational corporate strategies and network structures (UNCTAD 1993: chap. 7). The world economy seems to be evolving toward this more complex form of integrated international production, containing a multitude of buyer-driven as well as producer-driven commodity chains. Strategic alliances have expanded, particularly in industries with short product cycles and high research-and-development costs, while competitive pressures are forcing firms to seek cost savings from all segments of global commodity chains.

Latin America's experience in the 1980s shows that regional markets can be a step toward more extensive exports in the Third World. According to evidence from twenty-eight industrial sectors in thirteen Latin American and Caribbean countries in 1979 and 1989, the principal changes in this period concern the destination of exports. In both years, production was geared mainly to the domestic market, with only marginal exports to the regional market. In 1989, however, about one-quarter of these sectors redirected their exports to extraregional markets, without altering their primary focus on domestic markets. More competitive sectors in Latin America developed along different lines. During the 1980s, they shifted a majority of their output from domestic to external markets within the region. Of sectors that already were regional exporters in 1979, one-third used exports to Latin American markets as a training ground for subsequent entry into extraregional markets (ECLAC 1994b: 36–37). Thus, ISI production in Latin America is a platform for subsequent EOI, which in turn can expand from regional to global markets. East Asian firms, by contrast, have used their lengthy experience as global exporters to move along the EOI path to the sophisticated OEM and OBM export roles, which involve a much deeper pattern of functional integration in global markets.

The Asian region is at the forefront of both intraregional and interregional patterns of investment and trade. De facto regional integration in East Asia has been occurring through the strategies of Japanese, U.S., and European TNCs, largely in the absence of intergovernmental agreements. A regional division of labor has been fostered by the lowering of trade barriers, the shift of Japanese TNCs toward more offshore sourcing in low-cost production sites after the appreciation of the yen, and the emergence of new manufacturing centers in East and Southeast Asia. These tendencies are bolstered by geographic proximity and cultural affinities in the region. East Asia thus is characterized by a market-induced, rather than policy-induced, form of economic integration.

The cross-regional impact of FDI from East Asia into Mexico and the Caribbean is of growing contemporary relevance. Burgeoning investments from Japan and the East Asian NICs in North America are leading to a deepening of multilateral ties between the two regions. In anticipation of NAFTA, which took effect on 1 January 1994, Asian investors set up transplant factories in Mexico and the Caribbean Basin to gain preferential access to the U.S. market. NAFTA extends the regional division of labor to the poorest countries in the hemisphere, and it leads to a reevaluation of the impact of low-wage EOI strategies on Mexico and the Caribbean.

Today many of Mexico's traditional maquiladora exports are shifting to Caribbean venues, which are likely to become the favored locale for these low-wage activities. By the early 1990s, EPZs had become a leading source of exports and manufacturing employment in various Caribbean nations. In the Dominican Republic, for example, EPZs employed 142,300 Dominicans (primarily in garment assembly) in 1992 and generated $1 billion in trade, netting $300 million toward the balance of payments. In terms of employment, the Dominican Republic was the fourth largest EPZ economy in the world (the fifth if China's Special Economic Zones are included), and 11 percent of the more than three hundred EPZ firms in the Dominican Republic were Asian (see EIU 1993/94; Kaplinsky 1993; Portes, Itzigsohn, and Dore-Cabral 1994). Furthermore, East Asian projects were found to contribute more jobs, bigger investments, higher levels of local value added, and a greater utilization of skilled labor than the assembly-oriented sewing operations by other foreign firms (USITC 1989: 6/5).

Despite these gains, one should be skeptical of the longer-term role that labor-intensive EOI can play in the development of Caribbean nations. Although export-processing activities such as those that have grown so rapidly in Mexico and the Caribbean Basin in recent years have undeniable benefits in job creation, foreign exchange earnings, and the fostering of industrial experience, they do not by themselves constitute a sufficient basis for a long-term development strategy. Export-processing industries are best seen as a transitional phenomenon, the first stage in a process of moving to a higher level of industrial development, in which domestic inputs and diverse services also are required.

While many Caribbean nations are just now making the basic transition from farm to factory, Mexico is moving further up the industrial export ladder from clothes to complex components to computers. But these countries have a long way to go before matching the success of the East Asian NICs. The latter nations are shifting from being the principal suppliers of merchandise sold under foreign brand names in U.S. and European department stores to making goods for export under their own brand names with a growing emphasis on booming Asian markets. Hong Kong, Taiwanese, and Korean manufacturers thus are closing the buyer-driven commodity chains for items such as apparel, shoes, and consumer electronics (e.g., calculators, games, watches) by moving all the way from raw material supply through retailing within the Asian region, while the North American commodity chains are stymied by their weakest link—production. It is an open question whether Mexican or Caribbean manufacturers, or their U.S. or Asian counterparts, will step forward to fill this production gap for certain consumer goods in North America.

CONCLUSION

Globalization is not inevitable, nor is it an unmixed blessing in terms of development. Its foundations are political as well as economic and therefore far from stable. Globalization also generates substantial social and cultural resistance because of its uneven and in some cases marginalizing consequences within as well as between countries and regions. The tumultuous changes wrought by economic globalization affect all regions of the world. The East Asian nations, which probably have consolidated their position the most during the past twenty-five years, are in the midst of a radical transformation in their industrial and export profiles, as low-wage industries are being shed for a technologically sophisticated and more service-oriented image. For other regions of the world, however, problems remain as countries try to escape wage-depressing export strategies, low productivity, and marginal forms of integration to the world economy.

One of the central tasks in fashioning national development strategies is to determine how to plug into transnational production systems in a way that allows nations to increase their productivity and international competitiveness while generating a higher standard of living for the local population. An important lesson from the countries that have been successful in industrial upgrading and diversified exporting (such as the East Asian NICs) has been the prominent role of locally owned firms in their export-oriented industries. The vast majority of the exports in the East Asian NICs, with the exception of Singapore, are produced by domestically owned firms. Whether large industrial conglomerates, like South Korea's *chaebol,* or densely networked small and medium-size firms, as in Hong Kong and Taiwan, domestic enterprises have been the key to East Asia's international competitiveness.

In most of the East Asian NICs, the state has induced local private capital to take a mercantilistic approach to global markets, where overseas sales are equated with enhanced national security and prestige. Exporting is viewed as a matter of long-term necessity rather than short-term convenience. East Asian governments have used financial and other controls to exercise leverage over local exporters. Domestic exporters in East Asia thus have a far greater incentive than do foreign companies not only to export but also to establish more extensive backward linkages to local suppliers.

A major reason the East Asian NICs have been so successful in upgrading their export industries is that they have highly efficient networks of supplier industries for intermediate goods (e.g., plastics, textiles) and components (e.g., semiconductors, computer chips, auto parts). These supporting industries allow East Asia's exporters to receive high-quality inputs at world-market prices. In addition, the East Asian NICs have developed a full range of local design, financial, transportation, and communications services that give them major advantages over other Third World production sites. However, the directions the East Asian economies can move in terms of industrial upgrading are constrained by the availability of the natural resources on which these supplier industries depend. The importance of these raw material supply networks for successful export industries creates opportunities for resource-rich regions of the Third World.

Third World development involves ascending a ladder of industrial complexity that requires a dynamic enterprise base, appropriate state policies, and an improving set of skills and wages in the workforce. Whereas the least developed regions of the Third World have limited industrial experience, they are on a trajectory that many other countries with rich as well as poor resource bases already have traversed. The experiences of the most advanced regions in the Third World, like East Asia and Latin America, embody distinct pathways but with similar objectives. Reaching the status of core countries in the world economy is an ever receding frontier, but the gap can be closed by a combination of technological development and institutional learning from the best practices of successful nations around the world.

NOTES

The research for this chapter was partially funded by grants from Taiwan's Chiang Ching-Kuo Foundation for International Scholarly Exchange (USA), the Social Science Research Council's Korea Program, and the Arts and Sciences Research Council at Duke University. I gratefully acknowledge these sources of support.

1. For a detailed discussion of the preferential arrangements that have proliferated under GATT, see Finlayson and Zacher (1983).

2. The percentages used in this section come from the World Bank (1992: 222–223).

3. For a vivid illustration of this transition in Taiwan, see Gereffi and Pan (1994).

4. For an interdisciplinary investigation of Third World development strategies with a focus on the Latin American and East Asian cases, see Gereffi and Wyman (1990).

5. For evidence regarding convergence, see Gereffi (1990a) and Bradford (1990).

6. A fuller discussion of the natural limits of ISI and EOI development strategies can be found in Gereffi (1990b: 242–246).

7. For a polemical argument that these broad civilizations indeed are the fault lines for fresh conflicts in the post–Cold War world, see Huntington (1993).

8. This interdisciplinary volume illustrates the structure and dynamics of GCCs in a diverse set of industries, including agriculture, shipbuilding, apparel, footwear, automobiles, cocaine, and services.

9. World-systems theory is most closely identified with the work of Immanuel Wallerstein, who provided one of the earliest definitions of commodity chains: "A commodity chain is a network of labor and production processes whose end result is a finished commodity" (Hopkins and Wallerstein 1986: 159).

10. For a more complete discussion of this topic, see Gereffi (1994).

11. Henderson (1989) and Doner (1991) conducted exhaustive firm-level research that identified the structure and dynamics of regional divisions of labor in the East Asian semiconductor industry and the Southeast Asian automobile industry, respectively.

12. The Greater South China Economic Zone is a more specific subregional "growth triangle," which includes southern China's Guangdong and Fujian provinces, Taiwan, and Hong Kong (see Chen 1994).

13. Hong Kong offers an excellent illustration of this process. In the mid-1960s, low prices were the main competitive advantage of the Hong Kong garment industry. However, the imposition of quotas forced textile and apparel firms to upgrade. European and U.S. import quotas were calculated in terms of the quantity of goods shipped, rather than their value. This arrangement, chosen in part because it was easier to enforce by the importing countries, had an unforeseen effect: "It encouraged the Hong Kong manufacturers to move from textiles to clothing and then

from simple to fancy clothing, in order to generate more income and employment per square yard" (Lardner 1988: 46).

14. Besides the People's Republic of China (the new giant in high-volume exporting from Asia), other socialist economies in the region (such as Vietnam, Cambodia, Laos, and North Korea) also are becoming important production sites in the East Asian NICs' triangle manufacturing networks.

15. In the footwear industry, for example, the period of time required to set up successful export industries has grown ever shorter. While export-oriented footwear complexes took more than twenty years to develop in Japan and fifteen years or so in countries like Taiwan and South Korea, estimates are that China's footwear industry will be fully mature in ten years or less.

16. Nike creates over one hundred new models of athletic shoes every year to stay ahead of its competitors, who try to imitate Nike's best-selling styles as soon as they reach the stores.

17. The U.S. market remains most important for Taiwan (39 percent of total exports), followed by South Korea (35 percent), Singapore (30 percent), and Hong Kong (27 percent) (Dicken 1992: 37).

18. After controls were relaxed on Taiwanese investments in the People's Republic of China in the late 1980s, around five hundred footwear factories were moved from Taiwan to China in less than two years. Although China recently passed Taiwan as the leading footwear exporter to the United States (in terms of pairs of shoes), it is estimated that nearly one-half of China's shoe exports come from Taiwanese-owned or -managed firms recently transferred to the mainland (author interviews with footwear industry experts in Taiwan).

19. This section of the chapter draws substantially from Gereffi 1995.

Leo Panitch 5

Rethinking the Role of the State

The development of what came to be known as *the theory of the state* in the late 1960s and early 1970s marked an important departure for the discipline of political science. The purpose and effect of the new theory was to provide a nuanced counterpoint to conventional liberal pluralist and social democratic understandings of the state, which were founded on the notion that the liberal democratic polity had during the twentieth century freed itself from the determining power of capital. The new theory was concerned with demonstrating that, far from having become independent of capital, the contemporary state had become an ever more integral element in its development and reproduction. It did not deny the state's autonomy from immediate pressures from capitalists but, on the contrary, theorized such autonomy as a functional condition—given the competitive nature of the economy and the capitalist class itself—for the defense and reproduction of the system (Miliband 1968, 1977; O'Connor 1973; Offe 1984; Poulantzas 1973, 1978).

Indeed, the outstanding contribution of the new theory was to provide useful tools for analyzing both the variations and the limits of this relative autonomy of the state. It provided a framework for understanding the real effects that popular and working-class pressures could have, in terms of positive state responses to the demand for reform, while demonstrating the way these reforms could be limited and contained through the institutionalization of opposition and through the state's own reading of the conjunctural requirements of capital accumulation.

By the late 1970s and early 1980s a considerable reaction emerged against the growing influence of the new state theory. This involved a challenge to the notion of relative autonomy, stressing once again the state's independence from determination by the capitalist economy and class structure. The great irony of all these variants of the state autonomy approach was that they emerged just as limits of even the relative autonomy of the state were severely tested (Nordlinger 1981; Skocpol 1985; Korpi 1983). The instability of Keynesian policies and corporatist structures became more and more manifest in a new era of capitalist crisis from the mid-1970s on. By the early 1980s, with the rise of the Thatcher-Reagan regime, governments and bureaucrats proudly enveloped themselves in an ideology that proclaimed the necessity of state subordination to the requirements of capital accumulation and markets and even to the norms and opinions of capitalists themselves. During the decade, moreover, as social democratic regimes (including even Sweden's) found their freedom of maneuver restrained by the new limits to capitalist growth and a renewed ideological militancy on the part of capitalists, they soon abandoned all pretext that the mixed economy had not all along been a capitalist one and that the welfare state had not always been dependent on and necessarily contained within the limits of capital accumulation. Rarely has an academic theory been less apposite to its times than the one that asserted state autonomy against the theory of the capitalist state (Cammack 1989, 1990).

No one today can deny the immense structural power and global reach of capitalism as a system and of capitalists as a class. But very few embrace the insights and tools of analysis of the theory of the state as a way of understanding the role the state is playing in the construction of a global capitalism. Rather, we increasingly witness a claim that this global capitalism has now escaped the state, that it now operates beyond the state's control. To take one example of a new conventional wisdom, Held regards globalization as a distinctively new

> international order involving the emergence of a global economic system which stretches beyond the control of a single state (even of dominant states); the expansion of networks of transnational linkages and communications over which particular states have little influence; the enormous growth in international organization which can limit the scope for action of the most powerful states; the development of a global military order . . . which can reduce the range of policies available to governments and their citizens.

He concludes that, since this new global order has apparently escaped the control of democratic institutions located at the national level, "democracy has to become a transnational affair." Strategic priority must be given to "the key groups, agencies, associations and organizations of international civil society." Their capacity as agencies for democratic control must be extended through an appropriate recasting of the territorial boundaries of systems of accountability, representation, and regulation and fortified by entrenched transnational bills of social, economic, and civil rights (Held 1992: 32–34).

There are various problems in defining globalization this way and in addressing democratic dilemmas in the face of this concept. The premise that globalization is a process whereby capital escapes or overtakes the nation-state tends to be misleading in two senses. First, there is often an overestimation of the extent to which nation-states were capable of controlling capital in an earlier era. The undeniable evidence that has accumulated recently of the determining power of capital today becomes, paradoxically, the basis for asserting that the state used to be autonomous from capital, even a determining power over it, but that capital has managed to get out of the state's clutches by going global. And if the nation-state's modes of regulation are assumed to have once been an effective power over capital, this tends to encourage the idea that all that is needed is for similar modes to somehow be adopted at the global level. But even for those not given to such illusions, there is the problem of tending to ignore the extent to which today's globalization is authored by states and is primarily about reorganizing rather than bypassing them. A false dichotomy between the national and the international is promoted, which diverts attention from the need to develop new strategies for transforming the state, even as a means of developing an appropriate international strategy.

This reflects a continuing theoretical misconception that the state and capital must be seen as two independent spheres rather than as parts of a totality. The predominance of this misconception is due in some part to how little the theory of state has had to say about trends toward the internationalization of capital and the state. With a few important exceptions, contributions to understanding the specific role of the state amid the contemporary process of globalization have lagged far behind the process itself. After exploring three key theoretical contributions, this chapter will move to an examination of the role of the state in the context of the North American free trade initiatives. It will then consider the limits and possibilities of various strategic alternatives to globalization.

THE INTERNATIONALIZATION OF THE STATE

The apparent subjection of even advanced capitalist social formations in recent decades to the competitive logics and exigencies of worldwide production, trade, and finance has meant that the nature of state intervention has changed considerably but not that the role of the state has necessarily been diminished. Far from witnessing a bypassing of the state by a global capitalism, we see very active states and highly politicized sets of capitalist classes working to secure what Gill (focusing primarily on the European Union but pointing to much broader tendencies of this kind) aptly termed a "new constitutionalism for disciplinary neo-liberalism" (Gill 1992). In the few years past we have witnessed, at the world and regional levels, states as the authors of a regime that defines and guarantees, through international treaties with constitutional effect, the global and domestic rights of capital. This process may be understood in a manner quite analogous to the emergence of the so-called laissez-faire state during the rise of industrial capitalism, which involved a very active state to see through the separation of polity from economy and guarantee legally and politically the rights of contract and property. We may recall, with Corrigan and Sayer, the long "revolution in government" in England from 1740 to 1850: "We should understand . . .

what later became celebrated and dominant as 'political economy' to be simultaneously the discovery of economy (and 'the economy' argued for as a self-sufficient 'private' realm governed by the laws of the market) and a politicization of a moral code (entailing specific forms of 'policing') which makes that possible" (Corrigan and Sayer 1985: 105). Similarly, as regards the emergence of the modern corporation in the United States through the nineteenth century, Wolfe showed this could not properly be understood as "a triumph of laissez-faire."

> Laws could be changed only if the bodies that passed them were controlled; this meant that in order to take the corporation out of the public sphere and place it in the private one, the industrialists had to enter the public sphere themselves. Ironically, a political battle had to be fought in order to place an important—in the nineteenth century perhaps the most important—institution outside of politics. One had to have power in the state in order to make it impotent. Few clearer examples exist of how the struggle over legal parameters cannot be accepted as a given but becomes part of the activity of the state itself. (Wolfe 1977: 22)

We are living through something like this in our own time. Capitalist globalization also takes place in, through, and under the aegis of states; it is encoded by them and in important respects even authored by them; and it involves a shift in power relations within states that often means the centralization and concentration of state powers as the necessary condition of and accompaniment to global market discipline.

When the new theory of the capitalist state was developed two decades ago, two key contributions were made on the subject of the relation between capital and the state in the context of internationalization. In 1971 Murray offered a seminal contribution to what he termed "the territorial dialectics of capitalism" to the end of developing "a framework which would allow a more substantial approach to the problem of the effects of an internationalization of capital on existing political institutions" (Murray 1971: 84–108). Far from conceiving this as a process to be understood in terms of capital "escaping" the state, Murray demonstrated that as capital expanded territorially one of the key problems it had to confront was how to ensure that state economic functions continued to be performed. At issue was the structural role of the capitalist state in relation to "what may most aptly be called economic res publica, those economic matters which are public, external to individual private capitals." This included guaranteeing property and contract; standardizing currency, weights, and measure; ensuring the availability of key inputs of labor, land, finance, technology, and infrastructure; generally orchestrating macroeconomics; regulating conditions of work, consumption, and external diseconomies such as pollution; and providing ideological, educational, and communications conditions of production and trade. With the performance of these intranational functions there stood the function of international management of external relations pertaining to any or all of these dimensions. Any capital that extended itself beyond the territorial boundaries of a state that had heretofore performed these functions had to either take these functions on themselves or have them performed by some other public authority. Historically this was often accomplished through colonialism and then neocolonialism. In the contemporary era, and especially as regards the advanced capitalist states, it has primarily been a matter of "states already performing or being willing to perform the functions of their own accord." Thus, foreign capital came to be serviced on the same basis as domestic capital.

To speak in terms of functions is not necessarily improperly "functionalist" insofar as the range of structures that might undertake their performance and the conditions that might mean their nonperformance are problematized. Murray explicitly did this and addressed the possibility that "the contradictions of the international system will be such as to prevent their fulfillment at all." Yet he saw no reason why, despite the major increase in the internationalization of trade, investment, and finance capital in the 1950s and 1960s, the performance of both intranational and international state functions could not continue to be contained within the system of nation-states. Especially as regards "the *intranational* performance of public economic functions for extended capital," Murray stressed the positive advantages to capital in being able to play off one nation-state against another. "Thus," he stated, "even where there is extensive territorial non-coincidence between domestic states and their extended capitals, this does not imply that the system of atomistic nation-states is outdated. The [notion] . . . that 'multinational corporations and nations are therefore fundamentally incompatible with each other' is not necessarily true" (Murray 1971: 102).

On the other hand, Murray discerned the contradictions entailed in a process that was exposing exchange rates and national monetary systems to an international money market, easing the process of international speculation and opening sources of credit outside the control of national authorities. He said, "There is accordingly a tendency for the process of internationalization to increase the potential economic instability in the world economy at the same time as decreasing the power of national governments to control economic activity within their own borders." Attempts by states to correct balance of payments deficits in the context of this economic instability led to the adoption of policies that "further weaken the national capital and increase the domination of foreign capital within the national economy." Murray concluded that, precisely because capital was always a political opportunist that would take support from whatever public authority it could, "existing states often suffered a decrease in their powers as a result of internationalization . . . [yet] weaker states in a period of internationalization come to suit neither the interests of their own besieged capital nor of the foreign investor" (Murray 1971: 109). As if recognizing the unresolved ambiguities in his approach over whether the territorial dialectics of capital extended or diminished the role of the state, Murray ended his article by calling for an "elaboration of the connections between not only states, but the states and their capitals."

Three years later, in a brilliantly original analysis, Poulantzas took up exactly where Murray left off by explicitly problematizing the notion of states and "their" capitals. He insisted that "common formulations of the problem such as 'what can—or cannot— the state do in the face of the great multinational firms' [and] 'how far has the state lost powers in the face of these international giants?' are fundamentally incorrect" (Poulantzas 1974: 70–88).

Poulantzas's immediate concern was with understanding the dominant role U.S. capital had come to play in Europe, including the process whereby European states "take responsibility for the interests of the dominant capital." This involved not only granting the same type of concessions and subventions to U.S. capital as it did to indigenous capital but also acting as a "staging post" by supporting U.S. capital in its further extension outside Europe. This could "go so far as to help American capital circumvent the American state itself (the anti-trust legislation, for example). The international reproduction of capital under the domination of American capital is supported by various national states, each state attempting in its own way to latch onto one or other aspect of this process."

This did not mean (in contrast to Murray) that the state's policies weakened national capital. Rather, it meant that its industrial policies increasingly were concerned with promoting "the concentration and international expansion of their own indigenous capital" by linking it with the international reproduction of U.S. capital (Poulantzas 1974: 73). Nor did the concentration of power by transnational capital take power away from the state:

> The current internationalization of capital neither suppresses nor bypasses nation-states, either in the direction of a peaceful integration of capitals "above" the state level (since every process of internationalization is affected under the dominance of the capital of a definite country), or in the direction of their extinction by an American super-state, as if American capital purely and simply directed the other imperialist bourgeoisies. This internationalisation, on the other hand, deeply affects the politics and institutional forms of these states by including them in a system of interconnections which is in no way confined to the play of external and mutual pressures between juxtaposed states and capitals. These states themselves take charge of the interest of the dominant imperialist capital in its development within the "national" social formation, i.e., in its complex relation of internalization to the domestic bourgeoisie that it dominates. (Poulantzas 1974: 73)

Transnational capital's interpenetration with domestic bourgeoisies may have rendered the notion of a national bourgeoisie increasingly arcane. But even an internal bourgeoisie "implicated by multiple ties of dependence in the international division of labour and in the international concentration of capital" still maintained its own economic foundation and base of capital accumulation at home and abroad, as well as exhibited specific political and ideological features with autonomous effects on the state. Nor was this struggle one in which only dominant classes and fractions were at play: "While the struggles of the popular masses are more than ever developing in concrete conjunctures determined on a world basis . . . it is still the national form that prevails in these struggles, however international they are in their essence. This is due for one thing to uneven development and the concrete specificity of each social formation; these features are of the very essence of capitalism, contrary to the belief upheld by the various ideologies of 'globalisation'" (Poulantzas 1974: 78).

Poulantzas reminded us that the internationalization of the state was a development that could not "be reduced to a simple contradiction of a mechanistic kind between the base (internationalization of production) and a superstructural cover (national state) which no longer corresponds to it." Nor could the state be reduced to "a mere tool or instrument of the dominant classes to be manipulated at will, so that every step that capital took towards internationalization would automatically induce a parallel 'supernationalization' of states." If the focus of attention was on relations and struggles among social forces, we would see that these did not shift to some hyperspace beyond the state. Rather, global class interpenetrations and contradictions needed to be understood in the context of specificities of the nation-state's continuing central role in organizing, sanctioning, and legitimizing class domination within capitalism.

THE ANTINOMIES OF ROBERT COX

Only with Cox's *Production, Power, and World Order* (1987) did a full-scale study appear of the internationalization of the state founded on a historical materialist understanding of the role of "social forces in the making of history" rather than a false counterposition between globalizing capital and the power of states. The impact of Cox's book in challenging the dominant realist approach to the study of international relations has been comparable to that of Miliband's *The State in Capitalist Society* in challenging the pluralist approach to the study of comparative politics almost twenty years earlier. Writing over a decade later than Murray and Poulantzas, moreover, Cox was in a better position to analyze the changing modalities of the internationalization of the state induced by the new era of economic instability and crisis since the mid-1970s.

Cox's approach, like Murray's, is grounded in his understanding of the "indispensable functions" the state has to perform in a capitalist society, from guaranteeing property and contracts, to dismantling obstructions to markets, to ensuring the soundness of money (Cox 1987: 132–133). Cox is concerned, however, to go beyond this: "In order to comprehend the real historical world it is necessary to consider distinctive *forms of state* . . . [and] the characteristics of their historic blocs, i.e., the configuration of social forces upon which state power ultimately rests. A particular configuration of social forces defines in practice the limits or parameters of state purposes, and the modus operandi of state action, defines, in other words, the *raison d'état* for a particular state." Within these parameters, the state exercised power and choice in the organization and development of production and classes, although its actions "in these matters are, in turn, conditioned by the manner in which the world order impinges upon the state" (Cox 1987: 105).

Cox situates the internationalization of the state in the specific context of the rise and fall of the hegemonic world order of Pax Americana. Under the decisive shift in "relative economic-productive powers" in favor of the United States and its leadership outside the Soviet sphere after 1945, the "putting into place of the new order involved the transformation of state structures" from those that had existed in the prewar nonhegemonic system of nationalist/welfare states. The point is that the new order entailed a transformation, not a diminution, of the state—a reorganization of the state's structure and role in its external and internal aspects. Within the framework of interstate agreements forged at Bretton Woods, Pax Americana "was held in place by a configuration of different forms of state whose common feature was the role each played in adjusting national economic policies to the dynamics of the world economy." It was held also under the continued surveillance, incentives, and sanctions of new international financial institutions (the IMF and World Bank), which "behaved as accessories to U.S. policy." The process of establishing and internalizing a "notion of international obligation" to the world economy constitutes, for Cox, "the meaning given to the term *internationalizing of the state*":

> *First,* there is a process of interstate consensus formation regarding the needs or requirements of the world economy that takes place within a common ideological framework (i.e., common criteria of interpretation of economic events and common goals anchored in the idea of an open world economy). *Second,* participation in this consensus formation is hierarchically structured. *Third,* the internal structures of states are adjusted so that each can best transform the global consensus into national policy and practice, taking account of the specific kinds of obstacles likely to arise in countries occupying the differently hierarchically arranged positions in the world economy. (Cox 1987: 254)

Whereas Poulantzas proceeded from within ("states themselves take charge of the interests of the dominant imperialist capital in its development within the 'national' social formation"), Cox proceeds from the outside in:

He begins with international consensus formation, agreements, and obligations, to which internal state structures are then adjusted. To be sure, Cox is careful to say that this "was not necessarily a power structure with lines of force running exclusively top-down, nor was it one in which the bargaining agents were whole nation-states." Bureaucratic fragments of states were engaged in a process of bargaining, with the hegemonic power structure "tacitly taken into account" and, "through ideological osmosis, were internalized in the thinking of participants" (Cox 1987: 256–259). In the interwar era the state's political accountability was solely turned inward so that the state acted as a buffer protecting the domestic economies from external forces. But the internationalization of the state after 1945 involved establishing a compromise between the international and domestic obligations of states. The state now took the form of a mediator between the externally established policy priorities and the internal social forces to which it also still remained accountable. "The centre of gravity shifted from national economies to the world economy, but states were recognised as having a responsibility to both" (Cox 1987: 254–255).

The state was not less powerful in terms of controlling the national economy than before the war. State intervention, as Cox points out, had proved incapable of pulling the economy out of the 1930s depression; before the war no less than after, the state was primarily reactive, lacking "the ability to conceive and carry through an organization of production and distribution that would replace the market. It could tinker or 'fine tune'; it could not design" (Cox 1987: 189). Rather than a loss of power, the internationalization of the state after 1945 reflected a shift in power inside the state, entailing "a restructuring of the hierarchy of state apparatuses." In appearance there was "virtually nothing" to signal this change in structure; rather the goals pursued and the uses to which the structures were put changed. Agencies with direct links to the "client groups of national economy," such as ministries of labor and industry and institutions of tripartite corporatism that had developed in the interwar era, were not displaced. Indeed, they and the social forces attached to them remained "relatively privileged" and even "preeminent." But they were subordinated to prime ministerial and presidential offices, foreign offices, treasuries, and central banks in such a way that they became "instruments of policies transmitted through the world-economy linked central agencies" (Cox 1987: 214, 220–221, 228, 229, 266, 281).

A new stage in the internationalization of the state arose, however, in the wake of the crisis in the postwar order that emerged in 1968–1975. This crisis has led to the further expansion of "the breadth and depth of the global economy," even while undermining U.S. hegemony. The internationalizing of production and finance that grew through the 1950s and 1960s under the umbrella of Pax Americana, together with domestic inflationary pressures, industrial militancy, and declining profits under conditions of full employment, engendered this crisis. The Bretton Woods exchange rates arrangement was abandoned, and the limits of the domestic fine-tuning capacity of tripartism were severely tested. Although Cox thus sees the crisis as having been generated as much by domestic contradictions as international ones, he nevertheless once again portrays the reconstruction of the state in the new era from the outside in. A new doctrine redefining the role of states "was prepared by a collective effort of ideological revision undertaken through various unofficial agencies—the Trilateral Commission, the Bilderberg conferences, the Club of Rome, and other prestigious forums—and then endorsed through more official agencies like the OECD" (Cox 1987: 259, 282–283, 289). This doctrine, virtually identical as Cox portrays it to the governing philosophy of what he calls the Thatcher-Reagan hyperliberal state form ("the fullest, most uncompromising instance of a liberal state"), attacked the postwar compromise in both senses of the term: the domestic compromise that tied in labor and welfare interests and the international compromise of mediating between national interests and the global order. Inside the state, there is a further shift in power away from those agencies most closely tied to domestic social forces and toward those in closest touch with the transnational process of consensus formation. As summarized by Cox in a recent essay:

> There is, in effect, no explicit political or authority structure for the global economy. There is, nevertheless, something that remains to be deciphered, something that could be described by the French word *"nebuleuse"* or by the notion of "governance without government."
>
> There is a transnational process of consensus formation among the official caretakers of the global economy. This process generates consensual guidelines, underpinned by the ideology of globalisation, that are transmitted into the policy-making channels of national governments and big corporations. . . . The structural impact on national governments of this centralisation of influence over policy can be called the internationalising of the state. Its common feature is to convert the state into an agency for adjusting national economic practices and policies to the perceived exigencies of the global economy. The state becomes a transmission belt from the global to the national economy, where heretofore it had acted as the bulwark defending domestic welfare from external disturbances. Power within the state becomes concentrated in those agencies in closest touch with the global economy—the offices of presidents and prime ministers, treasuries, central banks. The agencies that are more closely tied with domestic clients—ministries of industries, labour ministries, etc,—become subordinated. This phenomenon, which has become so salient since the crisis of the post-war order, needs much more study. (Cox 1992: 30–31)

Cox had identified this same shift in power as the constitutive element in the reconstruction of the state in the Bretton Woods era. Although he does not make this explicit, it appears that now the corporatist and welfarist state apparatuses and the social forces allied with them lose the "preeminent" and "relatively privileged" position they had previously retained. But since they had already been substantively rendered "secondary" even in the post-1945 era (Cox 1987: 266, 283), the substantive change he has in mind in the post-1975 era appears related to the role of the already dominant state apparatuses of treasuries, central banks, prime minister's offices, and so on. They seem less and less to be in a bargaining relationship with the forces representing the global economy and more and more their agents.

Notably, for Cox, as for Gordon (1988), globalization reflects less the establishment of a stable new international regime of capital accumulation than an aspect of the decay of the old social structure of accumulation. As Cox puts it, the tendency to globalization is "never complete," and there is "nothing inevitable" about its continuation. "Any attempt to depict it must not be taken teleologically, as an advanced stage towards the inevitable completion of a latent structure. Rather it should be taken dialectically, as the description of tendencies that, as they become revealed, may arouse oppositions that could strive to confound and reverse them" (Cox 1987: 253, 258).

Even with this said, however, Cox's account of what is involved in the tendency to globalization still reflects to some extent the limits of the "outside in" orientation of his approach to the internationalization of the state. The notion of the state moving from being a buffer to being a mediator to finally becoming a transmission belt (Cox 1992: 30–31; 1987: 259) is too formal in its distinction of stages in the relationship between global and national economy. It is also (and against the spirit of Cox's approach) too "top-down" in its expression of contemporary power relations. I would argue that the role of states remains one not only of internalizing but also of mediating adherence to the untrammeled logic of international capitalist competition within its own domain, even if only to ensure that it can effectively meet its commitments to act globally by policing the new world order on the local terrain. It is in terms of the difficulty of such mediation that Cox's own insights on "the tendency toward limited democracy" as a means of limiting popular domestic pressures on the state can, in fact, best be appreciated. What needs to be investigated is whether the important shifts in the hierarchy of state apparatuses really are about bringing to the fore those most involved with the international "caretakers of the global economy" or whether a more general process is at work. This process is determined more from within the state itself, whereby even those agencies without such direct international links (but that nevertheless directly facilitate capital accumulation and articulate a competitiveness ideology) gain status, while those that fostered social welfare and articulated a class harmony orientation lose status. Whether that loss of status is considerable, or even permanent, however, depends partly on the transformations that these latter agencies are going through in terms of being made (or making themselves) more attuned to the exigencies of global competitiveness and fiscal restraint. Ministries of labor, health, and welfare are perhaps not so much being subordinated as being restructured.

As for the structure of power at the international level, a *nébuleuse* or a "governance without government" is not well captured through the notion of a "global centralisation of influence over policy" and the "transmission belts" that emanate from them. Indeed, in an insightful passage in *Production, Power, and World Order* Cox himself traced the "decline of centralized management characteristic of the world economy of Pax Americana" so that the world economy increasingly was better represented as "a system than as an institution." For the 1960s he could identify a set of institutions with the U.S. Treasury at the apex and its policy criteria being internationalized through the IMF, World Bank, and other such agencies. But "during the 1970s, private transnational banks assumed such an important role that the top management structure could no longer be convincingly represented exclusively in terms of state and interstate institutions." The key development here was that

> private international credit expanded for lack of any agreement on how the official intergovernmental structures in the system could be reformed. The impasse on reform was the consequence of stalemate between the United States and the European countries on the future role of the dollar. . . . In the absence of agreement on management by official institutions, dollar hegemony shifted to the financial market, that is to say, to the very largely unmanaged dollar itself. . . . Authority weakened at the apex of the international financial system. Crisis did not produce effective centralization. U.S. power was too great to be brought under any externally imposed discipline but was no longer great enough to shape the rules of a consensual order. (Cox 1987: 300–303)

Cox does not see this problem as having been resolved by the early 1990s. Indeed, he stresses in his 1992 essay the "parlously fragile condition" of international finance in a context where even the G7 governments have not been able to "devise any effectively secure scheme of regulation."

It becomes particularly clear here that there is an unresolved antinomy in Cox. On the one hand, there is an image of an increasingly centralized supranational management structure, founded on ideological consensus among the elites that populate transnational institutions and forums. He claims that the disintegration of the norms of postwar hegemonic order led to an intensification among the advanced capitalist countries of "the practice of policy harmonization [which] became correspondingly more important to the maintenance of consensus. The habit of policy harmonization had been institutionalized during the preceding two decades and was, if anything, reinforced in the absence of clear norms. *Ideology had to substitute for legal obligation*" (Cox 1987: 259). Is it this that transmits and links hyperliberal policy from country to country? On the other hand, there is another image of an unregulated system of international finance—which appears to be unregulated, moreover, in good part because of an inability to forge policy consensus at an interstate level. Does this system of international finance define the internationalization of the state in terms of hyperliberalism, making accountable national policy makers of whatever ideological orientation to the not-so-hidden hand of financial markets?

The antinomies in the Coxian framework have led one recent critic, looking for a more orthodox and neater pattern of determinations, to throw up his hands in frustration:

> [Cox's] frantic attempt to escape the twin evils of "economism" and idealism offers little more than a version of Weberian pluralism oriented to the study of the international order. . . . Variables which comprise a social order—the economy, the polity, the civil society—are given no overall structure but rather each has a real autonomy which preclude overdetermination. . . . This factor approach is reflected in Cox's analysis to the effect that in the interaction between material capabilities, ideas and institutions no determinism exists, and relationships are reciprocal. The question of lines of force is an historical one to be answered by a study of the particular case.
>
> However laudable in theory, the true consequence of this position is to produce a pluralist empiricism which lacks the power to explain either the systemic connection between values, social relations and institutions or the extent to which the historical appearance of capital as a social relation transforms the social order in such a way that all relations are subsumed under the capital relation as the basis for valorisation. (Burnham 1991: 77–78)

If the charge of a certain empiricism is perhaps not entirely off the mark, the general level at which Burnham demands primacy be given to "the capital relation" is hardly any answer. Indeed, Cox would readily grant determination at this level but then ask: so what? Certainly Burnham's additional critique of Cox for allegedly failing to recognize that "the state meets the interests of capital-in-general by enforcing the discipline of the market through the rule of law and the rule of money" is entirely misplaced. Cox explicitly recognizes this as regards both the liberal state of the mid-nineteenth century and the hyperliberal state of the late twentieth century (Cox 1987: 132–133). But he wants to know what disciplines the state to do this— and what makes it do it again in another form in another historical conjuncture? The role of the state is not best conceived as something given by the capital relation once and for all, but neither is it best conceived in terms of a transmission belt from the global economy to the national economy.

The role of each state is still determined by struggles among social forces always located within each social formation. Even though these social forces are also, to recall Poulantzas, "implicated by multiple tiers of dependence in an international division of labour and in the international concentration of capital," and although the struggles may be seen as "more than ever developing in conjunctures determined on a world basis," the specific national form still prevails in these struggles because of uneven development and the specificity of each social formation. (Is it really to international finance that governments in London and Ottawa are accountable when they prepare their budgets? Or are they accountable to international finance because they are accountable to the City of London or to Bay Street?) It is precisely in light of domestic as well as international concerns about the continuing salience of popular struggles at the level of the nation-state that we need to locate current attempts at constitutionalizing neoliberalism. The internationalization of the state in the 1990s appears to be taking the form, in the continuing absence of the ideological consensus or capacity to bring about a transnational regulation of capital markets, of interstate treaties designed to legally enforce upon future governments general adherence to the discipline of the capital market. This arises out of a growing fear on the part of both domestic and transnational capitalists, as the crisis continues, that ideology cannot continue to substitute for legal obligation in the internationalization of the state.

FORCED TO BE FREE:
THE CASE OF NORTH AMERICAN FREE TRADE

The North American Free Trade Agreement (NAFTA), which came into effect on 1 January 1994, most certainly fits the bill of constitutionalizing neoliberalism. Far more important than the reduction in tariffs, as Pres. Bill Clinton himself repeatedly intoned in the fevered run-up to the congressional vote on NAFTA, were the guarantees the agreement provided for U.S. investment in Mexico. As Robinson's incisive analysis demonstrates, international trade agreements like NAFTA not only "prohibit discrimination between national and foreign owned corporations [but also] create new corporate private property rights, possessed by both national and foreign investors. . . . It will function as an economic constitution, setting the basic rules governing the private property rights that all governments must respect and the types of economic policies that all governments must eschew" (Robinson 1993: 3; cf. Deblock and Rioux 1993; Grinspun and Kreklewich 1994).

NAFTA's investment chapter proscribes attempts by governments to establish performance requirements on foreign transnational corporations (TNCs) (except in the auto sector). It also defines investor rights that are protected under the agreement very broadly to include not only majority shareholders but minority interests, portfolio investment, and real property held by any company incorporated in a NAFTA country regardless of the country of origin. The monopolies and state enterprises chapter not only requires public enterprises to operate "solely in accordance with commercial considerations" and to refrain from using "anticompetitive practices" such as "the discriminatory provision of a monopoly good or service, cross-subsidization or predatory conduct" (all of which is the bread and butter of TNCs themselves) but also requires public enterprises to minimize or eliminate any nullification or impairment of benefits that investors might reasonably expect to receive under NAFTA. The intellectual property rights chapter (which grants copyright protection of up to twenty years to a vast array of trademarks, patents, semiconductor and industrial designs, trade secrets, satellite signals, and so on) goes furthest of all to "extend existing property rights by quasi-constitutionally protecting them against future democratic governments with the threat of trade sanctions . . . even though the effect of these rights is to restrict rather than enhance the free flow of ideas across national boundaries" (Robinson 1993: 22).

Taken together, these various provisions have the effect of redesigning the Mexican and Canadian states' relation to capital to fit the mold made in the United States by establishing and guaranteeing state defense of "new private property rights that go well beyond those recognised in Canadian and Mexican law, if not that of the United States" (Robinson 1993: 20). It is particularly important to stress that this is not something imposed on the Canadian and Mexican states by U.S. capital and state as external agents. Rather, it reflects the role adopted by the Mexican and Canadian states in representing the interests of their bourgeoisies and bureaucracies as these are already penetrated by U.S. capital and administration. As John H. Bryan Jr., president of Sara Lee Corporation, put it, the "most important reason to vote for NAFTA is to lock in [Mexico's] reforms" (*Business Week,* 22 November 1983: 94). This was all the more pressing insofar as there was a widespread awareness among North American elites (long before the Chiapas revolt on the day NAFTA came into effect) of popular discontent with the hyperliberal policies Mexico had adopted over the past decade, and a concern that any eventual opening up of Mexico's limited democracy might endanger the reelection of a PRI (Institutional Revolutionary Party) government. Shortly before the passage of the agreement, an article in the Toronto *Globe and Mail's Report on Business* (1 November 1993) quoted Alvaro Cepeda Neri of Mexico City's *La Jornada* as saying: "The booty of privatisation has made multimillionaires of 13 families, while the rest of the population—about 80 million Mexicans—has been subjected to the same gradual impoverishment as though they had suffered through a war."

The Mexican state was not only acting in terms of the interests of its domestic bourgeoisie, nor was it just concerned with providing further security guarantees to U.S. capital in Mexico. It was also, in Poulantzas's terms, "taking responsibility for the interests of the dominant capital" by endorsing NAFTA as an exemplary "staging post" for a renewed U.S. imperialism throughout Latin America and as a model for a similar constitutionalizing of neoliberalism on a global scale. The chairman of Salomon Inc. did not mince his words when he said that the defeat of NAFTA "would be a slap in the face to all leaders in the Western Hemisphere who have chosen the capitalist road over government-controlled economies"; nor did the Foreign Affairs Committee chairman in the House of Representatives, Lee Hamilton: "The question is U.S. leadership in the world" (*Business Week,* 22 November 1993: 35). What is especially notable, in fact, is that the greatest threat to the actual conclusion of NAFTA came not from Mexico or Canada but from the opposition within the United States itself. The side deals on the environment and labor undertaken by Clinton were designed to allow for the necessary compromises within the U.S. social formation; this succeeded to the extent that it divided the environmental movement. If the labor side deal failed to do the same it was because, not surprisingly, it did not go as far as the environmental side deal and did not allow for challenges to be made by Canadian or U.S. groups affected by NAFTA to challenge the nonenforcement of Mexican labor laws.

As regards the economic woes of the heartland of the empire, it is clear that the direct impact of NAFTA can only be minuscule. As Thurow (1993) pointed out, a worst-case scenario would entail the loss of 480,000 U.S. jobs over the next five years; the best case would see the addition of 170,000 jobs:

> The small stream of jobs produced or lost by NAFTA will not be noticed in a sea of 130 million American workers. . . . With a gross domestic product (GDP) only 4 to 5 percent of the United States, Mexico will not be an economic locomotive for America. . . . From 1973 to 1992 the per capita American GDP after correcting for inflation rose 27 percent. Yet over the same period average wages for the bottom 60 percent of male workers fell 20 percent in real terms. . . . Earnings prospects are collapsing for the bottom two-thirds of the work force. . . . After suffering two decades of falling real wages it is not surprising that Ross Perot can appeal to millions of Americans who lash out at the Mexicans in their frustration. . . . America is now a First World economy with a large, growing Third World economy in its midst.

NAFTA's predecessor was the U.S.-Canadian Free Trade Agreement (FTA), which served as the first staging post for hemispheric free trade and even for the Tokyo round of the General Agreement on Tariffs and Trade (GATT). The Canadian experience under the FTA certainly demonstrates that the constitutionalizing of neoliberalism exacerbates rather than contains the tendencies of the new global capitalism to generate successive social and economic crises. One study of Canadian employment trends since the inauguration of the FTA begins with a quotation from a currently popular Leonard Cohen song: "I have seen the future, brother; it is murder":

Official unemployment rose from 7.5% to 11.3% from December 1988 to August 1993. The ranks of the jobless swelled by 576,000, bringing the total to 1.6 million. Adding those who dropped out of the work force, the unemployment level rose to 2 million, doubling from 7.5% to 14%. If we include involuntary part-time workers which amounts to hidden unemployment, the "real" unemployment rate is currently at 20% of the work force. . . . Free trade supporters, though admitting that jobs have been lost in the low wage/low skill sectors of the economy, claim that the FTA is assisting the high-tech sectors, which comprise the emerging new economy of the 21st century, to grow and create high value added permanent jobs. The record of the first four years does not bear this out. . . . It is clear that despite positive signs in a few subsectors [only four—pharmaceuticals, computer services, accounting services, and management consultant services—to a total of 28,000 new jobs], the job creation numbers are minuscule. There is no sign of an expanding knowledge economy (either in manufacturing or services) to absorb the 434,000 workers displaced from the old and new manufacturing/resource economy, the 111,000 construction workers and the 104,000 workers displaced from the private sector, old and new, service economy, due to restructuring and recession. The public service sectors—education, health and social services, and government administration—absorbed 148,000 workers, but, given the extreme financial stress that these sectors are currently experiencing and the disinclination to change policy direction, even partial absorption by public sectors is not likely to continue in the future. The future is indeed bleak. (Campbell 1993: 1–6)

It was a mark of how deep the lines of U.S. imperialism ran in Canada that every issue, from social policy to defense to Quebec's status in Canada, was interpreted during the course of the 1988 federal election through the prism of the pros and cons of the FTA. All sides of the debate took the position that the free trade agreement was a historic departure, an epochal turning point for Canada. Either it would finally free Canadian business from the fetters of tariffs and regulation, expose it fully to the rigor of competition, and lay open a vast continental market for exports and investment or it would mean the end of Canada as we have known it for 121 years, shifting its economic axis southward, imposing the rule of business, destroying the welfare state, undermining Canadian culture, and subverting national sovereignty. Both views were misleading. The outcome of the free trade election marked not a new chapter but rather the punctuation mark in a very long historical sentence of economic and cultural integration with U.S. capitalism.

Canada had particular status as a rich dependency in the U.S. empire partly because of its geographic and cultural proximity to the United States. But also, as in the United States, the development of capitalism in Canada was predicated on a class structure that facilitated capitalist industrialization (Panitch 1981). A high-wage proletariat and a prosperous class of small farmers drew U.S. capital to Canada not only in search of resources (and not at all in search of cheap labor) but to sell to a market distinctly similar to the U.S. market. The national tariff designed to integrate an east-west economy and protect Canadian industry from competition from the south (and the flight of Canadian workers to the south) had the paradoxical effect of inducing the first U.S. TNCs to jump the tariff barrier and sell to Canada's (and sometimes through Canada to the British empire's) mass market. They were welcomed with open arms by the state as good corporate citizens and funded by Canada's substantial and powerful financial capitalists. During the first half of the twentieth century, Canada's status changed from that of a privileged white dominion in the old British empire to a state formally fully sovereign, but in substance quite dependent in a new kind of imperialism with a degree of direct foreign (U.S.) ownership unparalleled anywhere on the globe.

This status was still a privileged one, and Canadians shared in the spoils that went with U.S. hegemony in the postwar order. Any dependent country has a degree of autonomy. This is especially true of a rich country with a substantial industrial proletariat not as easily subjected to the same pressures as U.S. workers to accede to imperial demands of unswerving loyalty in a Cold War and therefore more open to socialist political ideas and mobilization. Canada's welfare state, however poor a cousin to those in northern Europe, eventually came to surpass what the New Deal had inaugurated in the United States. This gave Canada a badge of civility compared with U.S. society. Some public corporations and regulatory bodies took on the additional role of protecting what residual autonomy Canadian economy and culture could retain. But in doing this they did not so much challenge the fact of as negotiate the scope of Canada's dependency.

From this perspective we can see that the free trade treaty of 1988 was designed not to inaugurate but rather to constitutionalize, formalize, and extend Canada's dependence on the United States in a world now marked by economic instability amid rampant financial speculation and strong trade rivalries. Far from wanting to prove their entrepreneurial virility by taking the risk of becoming globally competitive, Canadian domestic capitalists sought to minimize the risk that Americans, when in a protectionist mood, might treat them, their exports, and their investments as merely "foreign." In turn, the Canadian government promised to give up those weak devices it had theretofore retained as a means of negotiating the scope of dependency. Margaret Atwood (following Antonio Gramsci) used a very Canadian metaphor to describe what the Mulroney government had done in entering into the FTA: in medieval bestiaries the beaver was noted for biting off its own testicles when frightened and offering them to its pursuer.

Even so, the free trade agreement failed to remove all restraints on U.S. protectionism. Many opponents of the FTA pointed this out, implying they might be content with the deal if it promised even fuller integration. But what most opponents were really objecting to was the whole dependent path of Canadian development; they wanted to avoid a punctuation mark being put at the end of Canada's long sentence of dependence. To defeat the deal would be to leave open the possibility of a "nevertheless" or a "however" —

which might yet be written at some point in the future. They were encouraged by the emergence of a visible strain of anti-Americanism, even of anti-imperialism. An indigenous cultural community had long been straining to define Canadian identity in the face of dependence. The labor movement, once a strong if subordinate sponsor of continentalism, had also experienced a shift toward Canadianization as the U.S. labor movement proved ever weaker and more abject in the face of economic instability. And considerable domestic ecology, peace, and feminist movements had emerged, often with socialists in leadership positions and with greater salience in relation to Canadian governments than such movements had in the United States.

The anti–free trade forces were encouraged as well by the fact that the Canadian electorate showed no great enthusiasm for the Thatcher-Reagan hyperliberal state model. Just as the 1980s began, Canadians had opted for a Liberal platform that promised to install a "fair tax" system rather than supply-side economics and to foster a Canadian capitalist class with distinctive national goals and ambitions through the National Energy Programme (NEP) and a strengthened Foreign Investment Review Agency. It had indeed been in reaction to all this, as well as to cries for protectionism in the U.S. Congress, that the business community launched free trade and pursued it with such remarkable unanimity. When the NEP was established, Canadian capitalists, no less than U.S. ones, were determined not only to get rid of it at the first opportunity but to disable permanently such interventions by the state. They feared that popular pressures were pushing the state to become not the handmaiden to business it had usually been but a countervailing power to it. Greed was at play here also. Some elements of Canadian business had become full players on a continental plane while others harbored ambitions that they too might reap substantial profits if Canada embraced its continental destiny. This demonstrated that the point had long passed when business in Canada was interested in "reclaiming" the Canadian economy.

The continuing political predominance of business, despite the mood of the electorate and the volubility of progressive forces, was seen when opposition from a unified capitalist class destroyed the tax reforms advanced in the 1981 budget. It was also seen when the liberal government responded to the recession of 1981–1982 by removing the right to strike from some one million of the three million organized workers in Canada. Yet the ideological impact of hyperliberalism still remained limited. In 1984 even the Conservatives sensed that they could not get elected on a Thatcher-Reagan platform. Brian Mulroney ran a typically Canadian brokerage campaign promising everything to everybody and declaring the welfare state a sacred trust. This did not make it a sacred trust, of course, given the powerful business pressures to which the government was beholden, but it emboldened people to defend the welfare state as soon as the Tories tried to undo it.

The decision to go for the free trade agreement, under considerable pressure from the Business Council on National Issues (a powerful lobby that comprised the most powerful domestic and U.S. corporations), thus took on a double purpose. The agreement was to make permanent the dominance of business by formalizing continental integration in the face of U.S. protectionism and Canadian economic nationalism and to introduce Reaganomics by the back door of the free market ethos and provisions of the free trade deal. A popular coalition, funded by the labor movement and led by the leadership of the abovementioned new social movements, marshaled against the FTA with remarkable fervor and determination to force the free trade election of 1988.

Alongside a trenchant critique of the details and implications of the FTA, the anti–free trade coalition took a different tack. And it proved a shrewd one. It chose to mythologize the Canadian state as if it had always been a repository of Canadian independence and social justice. This was myth indeed. But nationalisms are built on myths, and this one became uncontested in the election with remarkable ideological consequences. The small badge of civility that a welfare state lends to Canadian social life compared with that in the United States laid the basis for Canadian national identity to be defined in the 1988 election in almost Scandinavian terms, where pride in the welfare state was rather more justified. In this context, the outcome of the free trade election was, despite the narrow victory by the Tories and the subsequent introduction of the FTA, rather ambiguous. Certainly, the victory of the business forces confirmed the historical trend toward continental integration. An exclamation mark had been added to Canada's historical sentence of dependence.

Paradoxically, the election also confirmed the absence of an ideological mandate to carry through Reaganomics in Canada. The Tories and the business community accepted the anti–free trade forces definition of patriotism as at least involving a defense of the welfare state. The freedom to trade and invest by business was bought at the ideological cost of pledging allegiance to medicare and other social programs. Insofar as the popular coalition forged during the campaign against free trade set the terms of the debate and forced its opponents to adopt a defense of the welfare state as a central element in the definition of *Canadianism,* it provided a strong ideological basis for defensive struggles. The seeds of the destruction of the Conservative Party, reduced in the 1993 election to only two seats in the House of Commons, were sown amid the ambiguity of the 1988 victory on free trade.

But the anti–free trade coalition, and much less the opposition parties, never made clear what its alternative really was. The experience with the 1980–1984 Liberal government had already shown that a policy for more economic independence and social justice could not rely on the cooperation of business. Yet the anti–free trade coalition was afraid to spell out the conclusion that the alternative had to involve fundamental challenges to capital's power and radical democratization of the state. It was afraid to do so because the Canadian people had been so little prepared for such a departure, with the NDP's (Canada's social democratic party) failure in this respect particularly glaring. A defense of the welfare state promises only stalemate so long as the power and mobility of capital remains untouched. In the context of Canada's reinforced dependency amid global economic instability and financial speculation, a clear alternative to free trade and unbridled capitalist competition remains to be articulated.

A PROGRESSIVE COMPETITIVE ALTERNATIVE?

There are those who . . . believe that we can take on the challenge of competitiveness *and* retain our socialist values; indeed they believe that competitiveness will create the very economic success essential to sustaining social programs. They are mistaken. In the first place they are wrong because, in the particular case of Canada, there is no capitalist class with the interest or capacity to develop a strong industrial base. . . . But they are more than just mistaken. The framework for competitiveness they invite us to accept is ultimately dangerous. . . . Once it is accepted, its hidden aspects . . . such as attacks on social programs—quickly reassert themselves. Once we decide to play on the terrain of competitiveness, we cannot then step back without paying a serious price. Having legitimated the importance of being competitive (when we should have been mobilising to defend our social values), we would be extremely vulnerable to the determined attacks that will inevitably come in the name of "global realities." . . . The competitive model ultimately asks how the *corporate sector* can be strengthened. Our perspective asserts that it is the very strength of that sector that limits our freedom and belittles the meaning of "community." (Gindin and Robertson 1992: 32–33, 39)

The global recession of the 1990s is testimony to the economic failure of global hyperliberalism. Far from state policies having no effect, global trade competition among states has ushered in "an unstable vicious circle of 'competitive austerity'" whereby the cumulative effect of each state's policies is immense in the misery it causes. As Albo summarizes: "Each country reduces domestic demand and adopts an export-oriented strategy of dumping its surplus production, for which there are fewer consumers in its national economy given the decrease in workers' living standards and productivity gains all going to the capitalists, in the world market. This has created a global demand crisis and the growth of surplus capacity across the business cycle" (Albo 1994: 144–170). Unfortunately, however, the program for a more progressive form of competitiveness that has been advanced by most mainstream parties of the center-left does not constitute much of an alternative. For a considerable period through the 1970s and well into the mid-1980s, a large portion of the center-left (often represented in intellectual life by the "state autonomists") refused to acknowledge that the crisis of the Keynesian/welfare state was a structural one, pertaining to the very nature of capitalism and the contradictions it generates in our time. Their response to the crisis, clearly visible in the Canadian free trade debate, was to point to relatively low unemployment levels in Sweden as evidence of the continuing viability of tripartite corporatism in sustaining the Keynesian/welfare state (Panitch 1986, esp. chaps. 1, 4–6). This involved, however, ignoring or downplaying the very contradictions and conflicts that were undermining even the Swedish model. Eventually this naive stance was displaced by an attempt to emulate countries that were most successful in the export-led competitive race. But rather than allow mainstream economists, with their neoliberal logic of deregulation, free markets, privatization, and austerity, to dictate the terms of the race, a "progressive competitiveness" strategy is advanced whereby labor and the state are urged to take the initiative and seize the hand of business in running toward competitive success.

At the core of the strategy, still inspired largely by a different facet of Swedish corporatism, is to support and guide both workers and capitalists toward high-tech/high-value-added/high-wage production. The key to this is public policy promoting the widespread training of a highly skilled, highly flexible, and highly motivated labor force and encouraging enterprises to take full advantage of recent technological developments in microelectronics, to the end of producing high-quality commodities at high productivity levels through flexible production methods. Equally founded on an acceptance of the irreversibility of globalization, but convinced that its connection with hyperliberalism is only a matter of the ideological coloration of politicians too closely attached to neoclassical economists, this approach still wants to give strategic priority to the state. Once shorn of an ideology of free markets as the premise of state policy in the process of globalization, the progressive competitiveness strategy expects the state to be able to sustain a substantial social wage if it explicitly connects welfare and education to the public promotion of flexible production and technological innovation in sectors that can win in a global export-led competitive race. Relative prosperity (clearly based on an extension of the advantages of relative over absolute surplus-value extraction) would fall to states that can guide capital and labor to adopt this "smart" strategy.

That such a strategy is chimerical and dangerous is in fact demonstrated by the experience in North America of the Clinton Democratic administration and the Ontario NDP government elected in 1990. The progressive competitiveness strategy presents a program of vast economic readjustment for both labor and capital, with little regard for how, in the interim, the logic of competitive austerity could be avoided. It presumes that mass unemployment is primarily a problem of skills adjustment to technological change rather than one aspect of a crisis of overproduction. As well, it fosters the illusion that the rate of employment growth in high-tech sectors can be sufficient to offset the rate of unemployment growth in other sectors. Further, it either even more unrealistically assumes a rate of growth of world markets massive enough to accommodate all those adopting this strategy or blithely ignores the issues associated with exporting unemployment to those who do not succeed at this strategy under conditions of limited demand (and with the attendant consequence this would have for sustaining demand). Finally, it ignores the reality that capital can also adapt leading technologies in low-wage economies and that the competitive pressures on capital in this context push down wages even in high-tech sectors and limit the costs to it of the social wage and adjustment policies so central to the whole strategy's progressive logic in the first place. It is hardly surprising that Albo concludes from all this that even "the progressive competitiveness strategy will be forced to accept, as most social democratic parties have been willing to do, the same 'competitive austerity' as neo-liberalism . . . as a cold necessity of present economic conditions" (Albo 1994: 157).

Cox, who terms this strategy "state capitalist" and sees it as the only possible medium-term alternative to the hyperliberal form of state, makes it quite clear that it is, in effect, "grounded in an acceptance of the world market as the ultimate determinant of development":

> The state capitalist form involves a dualism between, on the one hand, a competitively efficient world-market-oriented sector and, on the other, a protected welfare sector. The success of the former must provide resources for the latter; the sense of solidarity implicit in the latter would provide the drive and legitimacy for the former. . . . In its most radical form, state capitalism beckons toward an internal socialism sustained by capitalist success in world-market competition. This would be a socialism dependent on capitalist development, i.e., on success in the production of exchange values. But, so its proponents argue, it would be less vulnerable to external destabilization than attempts at socialist self-reliance were in weak countries. (Cox 1987: 292–294)

Cox sees this option ("with or without its socialist colouration") as largely limited to late industrializing countries (such as France, Japan, Germany, Brazil, and South Korea) with strong institutional and ideological traditions of "close coordination between the state and private capital in the pursuit of common goals." He is well aware that this type of state capitalism, while incorporating that portion of the working class attached to the world-market-oriented sector or employed in the welfare services sector, would nevertheless exclude many people ("disproportionately the young, women, immigrant or minority groups, and the unemployed") who would remain in a passive relationship to the welfare services and without influence in policy making. Amid anomic explosions of violence from these groups, Cox expects that the state capitalist alternative's "historic bloc would be thin" and that this might entail the kind of repression and insulation from democratic pressures that would particularly make illusory the prospects the state capitalist strategy holds out for an "internal socialism." Still, as of 1992, Cox took the position that state capitalist strategies in Japan and Europe constituted "the only possible counterweights to total globalization at the level of states." He held out particular hope that the European Community, where the "unresolved issue over the social charter indicates a stalemate in the conflict over the future nature of the nation state and of the regional authority," might yet bring to the fore "a capitalism more rooted in social policy and more balanced development," one reflecting the continuing influence of social democratic and older conservative traditions. Given the limited medium-term options of those who are looking for an alternative that would go beyond choosing between rival forms of capitalism, Cox urges them to look positively upon "the ideological space that is opened by this confrontation of hyperliberalism and state capitalist or corporatist forms of development" (Cox 1992: 31, 41; cf. Cox 1987: 292, 297–298).

Yet what is the evidence of such a confrontation? Cox exhibits here an unfortunate tendency to turn juxtaposed ideal-types, constructed for the purposes of analytic clarity, into real-world confrontations for which there is all too little evidence. The institutional and ideological structures that Cox points to as the basis for a state capitalist progressive competitiveness alternative to hyperliberal globalization are in fact being subsumed as subsidiary sponsors of globalization in a manner quite analogous to the way he saw tripartite institutions of national economic planning as having become subsidiary elements in adjusting domestic economies to the world economy in the postwar order.

Both in Europe and in North America, ministries of labor (and the tripartite forums and agencies they sponsor), as well as ministries of welfare and education, are being restructured to conform with the principles of global competitiveness. However, their capacity to retain their links to the social forces they represent in the state depends on their ability to tailor this reconstruction along the lines of progressive competitiveness principles. In this way, social groups that would otherwise become dangerously marginalized and disaffected as a result of the state's sponsorship of global competitiveness may become attached to it by the appeal a progressive competitiveness strategy makes, especially through the ideology and practice of training, to working people who are unemployed (or who fear they soon might be) as well as the leaders of the unions, social agencies, and other organizations who speak for them. Insofar as they are successful in this, moreover, ministries may prevent their further loss of status in the hierarchy of state apparatuses and even recapture some of their previously foregone status. The progressive competitiveness strategy undertakes no greater challenge to the structure of the state or to the logic of global competitiveness than that of insisting that more state economic orchestration can be an effective and humane handmaiden to competition. Thus, this strategy ends up being not an alternative to but a subsidiary element in the process of neoliberal capitalist restructuring and globalization.

In North America, the most often cited guarantee that the progressive competitiveness strategy will not dissolve into the logic of competitive austerity is the European Community's social charter. It is pointed to as a model for other international agreements that would constitutionalize a high level of labor rights, social standards, and corporate codes of conduct. On this basis, Robinson argues: "If globalization can mean more than one thing . . . then the irreversibility of globalization no longer necessarily leads to neo-conservative economic and social policy prescriptions. In this light, national competitiveness, too, can mean more than one thing, depending upon whether it is achieved by cutting labour and environmental costs to TNCs, or promoting technological innovation and reducing the social, political, and environmental externalities associated with largely unregulated global market competition" (Robinson 1993: 44). This approach almost always involves vastly inflating the salience and significance of the European social charter. Robinson acknowledges its weakness but fails to inquire whether the reason "the most powerful labour movements in the world have made only very limited progress towards an adequate EC social dimension" is because of its incompatibility with even the progressive competitiveness strategy of global competitiveness. The trenchant critique made by Robinson of NAFTA's side deals as a cosmetic means of buying off domestic opposition is not apparently seen by him (and so many others) as entailing a deeper lesson regarding such incompatibility.

Lipietz has recently provided a chilling account of how moderate EEC social democrats "set up a Europe of traders and capital," hoping that a social dimension would follow but failing to understand that they had already "thrown away their trump cards by signing the Single Act of 1985":

> A single market for capital and goods without common fiscal, social and ecological policies could not fail to set off a downward competition between member states, each needing to bring its trade into balance. To deal with the threat of "social dumping," Jacques Delors counted on a push *after the event* by unions in peripheral and social democratic countries to impose common statutory or contractual bases throughout the community. This has not happened, despite the (half-hearted) protestations of the European parliament. . . . [A]ttempts to harmonise VAT failed . . . [and] lack of harmonization on capital taxation is much more serious. . . . Even more serious was the surrender over social Europe. In September 1989, the European Commission proposed an insipid Social Charter. . . . In December 1991, at Maastricht . . . legislative power in Europe was handed over to coordination by national governments; a state apparatus on auto-pilot. Social Europe was once more sacrificed, and reduced to a "zero-Charter," with Britain opting out. . . . In essence, as it is presently emerging, Europe will be unified only for the sake of capital, to allow it to escape from state control; that is, from the tax authorities and from social legislation. (Lipietz 1992: 156–159)

It is, of course, not really an escape from state control—Lipietz's account would make no sense if it were. The governments of Europe are not trying to assert control over capital at the nation-state level while trying to foreswear control at the regional level. The states, including those led by social democrats, as Lipietz avers, are the political authors of the Europe of traders and capitalists. Of course they reflect capital's domination in each social formation in doing so. But the notion that this capital is ready to sustain, as the basis of regional trade rivalries, a rival state capitalist form "rooted in social policy and territorially balanced development" is belied by all the facts before us. Indeed, Cox may have been closer to the mark when he suggested in 1987 that the decline of U.S. hegemony and the competitive pressures in the world system were acting on all states in such a way as to encourage an "emulative uniformity" (Cox 1987: 298–299). But his expectation at the time that this might involve common "adoption of similar forms of state-capitalist development geared to an offensive strategy in world markets and sustained by corporatist organization of society and economy" rings true only if we see state capitalism as a subsidiary element sustaining competitive austerity, even in Europe. As Albo notes: "It is not the Anglo-American countries who are converting to the Swedish or German models but Germany and Sweden who are integrating the 'Anglo-American model'" (Albo 1994: 168).

Even if U.S. hegemony in international institutions has declined somewhat, the continued direct imbrication of U.S. capital in Europe as a powerful social force with which the European bourgeoisies remain interpenetrated still induces an "emulative uniformity." Poulantzas may have been wrong in his estimation in 1974 that each of the European bourgeoisies were too enmeshed in a structure of dependence on U.S. capitalists to allow for a major extension of intraregional cooperation in Europe. But he was not wrong in insisting that U.S. capital must be seen as a strong presence within Europe rather than as standing outside it. Indeed, part of the reason for the failure of a "social Europe" has to do with the mobilization of U.S. firms in Europe against it from the early 1980s on (Lambert 1991: 16). The multidimensional spread of direct foreign investment, with mutual interpenetration among European, Japanese, and U.S. capitals, reinforces this tendency for emulative uniformity (Magdoff 1992).

CONCLUSIONS

It would indeed appear that there is no way of posing an alternative to neoliberal globalization that avoids the central issue of the political source of capitalist power, globally and locally: the state's guarantee of control of the major means of production, distribution, communication, and exchange by private, inherently undemocratic banks and corporations. It is inconceivable that there can be any exit from today's crisis without a planned reorientation and redistribution of resources and production on a massive scale.

Yet how can this be conceived as feasible, let alone made a basis for political mobilization?

This chapter has suggested that those who want to install a transnational democracy in the wake of the nation-state allegedly having been bypassed by globalization simply misunderstand what the internationalization of the state really is all about. Not only is the world still very much composed of states, but insofar as there is any effective democracy at all in relation to the power of capitalists and bureaucrats it is still embedded in political structures that are national or subnational in scope. Those who advance the case for an international civil society to match the *nébuleuse* that is global capitalist governance usually fail to appreciate that capitalism has not escaped the state but rather that the state has, as always, been a fundamental constitutive element in the very process of extension of capitalism in our time.

Picciotto, who himself wants to give strategic priority to international popular organization as the best way forward, is nevertheless careful to warn against "naive illusions that social power exists quite independently of the state." He calls for "more sophisticated analyses of the contradictions of the state and the ways they can be exploited to build the strength of popular movements, while remaining aware that the national state is only a part of the overall structure of power in a global capitalist society" (Picciotto 1991: 60). The international constitutionalization of neoliberalism has taken place through the agency of states, and there is no prospect whatsoever of getting to a more egalitarian, democratic, and cooperative world order beyond global competitiveness, without a fundamental struggle with domestic and global capitalists over the transformation of the state. Indeed, the contemporary era of the globalization of capital may have finally rendered the distinction between national and foreign capital that has underpinned the two-centuries-old search for a cross-class "producer" alliance between labor and national capital more or less irrelevant as a strategic marker for the left.

It is necessary to try to reorient strategic discussions toward the democratic transformation of the state rather than toward the transcendence of the state or the fashioning of a progressive competitive state. At the most general level this means envisaging a state whose functions are not tied to guaranteeing the economic res publica for capitalism. We have seen how the internationalization of the state entails a turning of the material and ideological capacities of states to more immediate and direct use, in terms of both intranational and international dimensions, to global capital. The first requirement of a strategy to counter globalization must be to seek the transformation of the material and ideological capacities of states so that they can serve to realize popular, egalitarian, and democratic goals and purposes. This does not mean attempting to take the state as it is presently organized and structured and trying to impose controls over capital with these inappropriate instruments. Nor does it mean trying to coordinate such controls internationally while resting on the same state structures. The point must be to restructure the hierarchy of state apparatuses and reorganize their modus operandi so as to develop radically different material and ideological capacities.

"One of principal tasks of the capitalist state," Harvey notes, "is to locate power in the spaces which the bourgeoisie controls, and disempower those spaces which the oppositional movements have the greatest potential to command" (Harvey 1989: 237). Any movement against globalization will need to take this lesson out of the book of capital to relocate power to the benefit of progressive social forces. The same might be said about the important role the state can play in the distribution of time as an aspect of power. Radical proposals for a statutory reduction in the working day to as little as four hours not only are directed at coping with the appalling maldistribution of employment in contemporary capitalism but, as Mandel and Gorz both note, are necessary to establish the conditions for the extension and deepening of democracy by providing the time for extensive involvement in community and workplace decisionmaking (Mandel 1992: 202; Gorz 1989: 159).

To emphasize the continuing importance of struggles to transform the state does not mean that territorial boundaries within which claims to state sovereignty are embedded ought to be seen as immutable. Poulantzas insightfully pointed to the regional disarticulations that resulted from the extended reproduction of international capital within the framework of existing nation-states. The integration of national with international capital upsets the old bases for national capital's unity. At the same time, regional discontents with state policies that are increasingly articulated with the needs of the global economy have provided fertile ground for a resurgence of old nationalisms with a separatist purpose. Right-wing nationalisms, and the parochialisms and intolerances they both reflect and engender, must be combated on every front. But it is not always necessary for the left to oppose the breakup of an existing state, just as it is not wise to dismiss out of hand attempts at international rearticulation of sovereignties through the creation of regional federations. The question is only whether the locus of power is thereby shifted to where democratic and inclusive movements oppositional to capital can expand their space and powers through a reorganization of sovereignties.

For instance, though many people are dismayed by the prospect of Quebec leaving the Canadian federation at the very moment when France is joining a federal Europe, it is by no means necessarily the case that the existing Canadian federal state lays a firmer foundation for democratic challenges to capital than would close and amicable cooperation between an independent Quebec and a restructured Canadian state. Indeed, more might be expected from two nation-states each of whose raison d'état was expressly more egalitarian and democratic in purpose rather than binational and territorial. (*"Ad mare usque ad mare,"* it has often been pointed out on the

Canadian left, does not quite match "Liberty, equality, and fraternity" as an expression of raison d'état.) A federal Europe does not have to extend democratic powers rather than disperse them more thinly in relation to a greater centralization of state powers oriented to fulfilling capital's res publica on a continental terrain. Moreover, a federal state composed of the existing states of Europe continues to rest on the modus operandi of these states. As every Canadian knows, capitalist forces are as capable of playing off the units of a federation against one another and against the center as they are of doing so with sovereign nation-states. Indeed, the process may be more easily obscured behind an interminable debate over the division of constitutional powers.

Lipietz, while taking as a starting point that "the struggles and social compromises are still settled at the level of the old-established nations of Europe," would like to see social and political unification as quickly as possible insofar as this would be democratically structured to overcome the terrible condition of competitive austerity. But he admits that though it "is better to have a Europe which is progressive (in the alternative sense of the word) than a France, a Sweden, etc., which are progressive in isolation . . . the present dilemma does not lie here. We are asked to choose between a Europe of *possibly* alternative states, and a united Europe which is liberal-productivist. My response is that if this is the choice, the first solution is better." He admits that in the short term it is unrealistic to expect a united Europe to be based on anything other than liberal-productivism. But it is no less unrealistic to expect that this will change in the future without a prior change in the configuration of social forces and restructuring of state apparatuses in the member countries (Lipietz 1992: 135–139).

A possibly alternative state to those sponsoring globalization amid competitive austerity today would have to be based on a shift toward a more inwardly oriented economy rather than one driven by external trade considerations. This in turn would have to mean greater emphasis on a radical redistribution of productive resources, income, and working time than on conventional economic growth. This could be democratically grounded only, as Albo puts it, insofar as "production and services [were] more *centred* on local and national needs where the most legitimate democratic collectivities reside." Democratically elected economic planning bodies at the microregional level should be the first priority in a program for an alternative state. These bodies should be invested with the statutory responsibility for engineering a return to full employment in their communities and funded through direct access to a portion of the surplus that presently is the prerogative of the private financial system to allocate.

This alternative could not be realized without at least some trade controls and quite extensive controls over the flow of capital. (Indeed, it is improbable that such capital control can be realized without bringing the financial system within the public domain and radically reorganizing it in terms of both its structure and its function.) Of course, this would require interstate cooperation to install managed trade (rather than autarky) and to make capital controls effective. Have we then gone through this exercise only to come full circle—right back to the internationalization of the state? Certainly not. International agreements and treaties between states will most certainly be required, but they will have the opposite purpose to the consti- tutionalizing of neoliberalism. They will be explicitly designed to permit states to effect democratic control over capital within their domain and to facilitate the realization of alternative economic strategies.

The feasibility of this alternative scenario rests entirely on conditions that still remain to be established. It is all too easy (and demobilizing) to pre- dict the immense pressure and exertion of naked power that would emanate from international capital and dominant states to a country that was even near the point of embarking on such a strategic alternative. Such a predic- tion ignores the prior material (including in the economic-technical sense) and political conditions that would bring the possibility of change onto the historical agenda. Even the technical feasibility of short-term capital con- trols is an open question today. Yet the instability of the world financial sys- tem is such that we are likely to see the discovery of means of control and regulation, whether before or after an international financial collapse. But it is, above all, the political conditions that need to be created. The impact of domestic and external resistance is unpredictable in abstraction from the character, strength, and effectiveness of the social forces within states that must mobilize to put the alternative on the agenda. Cox is extremely insight- ful on this when he insists at the end of *Production, Power, and World Order* that once "a historical movement gets under way, it is shaped by the mater- ial possibilities of the society in which it arises and by resistance to its course as much as by the . . . goals of its supporters." Yet this is why, he insists, "critical awareness of the potentiality for change . . . concentrates on the possibilities of launching a social movement rather than on what that movement might achieve. . . . In the minds of those who opt for change, the solution will most likely be seen as lying not in the enactment of a specific policy program as in the building of new means of collective action informed by a new understanding of society and polity" (Cox 1987: 393–394).

This will happen within states or not at all, but it will not happen in one state alone while the rest of the world goes on running with the bourgeoisie around the globe. Alternatives arise within international political time. The movement-building struggles arise in conjunctures that are more than ever determined on a world basis. Movements in one country have always been informed and inspired by movements abroad; this will surely prove to be the case as opposition builds to the evils globalization is visiting on peoples, including, increasingly, those in the developed capitalist countries. There is no need to conjure up an international civil society to install a transnational democracy. Rather we are likely to witness a series of movements that will be exemplary for one another, even though national specificities will continue to prevail. It is to be hoped, of course, that these movements will be solidaristic with one another, even though international solidarity movements cannot be more than critical supplements to the struggles that must take place in each state.

NOTE

A much earlier version of this chapter was originally presented as a paper at the seminar El Mundo Actual: Situación y Alternativas, at UNAM, Mexico City, in December 1993, and subsequently revised and published in *The Socialist Register 1994*. This extensively revised and expanded chapter has benefited greatly from the criticisms and suggestions of Robert Cox, Peter Damaskopolous, Stephen Gill, Bob Marshall, and Jim Mittelman.

Part 2

The Counterthrust to Globalization: Political and Cultural Resistance

Glenn Adler 6

Global Restructuring and Labor: The Case of the South African Trade Union Movement

At the end of the twentieth century the global division of labor (GDL) appears an irrepressible force—spreading new technologies and labor processes throughout the world, subjecting whole regions to powerful multinational corporate institutions, dissolving familiar divisions in the interstate system and undermining the sovereignty of states, remaking civil society and spurring subnational fragmentation. Before the onslaught of such impersonal and unaccountable processes, ordinary people appear quite powerless to defend themselves, much less to offer alternatives to the imperatives of global capitalist production. The collapse of "actually existing socialism" and the parallel impoverishment of Third World liberation movements as bearers of democracy and economic development contribute to a "politics of disillusionment" in which the possibilities for humane development are increasingly constrained, if not repudiated by the global system (Mittelman, Chapter 1).

Without denying the rather bleak possibilities open to individuals, groups, and movements in the Third World, it is curious that the emerging literature on the GDL generally overlooks important dynamics that suggest alternative directions. In particular, the literature pays limited attention to the impressive growth of labor movements in the newly industrializing countries (NICs) and to the expansion of working-class political and economic demands.

In large part this shortcoming derives from problems in the theoretical formulation of the GDL as a concept, which can be traced to the interpretation of the division of labor as an economic and technical process rather than as a contradictory and conflictual social relationship. Furthermore, much of the analytical work on the GDL operates from an elite and statist perspective, with a bias toward macroeconomic, rather than social and historical, variables. It thus becomes extremely difficult for the literature to explain movements emerging from civil society, particularly those that develop as a result of the industrialization process itself. Without taking labor seriously as an actor in the GDL it is difficult to assess where challenges are likely to emerge, as well as the substance of such challenges and their likelihood of success. However, the profound pessimism described here seems based less on an actual analysis of counterhegemonic projects than on an unfounded fatalism.

By contrast, this chapter begins from an interpretation of the division of labor as a creative process marked by social relations of inequality between capital and labor. The division of labor may give rise to collective actors (including labor movements) that are not just epiphenomena to be read off logically from economic structures. These actors are capable of self-conscious engagement in collective action, and just as they are affected by structures so too can they be a cause of structural change. As a result, collective actors growing out of the division of labor—in particular, the labor movement—must be studied in their own right as important components of the GDL.

An inability to account for how labor movements are generated and develop weakens our understanding of the GDL. This is especially true in addressing the supreme challenge of making economic revitalization compatible with democratization, as labor movements are not simply obstructions to be conquered and controlled but may be essential participants in economic policy and important bearers of democratic politics. They thus provide a bridge between these twin concerns; indeed, in many societies they are among the foremost advocates of such policies.

Surprisingly, these are not the actors that, a generation ago, radical analysts believed would bring change in the Third World. In place of peasant-based liberation movements and centralized vanguard socialist parties, labor movements in the NICs are contributing to a more incremental, reformist, and negotiated form of change in keeping with social democracy and corporatism rather than socialist revolution.[1] This suggests not only a more feasible politics of transition but, from the point of view of democratization, a more desirable one as well.

The first part of this chapter examines the theoretical status of the concept of division of labor and the forms of collective action it may engender. The second locates these more general arguments in the case study of the modern South African labor movement, as an empirical example of the processes of class formation and the possibilities for transformation in the NICs. South Africa is often identified as a unique case from which generalizations are difficult, because of the peculiar distortions caused by apartheid. But there are persuasive reasons to believe that developments there in fact describe an emerging pattern within globalization—at least within the NICs—which suggests the need for further research on similar trends elsewhere.

THE GLOBAL DIVISION OF LABOR:
WHERE ARE THE WORKERS?

The emergence in the late twentieth century of a global division of labor is of course not the first time that industrial capitalism has reconstituted the world system. The origins of modern social science lay in nineteenth-century efforts to make sense of the destabilizing social and political effects of the first wave of capitalist industrialization. On the eve of the revolutions of 1848 Marx and Engels described a capitalism that had established itself on a global basis:

> The bourgeoisie, by the rapid improvement of all instruments of production, by the immensely facilitated means of communication, draws all, even the most backward, nations into civilisation. . . . It compels all nations, on pain of extinction, to adopt the bourgeois mode of production. . . . In one word, it creates a world after its own image. (Marx and Engels, 1964: 64–65)

The spread of the capitalist mode of production transformed all manner of social and political relations in its wake.[2] In Marx and Engels's famous phrase:

> All fixed, fast-frozen relations, with their train of ancient and venerable prejudices and opinions are swept away, all new-formed ones become antiquated before they can ossify. All that is solid melts into air, all that is holy is profaned. (Marx and Engels, 1964: 63)

Despite the massive increase in productive capacity brought about by the new mode of production, Marx and Engels believed the lot of ordinary people subject to the new division of labor was one of increased pauperization, of alienation from the qualities that define workers as human beings.

For Marx, the capitalist mode of production was not an unfettered juggernaut but a process that generated its own opposition. At its heart was a division of labor that he conceived as composed of social relations between contradictory classes. The very success of the capitalist mode of production created the revolutionary working class that Marx optimistically assumed would lead to its downfall. Without accepting the teleological framework Marx constructs, the essential point is that the capitalist division of labor creates new forms of solidarity among those subject to its domination, and such solidarity can be the basis for dramatic—if not revolutionary—collective action.

Weber and Durkheim, no less than Marx, appreciated the injurious impact of the capitalist division of labor, though they both rejected the assumption of a teleological progression toward a revolutionary class-for-itself. For Weber, it was the capitalist market economy and its demands for precision, speed, and efficiency that provided the motive force behind the spread of bureaucratic rationality through all spheres of life. The minute division of labor, strict hierarchy, and impersonality of industry impose on all the stern discipline of ascetic Calvinism, the "cosmos of the modern economic order" (Gerth and Mills 1946: 215; Weber 1930: 181). The division of labor was thus the source of the profound disenchantment Weber identified as characteristic of the modern age, spawning "specialists without spirit, sensualists without heart" (Weber 1930: 182). Of course Weber did not view the division of labor as spontaneously generating class-based collective action. Such "communal action" flowing from class interests was far more likely where the contrast between the life chances of owners and workers was no longer seen as a given but as resulting from the structure of the economic order (Gerth and Mills 1946: 184).

Durkheim saw the development of the division of labor as the distinctive feature of modern society. The simple division of labor of primitive societies bound people together through commonality. All performed similar tasks and were linked through a common set of norms and values—the collective conscience—growing out of these common activities. Modern industry destroyed these bonds by transforming the division of labor through the growing specialization of function and occupations.

The differentiation of tasks, while allowing for the realization of human potential through education and skills development, did not automatically generate a new solidarity among workers. Indeed, the modern division of labor produced characteristic pathologies, such as anomie. In particular, it could lead to conflict among workers, especially when the assignment of tasks did not correspond to the natural distribution of talents—the forced division of labor—such as occurred when inheritance distorted people's life chances.

For Durkheim the central problem in modern society was the creation of a new form of solidarity articulating the diverse parts into a functional whole. He believed such solidarity would grow out of the division of labor itself, from the interdependence it created among workers. As it provides the source of solidarity, the division of labor would become the foundation of a new moral order.

In particular, the division of labor was the basis for new collective organizations that would constitute the rules for regulating and restraining human desires. The occupational group, or corporation, was to be composed of all the participants in a particular industry, who would themselves make the rules governing their collective life. It could be local, national, or international in extent, depending on the breadth of the occupation concerned. In the absence of a strong collective conscience, such rule-making allowed for the regulation of human activity in a particular field of endeavor. The occupational group was an end in itself:

A group is not only a moral authority which dominates the life of its members; it is also a source of life sui generis. From it comes a warmth which animates its members, making them intensely human, destroying their egotisms. (Durkheim 1930: 26)

The group thus could arrive at legitimate rules of behavior while linking disparate individuals in a common and meaningful entity.

For all three theorists the division of labor not only served as the source of the characteristic conflicts and cleavages in modern society, it also provided the integument from which new forms of solidarity would emerge linking workers (and, in Durkheim's conception, workers and owners) in meaningful and powerful new ways. None of the theorists approached the division of labor as a technical or purely economic phenomenon. For each, the division of labor was of interest as an essentially social process, composed of complex and contradictory relations among individuals and groups. While it dissolved old forms of associations and meanings, it was simultaneously the source of new, and potentially radical, forms of social organization. For both Marx and Durkheim these forms were not necessarily confined within state borders; both asserted the theoretical possibility (for Marx, necessity) of international solidaristic organization.

This social and relational aspect of the division of labor is overlooked in the GDL literature. The division of labor is more than a mechanical classification of countries in the international political economy according to their level of industrial production or the composition of their exports. As it entails structured relationships between producers, it describes relations between human beings, a division of laborers. Within a system of private property, it willy-nilly involves asymmetrical power relations between owners and nonowners, between capitalists and workers. By failing to grasp what Marx would describe as the social relations of production, the GDL omits as a theoretical problem the various possibilities for collective economic self-organization, which Marx, Weber, and Durkheim saw as distinguishing modern industry from its predecessors.

In the core, semiperiphery, and periphery, workers have developed the organized capacity to disrupt or contribute to economic growth, and their strength at the point of production has provided a platform for broader political initiatives. Recent analyses of labor in the NICS have identified organized labor's ability to challenge state economic development programs through its power to drive up wages, obstruct productivity drives, and resist austerity (Deyo 1987a).

This approach is taken furthest in a recent provocative critique of both pluralist and Marxist approaches to democracy by Rueschemeyer, Stephens, and Stephens (1992). They assert that trade unions (and the working class more broadly) have played a decisive role in the development of democratic polities and are perhaps the most important social force struggling for the extension of the franchise and the establishment and extension of the welfare state (Rueschemeyer, Stephens, and Stephens 1992).[3] For them, democracy is promoted not by the capitalist market nor by the bourgeoisie per se but rather by the revolutionary effect of capitalist development on the division of labor and the class structure. Indeed, they argue that democracy grows less out of consensus than out of class conflict, in particular from struggles by the bourgeoisie against landed oligarchs and in turn by the working class against the upper classes. Capitalism strengthens the working and middle classes while weakening the landed upper class. Thus, not only do workers have an interest in extending democratic political rights as a means to achieve their interests, but, relative to other subordinate groups, capitalists' dependence on their labor confers potential organizational capacity with which to press home their demands and to insulate themselves somewhat from the hegemony of dominant classes.

Trade unions and other working-class groups thus bridge economic and political realms and production and consumption, and they play vital roles in the most critical sectors of societies. They represent forces that are indeed taken seriously by states and that are often at the center of state-led efforts over development—as an ally or antagonist in the struggle for development, as an object of co-optation and/or repression.

Despite their centrality to politics, there is surprisingly little analysis in the GDL literature of labor movements as active agents capable of placing their stamp on the content and form of the national—and indeed international—political economy. Excellent research has illuminated the lot of unorganized workers, drawing particular attention to intra- and interstate migration (Mittelman 1994a; Sassen 1991, 1988; Harrod 1987; Cohen 1987). But many writers stop short of extending their investigations to the role of organized workers.

When writers on the GDL have addressed the question of working-class collective actors, they have tended to view such groups as less significant to political development than other social groups, such as the middle class or large capitals.[4] Texts that move labor to the center of the analysis invariably treat it as a more or less passive actor, controlled either by the bureaucracy of developmentalist regimes or by its own peak-level organizations that do the state's bidding under corporatist arrangements.[5] The working class and trade unions are seen largely as external to the main political conflicts among elites and as the objects of state economic policies and repression. Workers are not located in production but in the consumption realm, where they mobilize in response to the austerity programs that diminish their standard of living and occasionally burst into spontaneous protest and strikes.[6]

Austerity certainly affects workers as consumers, but the theories overlook the specific characteristics of workers in production and the way workers' place in production—hence their power—changes under capital-intensive industrialization. In leaving unexplored the impact of the GDL on workers in both production and consumption, these analyses also overlook workers' capacity to defend themselves against capital and the state and to develop alternative strategies for development.[7] Labor becomes an object of inquiry, but truly objectified, a thing subject to the conscious control of others—either state elites or the union bosses who control corporatist labor bodies. Workers do not appear as a conscious social force, capable of self-interested action.[8] Other writers, who accept in principle that labor may act as an autonomous social force, are skeptical about its capacity to counter the power of capital and developmentalist states (Haworth and Ramsay 1988, 1984; Enderwick 1985; Waterman 1984; Portes and Walton 1981).

Labor is thus generally treated in an economically reductionist, ahistorical manner, and often from an elite perspective. These theoretical problems result in an often static picture in which unions and labor movements are seen as passive, reacting to rather than causing change. Certainly, these shortcomings lead to difficulties in the understanding of labor anywhere, but they pose special problems in examinations of workers and their unions in the NICs, where the development of strong, militant industrial unionism—the "new unionism" in Latin America and elsewhere—is a very recent phenomenon.[9] Given the empirical evidence on the importance of labor movements in particular states, it is crucial to ask under what conditions labor can develop as a collective actor.

To answer this question it is fruitful to approach trade unions through the concepts developed by social movement theory. Such an approach allows for a more nuanced understanding of the double meaning implicit in the term *movement:* the visibly obvious forms of public protest suggesting movement as motion, mobility, and action toward certain goals and the less visible, though equally crucial, organizational considerations key to movements as campaigns, as more or less consciously directed social action.

By emphasizing the duality of movement as motion and as deliberate strategy (i.e., as mobilization), social movement theory helps overcome the tendency to view collective action as a mysterious reflex exploding, emanating, or otherwise arising unexplained from structural conditions. Too sharp a distinction between labor movements and other "new" social movements—the peace, green, women's, and religious fundamentalist movements—obscures important commonalities between these contemporary forms.[10] Indeed, late industrialization and political authoritarianism in the NICs produce powerful labor and political movements employing forms of action very similar to those identified by analysts of new social movements.

The concept social movement unionism has been usefully applied in South African labor studies to account for the development of the modern labor movement. Capitalist exploitation and apartheid meant that labor had to be both economically and politically engaged. Indeed, the union movement has been characterized by new social movement-type patterns of organization adapted to a struggle against an authoritarian enemy: local devolution of leadership and power; a repertoire of tactics and strategies of mass protest; and a willingness to align with community and political groups on a principled basis. The focus on social movement unionism brings together the two salient features of South Africa's modern development: deepening racial differentiation amid intensifying class stratification. It shows the necessity of linking class with other social processes.[12]

South African case studies will show how the transformative impact of the GDL on workers' conditions of life opened up potentials for collective action. Import substitution industrialization changed the scale of production in South African manufacturing, enhanced workers' skills, and raised the costs to capital of replacing workers. The collective organization that workers constructed enabled them to intervene in the GDL as an actor allied with foreign trade unions, international trade secretariats, and social movements to influence foreign governments and multinational corporations (MNCs).

However, the economic and political foundations of workers' collective organization have been profoundly affected by recent changes in the GDL as South Africa reintegrates into the international system, from which it had been excluded by sanctions. In particular, trade liberalization threatens the survival of import substitution industries in which labor is best organized and raises the prospect of painful (perhaps impossible) adjustment and widespread retrenchment. In this new context, labor has not operated simply as a constraining or negative force to be overcome by the state and capital but as a domestic actor influencing the development policy of the South African state. It has served as a source of counterhegemonic ideas for industrial development, economic reconstruction, and political democratization.

Thus, the labor movement, whose initial growth was stimulated by conditions in the GDL—in the form of import substitution industrialization—is now in a position to influence the country's responses to changes in the GDL that undermine that model of development. These two roles will be investigated through two case studies: analyses of the labor movement's involvement in the international campaign for sanctions against South Africa and in postapartheid policy formulation.

SOUTH AFRICAN CASE STUDIES

The New Labor Unionism

The first trade unions in South Africa were established in the 1880s by immigrant miners who rushed to the Witwatersrand goldfields.[13] These craft unions were extremely militant, and from the 1890s to the 1920s led a number of strikes culminating in the "Rand Revolt" of 1922. Industrial unions emerged as secondary manufacturing grew in the 1930s. Although they developed large memberships and economic power, these unions were racially divided in their membership, leadership, and even in organizational structure. With passage of the first national labor law in 1923, Africans were barred from the industrial relations system. African workers could enter tame unions "parallel" to white-led unions (and under white control), or joined vulnerable independent organizations led by leftists on the margins of the officially recognized movement.

South Africa first attempted to diversify from mining and agriculture in the 1920s through state-led industrialization policies. Despite these policies and industrial growth during World War II, South African industry was still relatively backward before 1960. Manufacturing was generally character-ized as low-skill and labor-intensive, based in small enterprises. It remained highly dependent on machinery and raw materials from abroad, which were financed from profits on traditional primary goods exports (Innes 1984: 169).

In the midst of the worldwide expansion of manufacturing in the 1960s, many leading South African corporations and government policymakers advocated the increased deepening of import substitution through a concert-ed program of import controls, government financial support, and tax incen-tives. Import substitution stimulated a sustained industrial expansion that marked a structural shift in the character of South African manufacturing. From the 1960s, capital goods manufacture increased in importance and rep-resented the most significant sectors of manufacturing, far outpacing older consumer-oriented industries. The shift brought with it an increase in the capital intensity in manufacturing.

The first employment effect was to create jobs in new enterprises with larger average workforces, more capital-intensive processes, and an empha-sis on semiskilled labor. The boom led not only to a massive increase in manufacturing employment but also to the expansion of the black proportion of the workforce—from 61 percent in 1948 to 75 percent in 1968 (Innes 1984: 188). What set the 1960s expansion apart from previous booms was not simply the absolute increase in black employment but the qualitative change in blacks' average skill levels. These increased as blacks occupied more highly skilled positions opening in the new industries or filled jobs that had previously been the preserve of whites under closed shop agreements or racial employment quotas. In 1956, Africans occupied only approximately 40 percent of semiskilled positions. In 1969 the percentage passed an impor-tant threshold when Africans filled more than half (55 percent) of all semi-skilled occupations; in 1979 the percentage had increased to nearly two-thirds (Schneier 1983: 28).

Finally, the growth of secondary industrialization and mechanization was not confined to urban manufacturing but extended into agriculture, with important consequences for both rural and urban social relations. The rapid capitalization and mechanization of agriculture in the 1960s and 1970s resulted in the massive expulsion from white farms of black migrants, labor tenants, and permanent workers (De Klerk 1984; Simkins 1984). Apartheid policies aimed at eradicating farms owned by blacks in white areas—the so-called black spots—further undermined the rural pole of African subsistence. The combination of mechanization and rural removals significantly limited black urban workers' exit option and consigned them to seeking survival within the opportunities available in South Africa's cities. The deepening of import substitution industrialization from the 1960s thus constituted a significant shift in the character of production in the South African economy as a whole and provided objective conditions for the development of industrial unionism.

The changes in the division of labor spurred by the growth of mass production assembly line industries are typical of import substitution around the world. However, in South Africa the impact of race on the division of labor produced specific grievances for black workers and provided an impetus for collective action. The employment relationship was deeply scarred by racism, and black workers experienced profound discrimination with respect to wages and working conditions, promotion, and the despotic behavior of supervision. The combination of intensified assembly-line work and direct racial oppression produced deep grievances and encouraged the view that the South African political and economic systems were unjust.

From the passage of the first national labor law in 1923 until 1979, African workers were prohibited from joining registered trade unions and engaging in formal collective bargaining within the official industrial relations system. Indeed, under the apartheid system an alternative framework of African representation was established under the direct authority of the Departments of Labour and Native Affairs. These administrative controls worked efficiently when strong repression in the 1960s forced black political and labor organizations into exile or quiescence. But the economic changes of the 1960s rendered them unworkable, and they were unable to cope with the massive increase in black worker militancy during and after the Durban strikes of 1973. African workers were granted full rights within the established industrial relations system only in 1981.

Throughout the 1970s and 1980s the official (white) labor movement was declining: membership was falling and white unions were unable to sustain white workers' standard of living. While one movement fell, another arose, as black workers built a new labor movement on a formally nonracial class basis. Unions organizing among blacks soon overtook the racist unions to become the central institutions of South African labor. Through their self-organization, black workers created new forms of worker organization, stressing democratic grassroots practices and merging shop-floor and broader political commitments in what has been described as social movement unionism. These innovations marked a fundamental departure in the history of the South African labor movement.

Though the 1973 Durban strikes vented grievances accumulated over the years of so-called labor peace during the repressive 1960s, they were not spontaneous eruptions. Student and worker activists had been organizing for two years before the outbreak occurred, and in its aftermath they worked to transform the workers' militancy into solid organizations.

In their organizational efforts these activists prioritized building decentralized workplace structures that could survive state repression. The strategy emphasized "the development of a cadre of shop stewards integrally linked into the constitution and decision-making structure of the unions" (Cheadle 1987:7). In this respect, the imperatives of careful organizing against an authoritarian state and under draconian labor legislation intersected with the structural economic changes that generated a mass of semiskilled workers with leverage in production. Taken together, these conditions provided the foundation for industry-based unionism and a shop steward system of union organization.

The unions that grew in Durban decided to build strong shopfloor structures in every factory, rather than rolling up high membership figures in a paper organization. This emphasis was captured in the slogan that it was "better to have a 1000 members in one factory than a thousand in a hundred factories." The collective strength on the factory flow "put pressure on their employer in a way that the dispersed membership in 100 factories could not" (Cheadle 1987:8).

The unions concentrated their organizing efforts on semiskilled operators in the most advanced import substitution sectors, such as metal, textile, and chemical industries. They also found that by targeting multinational corporations international pressure could be used to bolster organizing drives. The Durban unions soon formed the first trade union center since the 1960s repression drove the African National Congress (ANC)-aligned South African Congress of Trade Unions (SACTU) into exile. This center grew into the Federation of South African Trade Unions (FOSATU), with twenty thousand paid-up members in ten industrial unions. When African workers gained full trade union rights in 1981 FOSATU's membership increased almost overnight to ninety-five thousand.

In its stress on building industrial organization FOSATU eschewed political alliances with the leading organizations of the nationalist movement.[14] Furthermore, they stressed strategic and tactical flexibility in applying their principles of building a workers' movement and proved willing to participate in certain official institutions, when they could do so on their own terms and in ways that advanced their long-term interests. While advocating a radical vision, they pursued a strategy of reform, a strategic use of power that has been labeled radical reform (Adler and Webster 1995). The long-term goals of eliminating apartheid and inaugurating socialism were to be achieved—at least in the short- to medium-term—via legal means of struggle. The strategy of radical reform created numerous conflicts between FOSATU and emerging aboveground nationalist political groupings inside South Africa committed to revolutionary rupture, who misinterpreted FOSATU's position as one of co-optation and reformism. When these political movements began to launch militant trade unions after 1979, the differences often led to outright conflict between the industrial unions and the politically engaged unions, with sometimes disastrous consequences for both.

FOSATU nonetheless emphasized building broad unity, and in 1985 it helped form a new federation, the Congress of South African Trade Unions (COSATU), which would soon become the largest trade union center in South African history. In 1990 COSATU claimed more than 1.2 million members organized in fourteen industrial unions (Baskin 1991:448). COSATU emerged from a compromise between the industrial unions, grouped around FOSATU and the more politically oriented (but organizationally weaker) unions affiliated to the United Democratic Front, an internally based ANC-aligned political movement opposing apartheid. As a result, COSATU would be aligned with the ANC, while the political movement endorsed shop-floor-based industrial unionism as the most appropriate strategy for the labor movement (Fine and Webster 1989; Eidelberg 1993; Adler and Webster 1995).

The consolidation of the labor movement has occurred with a relatively limited amount of fragmentation on skill, regional, racial, or political grounds. Despite a history of strong white craft unions and militant African "all-in," or general, unions, industrial unions are the most common representative form today. The development of national industrial unions is in part accounted for by the industry-based structure of collective bargaining defined under the Labour Relations Act, as well as by the strategic choices of the new unions, which organized on the basis of "one industry, one union" to maximize their power (Eidelberg 1993).[15]

Furthermore, the new unions soon set about developing national coordinating structures and developed a model of strong national unions bound together in a tight federation to service the affiliates.[16] By 1994 nearly 40 percent of the nonfarm, nondomestic labor force was organized in trade unions; and despite a large number of independent unions and the existence of four other union federations, COSATU's membership is greater than the combined membership of the other federations and unions. In fact, the two next-largest federations have discussed merging with COSATU to form one superfederation (Macun 1995). A merger would create a massive trade union center as well as help overcome remaining political and racial divisions in the labor movement.[17] Thus, not only have the new unions been effective in organizing workers into powerful grassroots structures, but they have also developed tightly structured national coordinating bodies that offer workers unprecedented strategic power.

Unions and the International Sanctions Movement:
The Shop Floor Meets the GDL

As the antiapartheid struggle moved into its decisive phase in the mid-1980s, the international social movement for sanctions against South Africa won unprecedented victories. The enactment of various local and state divestment and sanctions laws in the United States prompted a trickle of corporate withdrawals from South Africa, which grew to a flood after September 1986 when the U.S. Congress passed the Comprehensive Anti-Apartheid Act (CAAA).[18]

Though these strategies were publicly supported by the new unions inside South Africa, they had many private misgivings about policies that could lead to the closure of firms and the loss of hard-earned membership. The actual withdrawals were hailed as victories for the antiapartheid movement, but the unions were caught without effective strategies for responding, especially since the disinvestments usually took the form of a buyout by South African capital or a merger with a non-U.S. firm. In these deals, worker rights were in jeopardy, especially where unprofitable companies used the restructuring of ownership as an excuse to reverse trade union gains. Workers feared that the assets of the company (which they had helped create) either would be repatriated or would fall under the control of a new owner who might repudiate their collective bargaining rights.[19]

It was especially difficult for South African unions to respond as the precise nature of such restructuring was usually obscure and because communication links between the internal unions and the external antiapartheid movement were poor. Unions' questioning of withdrawals was often misconstrued outside the country as opposition to sanctions. The sorts of demands appropriate to contesting corporate restructuring were unprecedented in South Africa and caused considerable confusion among workers. Demands for curtailing the decisionmaking power of capital (including assurances that vested interests, such as pension funds, would not be compromised), for opening the books, for rights of consultation, and for representation on corporate boards were entirely new. South African unions had traditionally followed a policy of "militant abstentionism," in which they refused such options out of a reluctance to "co-manage apartheid." Even if unions had raised such issues, South African corporate law and management hostility militated against success. At least initially, MNCs were much more sophisticated actors in the GDL than either nationally based unions or their international social movement allies.

In 1986 and 1987, unions were badly beaten in a number of prominent battles over sanctions, and their defeats prompted a thorough rethinking of strategy. COSATU reformulated its own disinvestment policy (which previously had said nothing about how firms should leave) by identifying a number of central demands focusing on curtailing managements' unilateral power over disinvestment decisionmaking. At its July 1987 congress COSATU redrafted its sanctions resolution to demand that corporations give adequate advance notice to enable negotiations to occur over the terms of withdrawal. The federation demanded that departing companies have a moral obligation to return profits accumulated under apartheid "so that the social wealth of South Africa remains the property of the people of South Africa for the benefit of all." Subsequent revisions of the resolution called for one-year's advance notice of withdrawal, full disclosure of the disinvestment plan, compensation, and recognition of union rights should the company be sold to either a local or an international corporation.

Unions paid close attention to building stronger ties to overseas organizations in the antiapartheid movement, allied unions and international trade union secretariats, and the U.S. media. During specific battles such links afforded South African unions greater purchase on the MNC head office. Some unions launched U.S.-style corporate campaigns to pressure MNCs to bargain over workers' disinvestment rights, while others explored the integrated use of strikes, negotiations, and local and international media blitzes.

These tactics came together in a powerful way in the COSATU-affiliated Chemical Workers' Industrial Union's "responsible disinvestment" campaign against Mobil, when the giant MNC sold its South African operations to a notorious anti-union mining house. The union sued the company in the South African courts to have the sale declared illegal, began a two-week strike of Mobil installations, picketed its corporate offices, and ran negative advertisements in local papers. It received support from the International Chemical and Energy Workers' Federation, as well as from U.S. labor and antiapartheid organizations. U.S. unions pressed Mobil in the United States to meet the demands, and antiapartheid groups presented resolutions at annual shareholders meetings condemning the company. This coalition of labor, church, and political groups targeted Mobil during Soweto Day (16 June) commemorations in major U.S. cities (Adler 1990). In the end, the combined pressures brought to bear on Mobil won significant concessions from the company.

The trade unions' social movement character facilitated these new strategies. Workers did not view the broad antiapartheid movement as alien to their interests; indeed, their own involvement in the labor movement was greatly influenced by desires for justice in a system that denied fundamental human rights. Workplace and broader political demands were merged in the development of "social movement unionism." Furthermore, the "movement" character of the trade unions meant that they were comfortable with the guerrilla-type strategies and tactics of corporate campaigns and other forms of international political struggle. These were not bureaucratic and office-bound unions unused to wars of maneuver.

Social movement unionism required a high degree of coordination among trade unions and between them and the formations of the anti-apartheid political movement both inside and outside of South Africa. The formation of COSATU greatly facilitated such coordination, as it created a single, national organization with legitimate decisionmaking structures through which the labor movement could make strategic decisions. Indeed, COSATU played an extremely crucial role in this process, as most political organizations had been formally banned during the mid-1980s state of emergency. The labor movement—though restricted in its open espousal of politics—was never formally proscribed, and it became the center of public resistance. Furthermore, COSATU's close links to the ANC (in contrast to FOSATU's stress on political independence) facilitated extremely close ties to the ANC-aligned international sanctions movement. Over time, the exiled African National Congress, the South African Communist Party, and the internal movements against apartheid formed an overarching body or broad front known as the Mass Democratic Movement to coordinate the last phases of the struggle against apartheid. Such institutions promoted the elaboration of common strategies against the apartheid regime both inside and outside South Africa.

In addition to more sophisticated strategies and tactics in contesting the terms of disinvestment, one extremely important variable emerged in the unions' campaign for "responsible" disinvestment. A union's existing strength on the shop floor emerged as a necessary condition for success in resisting the MNCs' unilateral decisionmaking. The two most prominent examples concerned workers from the National Union of Metalworkers of South Africa (NUMSA). In the first, workers' resistance to General Motors's 1986 disinvestment was broken after a three-week strike in the Eastern Cape city of Port Elizabeth. Support dissipated once the company threatened to dismiss the workforce and manipulated preexisting differences between African and coloured workers and weaknesses in the union's factory leadership. As a result of the union's defeat, the company (renamed Delta Motors after it was sold to its top management) embarked on a thorough rationalization and austerity drive, featuring extensive layoffs and the rooting out of unionists.

General Motors opened South Africa in 1926 as part of the company's first expansionary rush to establish assembly plants in the Third World (Adler 1994). From its founding, the South African operation was closely integrated with the parent company in Detroit; machinery, tooling, and designs were supplied either from the United States or from Opel in Germany, and top executives of the wholly owned subsidiary were seconded from either the head office or other foreign subsidiaries rather than developed locally. Its disinvestment was no less a part of a global strategy than was the original establishment of the plant. Though motivated by local political factors and the CAAA, the withdrawal was articulated to a comprehensive restructuring of the multinational during a period of profound crisis in the mid-1980s, which saw it close eleven plants and lay off nearly thirty thousand workers in the United States.

Furthermore, the method of withdrawal saw the first deployment in South Africa of the repertoire of corporate practices perfected in the global merger mania of the 1980s. GM engineered and financed a leveraged buy-out of its loss-making subsidiary to its own managers, who would maintain license links to Opel in Germany and Isuzu in Japan (respectively, wholly owned and GM-dominated companies) ensuring that the MNC retained its place in the South African market without falling foul of the provisions of the CAAA.

The autoworkers' union was completely mystified by this new and bewildering exercise in corporate camouflage, and it repeatedly raised inappropriate demands (such as for severance pay) on the mistaken assumption that the subsidiary would be closing down. Nor were the South African and international antiapartheid movements any better attuned to the sophistication of GM's strategy—they invariably hailed the company's compliance with the legislation. Indeed, the corporate consultants who engineered the scheme were canny enough to claim a substantial U.S. tax break for the parent company on the losses accumulated by the South African subsidiary; indeed, the sale was consummated as the loophole was scheduled to disappear.

By contrast, workers at Goodyear in the nearby city of Uitenhage successfully challenged the company's June 1989 sale to a South African conglomerate and redefined the terms of the transfer. Like GM, Goodyear had a long-standing presence in South Africa, having established a plant in Uitenhage in 1946 as part of the global expansion of tire and rubber manufacturing in the Third World paralleling the global extension of Ford's and GM's assembly networks.[20] The local subsidiary was consistently profitable, and indeed Goodyear's disinvestment was prompted by a move in the U.S. Congress the year before to eliminate protections against double taxation for U.S. companies operating in South Africa. Where GM sold an unprofitable firm and as a result managed to win significant tax gains, Goodyear was prompted to sell before sanctions-inspired changes in U.S. tax codes eliminated a source of profit and imposed new tax obligations on the parent company.

When workers learned about the proposed sale of the Goodyear subsidiary to a South African mining and manufacturing conglomerate, they immediately submitted a list of demands to the company. When these were refused, workers embarked on a legal strike in support of their demands. The company dismissed its workforce of twelve hundred after strikers spurned its ultimatum to return to work. NUMSA successfully organized a campaign through other COSATU affiliates to blacken Goodyear products, and workers at other tire companies donated a portion of their wages to a strike fund.

Most important, Goodyear workers successfully organized the highly politicized Uitenhage black townships to refuse to scab on the strikers—a direct
benefit of the trade unions' social movement character. After a ten-week
strike, the MNC conceded to the workers' core demands, including a commitment that conditions of service would be fully respected, granting ex gra-
tia payments to workers, and agreeing that the workers would be able to control their pension fund.[21]

The General Motors plant had always been a weakly organized affiliate
of NUMSA. Not only was the workforce deeply divided between African
and coloured workers, but management was out of step with best practice
standards in South African industrial relations. Furthermore, the workers
had never fought and won a protracted strike. By contrast, in 1989 Goodyear
was an extremely well organized factory. Though in the early 1980s it had
been the site of internecine conflicts between progressive unions, NUMSA
had mounted an effective campaign from 1985 to reorganize the workforce
on a solid basis; strong shop stewards worked to overcome differences
between coloureds and Africans. The organizing gains were consolidated in
a series of disputes in 1988 around management's disciplinary abuses, culminating in a successful month-long strike in May.

Workers at General Motors had been the first to enter the new and con-
fusing terrain of industrial struggle over international sanctions and did so
amid rank-and-file divisions and little experience in strike action. Goodyear
workers, however, conducted their strike three years later, after more sophisticated domestic and international strategies had been developed, and did so
with battle-tested factory organization.

In the context of these two strikes, ordinary shop-floor workers became
important actors in a drama of international political economy, engaging in
tests of strength with powerful MNCs. The shop floor became a terrain of
conflict in the global division of labor, upon which workers' self-conscious
organization held out the possibility of checking the awesome power of
international capital. As a result, the normally mundane and provincial (from
the point of view of the GDL) concerns of factory organization, community
networks, and even the personalities and strengths of individual shop stewards had important ramifications for processes at the level of the world system.

Unions and Reconstruction:
The Future of South Africa's Location in the GDL

As asserted earlier, development in the NICs creates new social forces that
can challenge the political and economic basis on which they themselves
emerged. Labor movements in particular are not static phenomena; different
movements, with different organizational bases and different strategies,
emerge at different times, in part as a consequence of development. These

movements in turn may become self-conscious actors addressing the broad policy questions of the day. In recent years the labor movement in South Africa has come to play an increasingly central macroeconomic role and has in fact become recognized by big business and sections of the state as the source of the most innovative thinking on development.[22]

The labor movement's long-standing commitment to militant abstentionism (the refusal to collaborate in state and management structures) shifted in the late 1980s to a policy of conditional participation (Von Holdt 1991).[23] This shift was dictated by a major threat to the unions' survival when the government attempted to reverse the liberalization in labor relations by passing the repressive Labour Relations Amendment Act (LRAA) of 1988. The unions chose to fight the LRAA through social-movement-style mass action as well as negotiation with business elites and ultimately with the state. These efforts led to the eventual repeal of the LRAA and the passage of a new labor code drawn up by the leading union federations and capital.

Though promulgated before the full transition to democracy, the new Labour Relations Act was immediately labeled the first piece of post-apartheid legislation and was widely seen to have ushered in a new era characterized by the politics of reconstruction (Schreiner 1991). In the process, the labor movement logically extended a strategy of negotiation backed up with industrial action first developed on the shop floor to contest managerial authority.

This strategy has been increasingly employed to influence broad state policy, motivated by a desire to address the macroeconomic and political conditions that determine the traditional union bargaining issues of wages and working conditions. COSATU was thus the primary force behind the creation of the National Economic Forum (NEF), a tripartite negotiating body where economic policy could be discussed with capital and the state in a more coordinated, global manner. After the 1994 elections the NEF was reconstituted as the National Economic Development and Labour Council (NEDLAC), a statutory body in which labor, business, the state, and representatives of civil society formations are meant to reach negotiated agreements on macroeconomic policy. NEDLAC's first brief was to devise a new labor law, and after months of bargaining it forwarded a bill to the minister of labor that powerfully entrenches labor's power while moving the industrial relations system in the direction of codetermination.[24]

The new bill grants labor statutory organizing rights that should greatly facilitate the enrollment of new members. It also for the first time in South African history grants all workers—including farm laborers, domestic servants, and civil servants—similar rights within the same industrial relations framework. Furthermore, new provisions greatly ease historic restrictions on the right to strike (as well as employers' right to lockout) and encourage (though do not compel) centralized bargaining through industrywide statutory councils. The most innovative feature, the establishment of workplace forums (modeled in part on German-style works councils) provides worker rights for consultation and joint decisionmaking on crucial enterprise issues. These reforms grant labor considerable new powers to influence development from the shop-floor and enterprise levels, to sectoral and macroeconomic policymaking.

Trade union leaders have also been playing an extremely important role in the political transition. They were prominently placed on the ANC's election list, and many who began their union involvement in shop-floor movements are now sitting on the front benches in Parliament and taking up important ministerial portfolios in the new Government of National Unity (GNU).[25] This electoral role does not exhaust the labor movement's involvement in politics. Local, regional, and national labor leaders have played a central role in peacekeeping and dispute resolution structures across the country. A further movement of labor leaders into politics occurred after the November 1995 local government elections, as shop stewards and union activists who played prominent roles in community development were drawn into formal government positions (Buhlungu 1994a, b).

After the creation of the National Economic Forum, labor sought similar participation in negotiating forums dedicated to education, housing, and local government policy. These societal corporatist-type arrangements developed in the interregnum between the collapse of apartheid and the installation of a majority-rule government, and they increasingly define a new mode of interest representation and policy formation. As a result, the labor movement has operated at the center of debates and struggles at every level of the society about the form and direction of social change and has been one of the central participants in processes to promote an autonomous and strong civil society. Since the 1994 elections, labor has been one of the strongest critics of undemocratic tendencies in the ANC-led GNU.[26] It has also led a series of strikes against prominent employers and has successfully fended off criticisms from employers (and even from sections of the ANC) that mass mobilization for workers' rights is an inappropriate "sectional" indulgence in a period of reconstruction.

Despite developing this interventionist role, there is a growing sense that the labor movement is living on borrowed time and that in the future its position could worsen considerably. In part this is due to difficulties related to the rapid growth of membership in the context of an organizational culture hostile to bureaucratic forms of management. In addition, the advance of key intellectuals into government service and business has deprived the movement of important strategists at the very moment when strategic innovation is most needed. However, the most profound difficulties for the movement come from the context in which it operates, as the South African political economy comes under increasing pressure from globalization.

Ironically, the South African transition to democracy has been accomplished in large part through organizations such as labor that drew their strength from the country's isolation from the GDL. Not only did labor grow in import-substitution manufacturing industries, but the sanctions strategy proved extremely costly to both business and the state, while material resources generated through international solidarity fueled the development of mass opposition organizations. Having accomplished democratization— if only in its infancy—the labor movement now faces a considerably less hospitable global context.

Globalization poses an immediate challenge to the viability of core manufacturing sectors, most prominently automobile and components, textile, chemicals, and consumer appliances. Many of these are currently uncompetitive in international terms and are characterized by low productivity, low output and overcapacity, and a poor record of employment creation (Joffe et al. 1995). Coincidentally, they are also among the sectors with the highest union densities and form the backbone of the labor movement's industrial muscle (Macun 1993). The GNU's acceptance of the free trade principles established in the recent GATT agreement has reversed generations of protectionist industrial and trade policies and has put the viability of such industries in doubt. In the automobile sector, for example, protection will be reduced from an effective 115 percent at present to 40 percent in 2002. In a variety of industries bipartite and tripartite forums have been established to restructure the trade regime to bring tariffs in line with international norms and to develop adjustment policies to avoid deindustrialization and job loss.

While trade liberalization threatens the material basis of the labor movement, the cultural and intellectual impact of globalization has affected the very terms on which development is discussed in the country. Arguments supporting free trade, fiscal prudence, and a more limited development role for the state have gained currency in intellectual circles of the erstwhile opposition and have shaped the policies adopted by the GNU itself (Adelzadeh and Padayachee 1994). Labor's historic commitment to nationalization, worker control of the means of production, and a strongly interventionist state have met, not surprisingly, with little favor in a context of cross-class GNU (with representation from powerful groupings from the old regime) quickly "normalizing" South Africa's relations with the GDL.[27]

Nonetheless, labor has attempted to influence this development debate, guided in part by an impressive policy review that COSATU sponsored between 1991 and 1994. The work of the Industrial Strategy Project of the Economic Trends Research Group has shifted the terms of the development debate by inserting a working-class perspective into policymaking, raising issues of productivity and international competitiveness while prioritizing employment creation, job security, and training.[28] These policy formulations are contested by capital and have met resistance even within the labor movement, where they are the subject of continuing debate, particularly for their qualified acceptance of trade liberalization and a high-value-added export-oriented growth strategy (Etkind and Harvey 1993). Nonetheless, they constitute a portion of the labor movement's contribution to debates over the transformation of South Africa's economy and society.[29]

In 1993 these ideas shaped the content of the Reconstruction Accord originally advocated by COSATU, a broad statement of economic and social policies to guide future development. The program, as well as the federation's positions advanced in the various policy forums described earlier, do not represent the interests of a relatively well-off, relatively skilled, emergent aristocracy of employed workers. Rather, the labor movement's formulations have been aimed at the broad interests of the working class—employed or not—and at policies to satisfy the basic needs of the population.

After being debated and rewritten by COSATU and its alliance partners (the ANC and the South African Communist Party), the document emerged as the Reconstruction and Development Programme (RDP), the alliance's core policy program and the centerpiece of its campaign in the April 1994 elections.[30] The package of macroeconomic and social targets was meant to guide policy in the new government (Cargill 1993).

Though not a socialist document, the RDP represented a significant attempt to move policy beyond socially and economically conservative goals by taking as its point of departure people's basic needs. A central idea underlying the program was that social movements such as labor, women, youth and student organizations, and associations of the unemployed and the aged would be part of an organized pact to reconstruct society. Democracy, the document promised, would not be confined to periodic elections but was viewed rather as an active process enabling formations of civil society to contribute to reconstruction and development.

Notwithstanding the claims made for the RDP as an election manifesto, it has evolved into a rather different document in the process of being transformed into a white paper and official policy in the GNU. In its most recent form, the document has placed far less emphasis on state intervention, has granted wide latitude to the fiscally conservative Finance Ministry while affirming the independence of the monetarist South African Reserve Bank, and has lost the central emphasis on transparency and participation in policymaking.[31]

Against this thrust the labor movement has developed what one analyst has described as a "creative challenge to the global agenda of neo-liberalism" (Webster 1995). While accepting "the constraints imposed by the need to maintain international competitiveness in a capitalist world economic system," Webster argues that the labor movement can exert pressure on the GNU "towards redistributive policies by mobilising pressure from civil society, communities and the workplace." Such pressure depends on labor's ability to maintain a strategic balance between mobilization in civil society (the deployment of social-movement-type activity) alongside participation in tripartite institutions.

It remains an open question whether these efforts can hold neoliberalism at bay. It is certain, however, that South Africa's reaction to globalization will be profoundly shaped by labor and other social movements, actors that have historically received little attention within the academic literature on the subject. Any assessment of the country's changing location in the GDL must take labor into account, not simply as an object to be repressed in pursuit of developmentalist goals but as a self-conscious actor in its own right pursuing economic growth and democratization.

CONCLUSION

This chapter began with the observation that the literature on the GDL overlooked labor movements as self-conscious actors in the political economies of Third World states. Such an oversight appeared surprising considering the growing importance of labor movements in a number of NICs. In overlooking such processes, it was asserted that the GDL literature risked ignoring certain creative possibilities for bringing about sustainable economic growth and democratization.

It may be true that the South African case represents an unusual form of labor movement organization and political, economic, and social intervention. Perhaps the unique combination of economic and political grievances caused by apartheid generated a peculiar set of struggles, which may not be replicated elsewhere in the NICs, let alone in the more impoverished regions of the periphery.

It is likely, however, that these criticisms are misplaced. Globalization—the rapid development of import substitution industries from the 1960s fed by both foreign and domestic investment—helped create the structural conditions that spawned the modern labor movement. Furthermore, the labor movement has been able to develop the intellectual, strategic, and tactical resources and, perhaps more important, the political power to shape the country's response to contemporary changes in the GDL, particularly those that have undermined the foundations of import substitution. The labor movement has pioneered new societal corporatist arrangements and has promoted the development of a strong civil society—a necessary condition of democratization. To state these innovations does not suggest that labor's responses will be successful, nor that the labor movement will avoid becoming an isolated aristocracy; rather, at least for now, South Africa's development cannot be understood without recognizing the central role labor plays as an actor in national policy making.

The same global conditions that helped create the labor movement in South Africa stimulated vigorous labor movements elsewhere in the world, most notably in Brazil but also in Mexico, South Korea, and elsewhere in Latin America and East Asia. These organizations have exerted important influence on both economic and political transition in these countries. Their absence from discussions of globalization does not suggest their irrelevance but rather indicates a major gap in the scholarly literature that will need to be addressed in the years to come. A comparative research agenda on labor movements and economic and political transition in the NICs may yield major insights into the dynamics of opposition in these countries, as well as into the challenges being generated to the GDL, their content, and their likelihood of success.

The South African case study suggests that labor has played a significant role in economic reconstruction and democratization. This chapter has attempted to identify the emergence in South Africa of a codeterminist, tripartite process that opens possibilities for counterhegemonic development policies. If labor can play such a role and such institutions can develop in South Africa, it is incumbent upon analysts of the GDL to assess where else in the Third World similar process may already have gained a toehold.

NOTES

I wish to thank Ann Griffiths, Diane Singerman, and Jim Mittelman, as well as the participants at the workshop Globalization: Opportunities and Challenges, for extremely valuable comments on an earlier draft of this chapter.

1. Haggard (1990) seems to recognize such possibilities when he very tentatively suggests that social democratic forms of representation may hold out the promise of an efficient, yet more humane, growth path in the NICs. However, the insight is not pursued.

2. Though Marx and Engels were certainly mistaken about the bourgeois mode of production creating replicas of European capitalism, they clearly grasped the historically transformative impact of capitalism on the periphery. Their arguments alert us to globalization as a phenomenon of long duration and broad historical sweep, insights often lacking from discussions in which contemporary forms of globalization are seen as a historically unprecedented event.

3. In an argument that carefully examines the influence of the state and transnational power relations on democracy, the authors place social class at the center of their analytical framework. In asking what benefits and losses different classes could expect from extensions of political inclusion, they turn both Leninists and pluralists such as Barrington Moore on their head. The bourgeoisie may favor (and be able to win) an extension of political representation from a landed aristocracy, "but it rarely fought for further extensions once its own place was secured," as such a move could well threaten its newly won prerogatives. They conclude that the working class is the most frequent proponent of full democratization "because this promised to include the class in the polity where it could further pursue its interests." Their conclusions are drawn from a fairly unique comparative research framework, analyzing cases drawn from Western Europe, the Caribbean, and Latin America (Rueschemeyer, Stephens, and Stephens 1992: 6, 8, 46, 50).

4. The otherwise excellent work in Gereffi and Wyman (1990a) demonstrates this tendency.

5. The contributors to the extremely valuable collection edited by Bergquist refreshingly place labor at the center of development struggles in the Third World, yet they fail to escape from a reductionist treatment of workers and their organizations characteristic of the structuralist world-systems approach they criticize (Bergquist 1984). A similar weakness befalls the contributions to debates on labor in the changing international division of labor (Boyd, Cohen, and Gutkind 1987), as well as some of the early works by the new generation of writers on Latin American labor (Middlebrook 1981; Erickson 1977; Mericle 1977).

6. Haggard's sweeping comparative analysis of industrialization in the East Asian and Latin American NICs is unusual in its recognition of labor's central role in development. Yet in his framework labor is generally an object to be controlled and/or co-opted by state elites in their pursuit of "insulation" from the constraining forces of civil society. He often takes as given the state's power to restructure labor relations and to repress unions and workers; however, his own evidence shows that labor continually regroups and challenges elites. The obvious tensions and outright conflicts between the state and capital, between states, and between foreign and local capital somehow dissipate when these actors confront workers, who remain noticeably unable to exploit such divisions among their adversaries. Without one focusing on labor as an autonomous actor, these continual reassertions of militancy are impossible to understand and seem to arise out of the blue (Haggard 1990). Martin (1990) demonstrates how political struggles by antisystemic movements (including labor movements) are integrally related to the development of the semiperiphery, though none of the authors in this edited collection explicitly focus on trade unions.

7. See Bergquist's criticism of Latin American structuralist treatments of labor (Bergquist 1986: 2–14). There are important exceptions. Becker shows how the development of capital-intensive mining and the increasing penetration by foreign capital in Peru contributed to the growth of an industrial proletariat with the skills and capabilities to organize independent unions to protect its interests (Becker 1983). Similarly, studies have demonstrated how the development of semiskilled operative labor under import substitution industrialization transformed the basis of the labor movement in a range of Latin American countries, creating the conditions for the self-organization of a new, militant force for economic advance and political democratization (Keck 1992; Middlebrook 1987; Winn 1986; Humphrey 1982).

8. The major exception is the excellent work by Deyo (1989, 1987a).

9. Indeed, the overriding theme of the work presented in Nash and Fernandez-Kelly (1983) portrays trade unions as corrupt, bureaucratic, and defensive of insider (largely male) workers' interests. While this portrait is certainly accurate with regard to official unions, the contributions to that volume do not generally examine the practices of the new unionism in the Third World. In Brazil especially, but also in Mexico, South Korea and elsewhere, trade unions emerged in import substitution industries in the 1970s and 1980s with a number of common characteristics. These unions were usually shop-floor based, prioritizing decentralized structures and democratic practices emphasizing the role of factory leaders such as shop stewards; they also prioritized the importance of worker control over production as well as over their own organizations. As a result, they invariably grew in opposition to established unions locked into the classic state-corporatist structures of interest mediation and asserted (by contrast to the often corrupt official unions) an authenticity in their representation of worker interests. Finally, these unions were often enmeshed in complicated relations with other oppositional social forces and pro-democracy movements, often struggling to assert alliances based on mutual interest between independent organizations. In the face of more populist tendencies in opposition political groupings, unions' claims to independence were often misconstrued (by political activists and scholars alike) as assertions of a labor aristocracy. For works

analyzing the new unionism, see Seidman (1994); Keck (1992); Middlebrook (1987); and Roxborough (1984).

10. An overdrawn contrast is often made between new and old social movements (Touraine 1982; Inglehart 1990; Rucht 1992). Klandermans and Tarrow argue convincingly for an approach that sees similarities between these movements and attempt to synthesize theoretical traditions in social movement studies (Klandermans and Tarrow 1988: 17; Tarrow 1991: 63–66). Olofsson (1988) has written a strong critique of new social movements theory.

11. Waterman (1991) and Munck (1988) developed the concept and applied it to Third World labor movements. Webster (1988) first applied the concept to the South African labor movement. Seidman's (1994) comparison of labor movements in Brazil and South Africa shows that social movement unionism can help account for militant industrial unionism in the authoritarian NICs, even in what appear to be dramatically different cases.

12. South African sociologists and historians have used insights drawn from social movement literature to explain the development of industrial and political organization. Sitas (1984, 1985) has studied union formation among migrant workers in the single-sex hostels of the East Rand metal industry, where union organization occurred through regional or clan affiliations. He labels these cultural formations "defensive combinations," which provided protection for workers in the harsh environment of the hostels and foundries; these same informal social networks provided the base for collective organization by the Metal and Allied Workers' Union. For an analysis of the ways rural associations provided the foundation for popular protest in formal political organizations, see Delius (1993). For an overview of the development of theoretical and methodological approaches to labor in South Africa, see Webster (1991).

13. The material in this section was developed in my doctoral thesis (Adler 1994) and in a recent collaboration with Eddie Webster (Adler and Webster 1995). For overviews of trade unionism in South Africa, see Seidman (1994); Baskin (1991); Friedman (1987); Webster (1983).

14. The position was motivated by a tactical fear that such involvements would jeopardize hard-won gains by provoking a state reaction before structures could be consolidated, as well as by left-wing class-based criticisms of nationalist politics.

15. At the time of its launch in 1985, COSATU comprised thirty-three separate industrial, general, and white-collar unions. The industrial union policy saw these consolidated within three years into the present fourteen.

16. In addition to offering a forum to address common problems and to resolve differences, the federation provides educational services for the affiliates, finance, and legal support. It is the venue where common positions are developed, including political alliances, policies regarding sanctions and general opposition to apartheid, and, more recently, reconstruction and development. FOSATU pioneered practices to guard against oligarchic tendencies in federations by entrenching the constitutional position of the shop steward as a locally and directly elected worker leader. Elected officials at all levels of both the unions and the federation must be employed workers (in practice, shop stewards); all structures, from local branches to the national congress, must be composed of numerical majorities of workers; and full-time officials are not voting members of these bodies (Baskin 1991).

17. The two federations are the National Council of Trade Unions, which organizes black workers on the basis of a political program at odds with COSATU (one combining black consciousness and pan-Africanism rather than nonracialism) and the Federation of South African Labour, which has traditionally organized white workers in the public sector.

18. The evidence for this section relies on Adler (1990, 1989).

19. Indeed, the National Union of Metalworkers of South Africa alleged that in 1985 Ford Motor Company used monies from the workers' pension fund (on which the union had no representation) to finance its merger with another South African motor assembler.

20. In contrast to the terminal automobile industry, where only the final assembly stage was transferred, technical considerations allowed tire and glass companies to locate the entire manufacturing process close to the point of sale where they could easily service the automobile assembly plants. In Latin America, for example, the first tire plant was opened in Argentina in 1931, and by 1947 there were nineteen tire plants operating across the continent as either subsidiaries or licensees of the major international producers (Chandler 1989). The first South African tire plant opened in 1935 when Firestone began operations in Port Elizabeth (Adler 1994).

21. The pension agreement was an unprecedented concession in South Africa, as workers have historically been excluded from the management of such funds; at the time, the fund's actuarial reserve was estimated to be nearly $20 million. This was an extremely important gain, not only for the principle of worker control but because of the union's previous experience at Ford.

22. The leading South African management consultant described the unions' researchers' work as "thorough and uncomfortably realistic, and far more sophisticated than business policy work" (Andrew Levy and Associates 1993). On the labor movement and economic policy making, see Joffe, Maller, and Webster (1995).

23. Many of the ideas that follow are drawn from Adler and Webster (1995).

24. The legal drafting team was led by Halton Cheadle, one of the most prominent labor lawyers in South Africa and a long-standing legal strategist and adviser to COSATU.

25. The Government of National Unity comprises a coalition of the parties receiving the largest shares of the vote in the April 1994 elections. Created through multiparty negotiations in 1993 and 1994, the GNU rules under an interim constitution, which will be in force through elections scheduled for 1999. In the meantime, a Constitutional Assembly, drawn from the new Parliament, is drafting a final constitution.

26. For example, labor has been a vociferous opponent of high salaries paid to ministers, senior civil servants, and members of parliament (MPs) and an advocate of transparency in policymaking and appointments processes; it has also championed a code of conduct for parliamentarians and civil servants. The labor movement has also played a behind-the-scenes role with the South African Communist Party and socialist-oriented ANC MPs attempting to bolster the position of the parliamentary caucus against the cabinet. More recently, labor was the strongest critic of the 1995 budget, lodging a critique of its neoliberal agenda while attacking the absence of "transparency" in its creation.

27. This intellectual debate has been materially affected by the reestablishment of public links between the GNU and the World Bank and the IMF, as well as other bilateral and multilateral international institutions. At the same time, many leading labor intellectuals have become MPs and have taken up top policymaking positions in civil service, which has been seen by some commentators as the beginning of a degenerative "brain drain" from the labor movement (Buhlungu 1994b). The latter does not mean that such intellectuals will inevitably be co-opted; it is also possible that they will exert an important labor-oriented influence on government policy. However, taken together these two developments might indicate the beginning of a reduction in labor's intellectual influence in national development policy debates.

28. The Industrial Strategy Project emphasizes the linkages among productivity growth, redistribution, and social welfare. Its framework for redressing productivity problems is built around "the active participation of workers in both the

conception and execution of production" (Joffe et al. 1993: 96; Joffe and Lewis 1992).

29. For further discussion of labor's impact on the political transition, and the revisions this suggests in established theories of transition to democracy, see Adler and Webster (1995).

30. The RDP drafting team included as well representatives from the South African National Civics Organisation and the National Education Coordinating Committee.

31. Two leading critics of the RDP white paper have argued that it "represents a very significant compromise to the neo-liberal, 'trickle down' economic policy preferences of the old regime, despite assurances from key economic ministers in the GNU that only the language of the W[hite] P[aper] has been changed to accommodate a wider constituency of interests" (Adelzadeh and Padayachee 1994: 2).

Fantu Cheru 7

New Social Movements: Democratic Struggles and Human Rights in Africa

As we enter the twenty-first century, the world is witnessing revolutionary changes in the way human beings are organizing production, consumption, and other aspects of social relations. This compression of the time–space aspects of social relations—allowing the economy, politics, culture, and ideology of one country to penetrate another—is called globalization (Mittelman, Chapter 1). This rapid interpenetration of social relations, involving world factories, labor flows, lending facilities, communications, new knowledge and information technologies, and new cultural norms, is making national borders less relevant while severing family ties, undermining established authority, and straining the bonds of local community.

The key agents of globalization have been a few hundred industrial and financial corporations. By developing the arts of planning, production, and marketing, the global corporation is rushing into the vacuum left by the increasing inability of national governments to offer vision. This growth in the structural power of capital indicates the shift in the balance of power in the world economy from territorially based governments to companies that roam the world (Barnet and Cavanagh 1994). This process is also facilitated by the global drive for liberalization of markets and the rapid reduction of the commanding role of the state in national planning. In short, the state itself facilitates globalization, acting as an agent in the process. Despite talks of structural economic reform by governments across the globe, no government can realistically provide economic stability, development, and social progress within its borders on a sustained basis unaffected by the forces of globalization. Globalization, therefore, encompasses contradictory trends, with varying degrees of pressure on the state, society, and the economy.

But if the outcome of globalization is more hardship and further marginalization for the majority of poor African peasants and the Third World as a whole, one must ask what the losers can do to defend themselves from the remote forces of globalization and domestic social forces that facilitate it. Why do ordinary people decide to engage the state through the "exit" option, and how can localized "everyday forms of resistance" be channeled toward establishing a more just political and economic order? This chapter attempts to respond to these questions by examining the various forms of resistance being waged from below (independent of traditional political parties) and outside the state. It also examines the extent to which donor-driven democratization initiatives deflect the projects of popular groups from below and splinter civil society.

GLOBALIZATION TENDENCIES
AND THE AFRICAN CONDITION

The 1980s have been characterized as the "lost development decade" for Africa. This is reflected in weak growth in the productive sectors, poor export performance, mounting debt, deterioration in social conditions, environmental degradation, and increasing decay in institutional capacity. Of the forty-seven countries classified by the UN as least developed, no fewer than thirty-two are found in sub-Saharan Africa. Zambia, Zaire, and Madagascar were added to the list in 1992 by the UN General Assembly. Only diamond-rich Botswana has managed to become the first country to graduate from the club of the destitute (Harsh 1992; UN 1991a). The possibility of other African countries following in the footsteps of Botswana is exceedingly dim. Most countries may instead experience the same tragic fate of Somalia and Rwanda, which have descended into a desperate spiral of anarchy, looting, famine, and self-destruction. These developments are taking place against the background of unprecedented changes in global economic and political relationships in which Africa will have a very marginal role to play.

Africa's current economic and political crisis is said to be the result of a combination of numerous economic and financial factors, both internal and external, often cited with varying degrees of importance. Included among them are the two rounds of oil price hikes, the world economic recession, the deterioration in the terms of trade, and the absence of an "enabling" domestic political environment (World Bank 1989a). While these factors have played a role in aggravating Africa's economic problem, the discussion along these lines fails to take into account the negative impact of powerful forces in the world economy. Some of the key components of the globalization drive are evident in five areas:

1. Advancement in biotechnology and microtechnology
2. Increasing differentiation among developing countries
3. Decreased diffusion of investment
4. Structural adjustment as an ideology of development
5. Competing trading blocs

The first broad change shaping the world economy is the advent of quantum advances in biotechnology and microtechnology. The establishment of a global communications network, new patterns of industrial organization, the development and spread of microelectronics (including automation), and the development of advanced or synthetic materials are affecting world economic ties. This change was largely responsible for the emergence of a global production network wherein pieces of a once continuous assembly line were divided internationally, most often to take advantage of lower labor costs for unskilled work in developing countries. With less labor involved in automated processes now possible through microelectronic technology, multinational corporations (MNCs) are already beginning to move their production facilities closer to Northern consumer markets.

Except where changes in existing patterns of production would be costly, where patterns of production are firmly established (as with car parts in Brazil and Mexico), and in newly industrialized countries (NICs) and some of the second-tier developing countries where investment will remain fairly attractive, MNCs will probably move away from further Third World production. For this reason and because the rampant political and economic instability in Africa is inimical to investment, Africa does not really have a comparative advantage in either low-cost labor or agricultural commodities anymore. South Asia, for example, provides a stable investment environment, low-cost labor, better infrastructure, and a more highly educated work force.

A second major trend in the world economy is an increase in the differentiation among so-called developing countries, as well as different communities within developing countries. While some social groups with particular skills or capital benefit from their links to global production systems, others lacking similar skills will remain detached from the world economy. Though this phenomenon is especially apparent worldwide, it is applicable to Africa, with some countries doing better than others. We will increasingly witness more "black holes" in the emerging global economic landscape.

The increasing differentiation among developing countries means that only a handful of African nations may be able to attract small amounts of investment (e.g., Egypt, South Africa, Zimbabwe, Kenya). But this will in turn increase regional disparities. These forms of polarization could become major impediments to regional integration and harmonization of development policies in almost all spheres. Further, regional polarization is exacerbating the migration of millions of skilled and unskilled Africans to growth centers such as Johannesburg, Nairobi, Harare, Lagos, and other emerging centers linked to the forces of globalization.

This differentiation among countries brings us to the third global trend, that of decreased diffusion of investment to certain developing countries. As Frank (1991) points out, "The real struggle is between the U.S., the EU, and Japan." These three power blocs are the major global investors, but they are also the major recipients of investment. Fully 80 percent of investment worldwide is among this economic power triad. As investment becomes concentrated among these powers, few developing countries, other than some of the NICs and second-tier countries, will benefit. The solidification of investment patterns that exclude Africa means that there will be little hope for most African nations to attract foreign investment (UN 1991b).

A World Bank report stated that new flows of external finance to developing countries rose by 13 percent in 1993 to $177 billion, up from $153 billion in 1992 (World Bank 1993). Despite the flurry of news reports about McDonald's setting up shop in Moscow or IBM investing in Eastern Europe, Asia was the largest recipient of foreign direct investment (FDI), followed by Latin America and the Caribbean. China, Mexico, Argentina, Malaysia, and Thailand accounted for almost 60 percent of the $47 billion FDI flowing to developing countries in 1993. The report also stated that 70 percent of U.S. private investment during 1990–1992 went to Latin America and the Caribbean, 18 percent to East Asia, and only 7 percent to Europe and Central Asia. The regional pattern of FDI flows is increasingly affected by preferential trade schemes and regional economic integration. Africa's share was almost negligible. And much of the direct investment is made up of high-technology investment in telecommunications and transportation, implying a significant shift of FDI from manufacturing to services.

The fourth major trend in global relations is the widespread and one-sided application of structural adjustment as a response to the new international conditions of the 1980s and 1990s. We have witnessed a shift in development paradigm from development planning and an active and commanding role for the state to devaluation, deregulation, liberalization, and privatization—in short, installing market fundamentals under the iron discipline of the International Monetary Fund (IMF), the World Bank, and the General Agreement on Tariffs and Trade (GATT). African countries are told to "adjust" to a virtual cessation of bank lending, less aid, the lowest commodity prices in years, ever more stringent expectations on the part of the multinational corporations about appropriate investment climate, and, although this remains unsaid, increased threats of economic sanctions by the Group of Seven (G7) countries if a country violates the rule of the game.

In fact, structural adjustment and global integration are mutually reinforcing. While the process of globalization gave birth to structural adjustment as a response to the world economic crisis, the adoption of reform measures has in turn widened and deepened the thrust toward global integration. Although neither the IMF short-term stabilization programs nor the World Bank longer-term structural adjustment programs (SAPs) have met with much success, "African states cannot now avoid adjustment conditionalities as they have become the sine qua non of short term economic (and regime!) survival" (Shaw and Nyang'oro 1992; World Bank 1994). Nevertheless, SAPs are likely to lead to conflict between the state and civil society (Beckman 1992: 83–105). In reality, economic reform programs require more flexible domestic and international political structures to deal with increasingly autonomous groups in civil society—families detached from the farm, workers who have lost their jobs, export producers whose products have declined in value as a result of artificial substitution, and elements in society that are integrated closely in the world economy and that benefit from trade. For weak African states, the challenge for the next decade is how to expedite the democratization process while revitalizing the economy.

I see no long-term improvement for most Africans in the free-market policies now in vogue from Zimbabwe to Senegal. The current boom in a handful of countries implementing IMF-mandated economic reform cannot be sustained as long as it is based on depressed wages for the masses and the sale of state industries at bargain-basement prices. The task for social movements is to renounce these externally imposed policies and to offer alternatives that are designed to better the lives of the vast majority of the African poor. Social movements must coordinate their activities to attack a form of conditionality that sees social services and minimum wages as inefficient while bloated military expenditures, political repression, and presidential looting of the public treasury are decidedly ignored.

The emergence of three trading blocs—the North American Free Trade Agreement (NAFTA), the European Union, and an incipient East Asian bloc under the leadership of Japan—signifies the consolidation of the North-South divide, although Mexico and the Southeast Asian countries are generally regarded as part of the South. This will intensify Northern protectionism, especially through the proliferation of nontariff barriers (e.g., intellectual property rights, food safety standards, etc.). Africa will find itself ever more vulnerable and isolated if it chooses (or is obliged) to remain a collection of fifty small, competing exporters dependent on these regional giants to purchase its output and to supply its needs (Lang and Hines 1993). There is a compelling need to reverse this state of vulnerability, to strengthen regional markets, and to rationalize existing resources by establishing viable subregional economic integration schemes.

Yet economic cooperation within and among groups of African nations has been difficult to achieve. The Southern African Development Community (SADC), the Economic Community of West African States (ECOWAS), and the Preferential Trade Area for East and Southern African States (PTA), now renamed the Common Market Area for East and Southern African States (COMESAS), represent feeble efforts at such cooperation. In fact, intra-African trade barely accounts for 6 percent of total African trade with the rest of the world (Cheru 1992a). Countries that are not linked to any of the three major trading blocs will be completely shut out from effectively participating in global trade. The general rule seems to be that the door to Europe is open but certain countries are not going to be let in! With the successful conclusion of the Uruguay Round of trade negotiations in 1993, nontariff barriers to trade such as in standards and intellectual property rights will be effectively used to bar commodity-producing African countries from exporting to the major trading blocs. This news comes on top of rapid advances made in biotechnology, which are making traditional African exports useless as a result of substitution (such as fiber optics for copper and corn syrup for sugar beets) (Raghavan 1991).

The marginalization of Africa will extend to the diplomatic arena as well. Hutchful (1991) strongly argues that the dissolution of the Soviet Union and the socialist voting bloc in which some African countries participated, especially in the UN, means the further geopolitical isolation of Africa. This marginalization was evident during the UN Conference on Environment and Development (UNCED) negotiations, as well as the Uruguay Round, where African needs were never addressed. In the UNCED process, for example, issues of particular importance to Africa, such as the dumping of toxic waste, debt and commodity prices, and desertification, were given scant consideration. This is in stark contrast with the considerable international concern expressed over deforestation, ozone depletion, and global warming (Khor 1992b; Shiva 1992). Marginalization was aggravated by the inability of African countries to organize themselves effectively at the caucus level. In short, the UNCED process underscored Africa's marginalization within multilateral forums.

One issue that will keep Africa at center stage of the G7 strategy is the debt equation. The debt will be a mechanism to keep Africa within the emerging international economic order. This link with the world economy through dependence on exports to generate foreign exchange to pay the debt is creating a situation where weak African states are managed by trade instead of managing trade. As a result, developing countries are accountable more to foreign creditors and investors, international financial institutions, and industrialized countries than to their own people. In much of Africa, governments have increasingly ceded sovereignty to supranational institutions (e.g., the IMF, World Bank, GATT) while losing the capacity to manage domestic affairs on their own (Gill and Cheru 1993).

This new economic and political conjuncture should not necessarily be viewed negatively. It could instead provide a compelling occasion to redirect African foreign policy away from global integration and toward self-reliance and new regionalism, to recognize informal economies, and to encourage informal politics, particularly civil society at a regional level (Shaw 1994). The flag bearers of this new renaissance are based in the church, the informal sector, human rights movements, environment movements, and development communities that have sprung up all across Africa in the last decade to articulate alternative visions of survival and democratic governance. Needless to say, the vibrancy of these new institutions in civil society contrasts with the paucity of their strategic power and resources. The biggest challenge in the coming decades will be how to strengthen these internal forces, which are best placed to defend the democratic project in their respective communities.

The crucial challenge for African social movements is therefore how to develop a long-range strategic and sustainable economic agenda and to generate the necessary resources needed to fulfill this objective. This requires the rehabilitation of both states and market at the national level, the democratization of civil society, capacity building and institutionalization, and the continued coordination of activities with other social movements at the regional and transnational levels (Shaw and Nyang'oro 1992). This is necessary because problems that affect the poor and the marginalized cut across national borders. The North-South popular alliance becomes even more crucial when viewed in the context of the considerable power held by elites and firms that underpin the globalization process.

Learning from the Past:
The Burdened History of African Peasants

The postindependence history of Africa is replete with examples of broken promises and unfulfilled dreams. Since the 1950s, African society has gone through three different political and social experiences, all of them to the detriment of the urban poor and peasants. Broadly speaking, the three phases include the independence struggle, the postindependence experiment with development and nation building, and the post-1970s experience with economic reform, dominated by the policy of structural adjustment and debt crisis management. We are now in a fourth phase, characterized by an unprecedented drive for democratization. Peasants and the urban poor saw their living conditions deteriorate and their democratic rights evaporate during the first three phases, and phase four is unlikely to bring substantial economic and political changes to the majority, except maybe in South Africa, where civil society is vibrant and strong.

To begin with, one observes a striking similarity between the movement for democracy today and the mass mobilization campaign for independence that took place in the 1950s. Issues of landlessness, taxation without representation, exploitation of peasants by parastatal boards, lack of basic services, and the denial of fundamental rights and community control of decisions are all pressing today, just as they were thirty-five years ago. Similarly, the democracy movement has drawn people of diverse social and political backgrounds under the leadership of the middle classes, which was also the case in the independence struggle.

While the slogan of "second liberation" implies a vision of social development and political change fundamentally different from the first liberation, the lack of a broad-based program of economic and social reform and the exclusion of civil society by elite-led parties points to the limitations of the present democratization project. There exists widespread fear that the second liberation might turn out to be as disappointing as the first and that the "new democrats" might turn their backs on the poor majority, as the leaders of the nationalist movements had done. Elections in Zambia, Kenya, Cameroon, and elsewhere have turned out to be ineffectual.

It is common knowledge that the vast majority of Africans are peasants and landless agricultural workers. Without peasant production, one cannot talk about any meaningful development in Africa. Yet the postindependence development model has been very similar to the colonial development model, which stifled peasant autonomy and production. The last thirty years in Africa can best be characterized as a period of pacification of African peasants by both socialist and capitalist regimes and the social classes whom they represent as they attempted to push through ambitious development programs (Cheru 1989; Sandbrook 1985). As the state extended its administrative and regulatory wings to the furthest rural outposts, the capacity of peasants to initiate grassroots development autonomously on the basis of local reality was severely circumscribed. Like the colonial system, neither participation nor accountability has been passed on to local structures (Hyden 1983; Coulson 1980; Rahmato 1985). Under the guise of "development and nation building," elite bureaucrats and party loyalists, far removed from the reality of rural life, began to dictate what peasants can and cannot produce, for whom they can sell their outputs, and at what price (Bates 1981; World Bank 1989a). In some instances, the forced removal of peasants and pastoralists from fertile areas to marginal lands to make way for export plantations has been justified by the authorities on the grounds of advancing the national interest (Cheru 1992b; Rosenblum and Williamson 1987). The onset of drought only compounded rural poverty and hunger. Rural people now constitute the largest single group of refugees and displaced persons (Timberlake 1986).

By the mid-1970s, the euphoria of independence had long disappeared and the military had entrenched itself as the sole conductor of state politics in many parts of Africa. The much publicized development decade had given way to greater disillusionment, and many people found themselves on the brink of starvation (Sandbrook 1985; Barraclough 1991). Various indexes of economic development registered a decline. Agricultural stagnation, poor export performance, underutilization of capacity in industries, growing indebtedness, and significant social erosion characterized the continent (World Bank 1989a). Not only were development policies antipeasant and antipoor, but even projects and programs designed to help the poor with assistance from the new "lords of poverty" ended up marginalizing them (Hancock 1989). The familiar cry from the poor became "Please don't develop us!"

When Africa entered the 1980s, new pressures were placed on impoverished and disillusioned African masses. Since the demands of the postcolonial state for more revenues have steadily increased since the mid-1970s to pay foreign debt, expensive oil imports, bloated military expenditure, and presidential looting of the public treasury, peasants and the urban poor were expected to sacrifice once more for the extravagant mistakes of the powerful. "Tighten your belts, eat less, and pay more" toward the national debt became the order of the day. As IMF programs began to take a bite (through drastic reductions of social expenditures), large numbers of peasants began to drop out of the formal economy to guard against threats to their subsistence (Onimode 1988; Rau 1991). This is logical because, for peasants, the future is not necessarily more knowable—they prefer security and subsistence over uncertain progress (Gran 1984; Berry 1994).

It is no wonder that governments in Africa have not been able to mobilize the population for development in a constructive manner. As many people began to draw a direct connection between their economic plight and the paucity of basic liberties, local grievances very quickly escalated into popular challenges to the established systems of government. Ordinary people now want to construct a new political and economic reality on their own terms, with a future based on participation, local control, and the meeting of basic human needs (UNECA 1990). This has created tension between peoples and states (Chazan and Rothchild 1988; Beckman 1992). In response, the state has tried to keep control over informal organizations through co-optation of their key spokespersons.

Democracy in Africa: One Step Forward, Two Steps Backward

While democracy as an idea has triumphed in much of Africa, in practice it is in profound trouble. Although there are many reasons for this state of affairs, two elements stand out. First, participation of citizens in the political process cannot be ordered from above, or even from outside. Second, participation cannot function under conditions of absolute poverty and visible inequality. For democracy to emerge, there must be significant social reform and a reduction of economic inequalities (Nyong'o 1987; Cheru 1989). Satisfying basic needs and providing education are important prerequisites for this. In the absence of real change in people's lives, zero-sum mentalities and destructive competition will prevail instead of moderation, thus undermining the chances of democratic transitions. Yet much of the debate on democracy in Africa has paid only lip service to fundamental social reforms.

There exists an intense suspicion of the state and the parties in much of Africa. All too often, elections deteriorate to the formal legitimation of autocratic rule and diminish the role of civil society. Instead of being liberating, multiparty systems might lead to new forms of old hierarchies. Political leaders seek time to pursue power and profit by patterns of bargaining, manipulation, and deceit. This does not build local capacity or national purpose.

Kenya is a good example of a country where the institution of formal democracy has failed to broaden popular political participation in a meaningful way. The collapse of one-party states is rarely accompanied by a substantial reorientation of power relations, the rural-urban dimension in particular. Social reform agendas that could have established the basis for broader popular participation and greater social justice have been abandoned. Furthermore, a multiparty system, with the old guard at the helm, is not going to change the ubiquitous corruption, marginalization of rural people, and ethnic identification patterns. Therefore, in Kenya, participation is without empowerment.

Adding fuel to the fire is that Western governments and donors have been insisting that aid must be conditioned on the implementation of free elections and free markets without realizing that the full expression of democratic values requires more than a procedure for electing officials. Democracy is a way of life, with a set of traditions and institutions. More important, it requires an independent judiciary that can enforce rights, protect the opposition, and ensure not only that elections are democratic but that daily life is democratic as well.

The "new" political conditionality the Western donors have been insisting that African governments implement tends to contradict the economic reform coming under the rubric of IMF/World Bank structural adjustment. Repression and authoritarianism have represented the flip side of donor-driven structural adjustment programs (Beckman 1992: 83–105). In a bid to gain external legitimacy, African governments were willing to suppress domestic opposition to austerity measures. This in turn has backfired and created popular resistance against newly elected democratic regimes. In Zambia, for example, when the Movement for Multiparty Democracy (MMD) became a party in power, it strengthened the structural adjustment policy that hits hard against the urban poor. In addition, the new government introduced an aggressive antisquatter policy and bulldozed some housing areas right after the election (Schlyster 1993). Seen in this context, African democratization is cosmetic and temporary.

The challenge in Africa and elsewhere today is how to make economic revitalization compatible with democracy. While multiparty elections and universal suffrage are important formal criteria, they are by no means sufficient to judge the democratic qualities of a society. In impoverished societies such as in Africa, democracy must go beyond free expression and the inclusion of diverse groups in national politics. There must be an organic link between political freedom and freedom from hunger, ignorance, and disease. Therefore, people must see the results of democracy in an improved standard of living, better education, better housing, and access to health care. In the absence of real changes in people's lives, zero-sum mentalities and destructive competitions will prevail instead of moderation, thus undermining the process of democratic transitions. In short, the popular movement for political change in Africa was generated by a quest for basic consumption items and everyday survival rather than for a multiparty democracy. The meaning of multiparty democracy on a local level remains rather confused.

SPEAKING TRUTH TO POWER: DEMOCRACY AND SOCIAL MOVEMENTS IN AFRICA

In reaction to top-down democratization initiatives, a challenge to democracy as an ideology of domination has emerged from the mobilization of social movements seeking to reassert popular control. This terrain has increasingly been occupied by civic associations, women's groups, peasant associations, environmental groups, and human rights organizations, pressing demands on the state through the "politics of claims," nonpayment of taxes, open peasant insurrection, urban riots, or collective actions to find solutions to common problems (Pradervand 1989; Rau 1991; Scott 1993).

The new social movements advance the idea that development is a human right whose achievement requires popular participation and control. The desire to define issues in these terms has forced local social movements to link up with other groups elsewhere in the world that are grappling with similar problems. These global networks are being facilitated by the various communications and transportation hardware that are also a result of the conditions for globalization (Ekins 1992; During 1989). This has profoundly changed the nature of social organizing.

At this point, a note of caution is in order. Despite the critical role social movements are playing, we must not romanticize them, for they presently lack a coordinating mechanism. The emerging civil society in Africa, as in Eastern Europe, is riven by deep cleavages and tensions, which can threaten both economic restructuring and political liberalization. The real danger is that pro- and antidemocratic forces coexist side by side. These forces may be either elitist or populist, atavistic and divisive or constructive and cohesive elements projecting a vision of an alternative order (Mittelman, Chapter 1). For example, can we equate the spread of nongovernmental organizations (NGOs) with democracy? After all, NGOs do not have electoral constituencies and thus are not accountable to anyone except the agencies that fund them.

Is the vibrancy of independent social movements an indication of the growth and development of a strong and viable civil society that can serve as a base for democratization? Is the space that exists somewhere between the "private" realm and the organization and institutions constituted by the state (i.e., the public realm), where everyday life is experienced, discussed, comprehended, contested, and reproduced and where hegemony is built and contested? Future research must examine these important questions if we are to understand popular challenges to globalization.

What distinguishes progressive social movements from others is that they are inclusive and articulate the demands of poor people and politically disenfranchised groups; they represent alternative forms of political articulation; they are often at odds with their own governments; and they always seek to attain objectives that entail other paths to economic development, political control, and social organization (Stavenhagen 1992). The most promising elements with the capacity to initiate fundamental change are the informal sector, ecology movements, peasant movements, church organizations, and human rights movements. These groups not only pursue single issues but are increasingly conducting interactive campaigns, focusing on matters of a structural nature. For example, environmental groups now focus not only on issues of resource management and pollution control but also on trade, debt, immigration, human rights, and other issues that the first-generation environmental movements would not have considered because they were presumed to be outside the realm of ecological campaigns.

The Informal Sector

The predominance of informality in African urban centers is beyond dispute. The retreat of the state in key areas of social services has left enormous gaps that have been filled by local initiatives. From Johannesburg to Dakar, large numbers of people are now engaged in the parallel economy: shelter, employment, law and order, transportation, garbage collection, catering services, trade, and even household credit supply (Mabogunje 1991). Therefore, the informal sector and social networks in urban sectors are neither exotic nor pathological. They constitute a dynamic and enduring force that has shaped African cities.

Squatter settlements, for example, represent not simply a shelter entity or a mere collection of shacks. They are sociopolitical entities, with their own rules, forms of organization, and internal hierarchies. While they may be functional to capital in the role they play in supplementing the reproduction of labor, they also constitute a node of resistance and defiance against state domination. The same applies to unregistered markets, street vendors, backyard artisans, pirate taxis, and the entire arena of social reproduction for the majority of the urban population. Under the apparent chaos in this sector is a substantial degree of order.

What explains the resilience and dynamism of the informal sector? Research has demonstrated that they are maintained by the solidarity and the organic nature of the institutional and organizational superstructure embedded within this sector. There is a high degree of participation, accountability and commitment and a sense of obligation in informal sector activities

(Jules-Rosette 1981). Over time, new types of voluntary associations develop that often blossom into different kinds of political and social movements, whose importance spreads beyond the limits of the specific local shantytown or settlement (e.g., the *matatu* taxi drivers in Kenya, the market women of Ghana).

The Church

The challenge to the state from below is further being strengthened by the growing fundamentalist movements in largely Islamic countries and the growth of indigenous churches whose appeal to a broader base of African society is growing everyday. Church involvement in development activities has been contributing for good measure to the strengthening of the popular sector (Hyden 1985). Both Islam and Christianity are now at a political crossroads—choosing a path, seeking change in the material conditions of their followers, or ignoring political and economic conditions in expectation of a better life in the spiritual hereafter. Islamic fundamentalism and indigenous Christianity have developed into institutions that can offer viable opposition to government policy and have continued to do so despite government pressure and coercion (Mazrui 1990). Is the world prepared to accept these movements as legitimate expressions of public dissent? Or will it simply disregard them because they adhere to Christianity or Islam?

Peasant Resistance

Ordinary peasants know that the postcolonial state has lost its role as an instrument of development. Instead of becoming more effective, the state in Africa has become the main obstacle to development. The relations between the state and the peasantry are thus characterized by mutual suspicion and distrust.

The peasants have realized their powerless situation and have drawn conclusions: it is better to avoid the state altogether and withdraw within their local communities on a subsistence basis and by engaging in collective action to find alternative strategies of survival. Small farmers now market their produce through their own channels, disregarding political boundaries and marketing boards (Cheru 1989; MacGaffee 1983). Having been victims of state-sponsored development, they attempt to bypass formal agencies and link up with different kinds of NGOs at the local level. In many communities, the emphasis has shifted from export crops to food crops for local consumption.

In Kenya, for example, farmers have almost totally abandoned coffee production, and tea and sugar growers have on occasion neglected their crops to demonstrate their anger at the perceived hostility of the official buyers toward them (Kimenyi 1993). In Nyeri, Central Province, about eight hundred members of the troubled Mathira Coffee Farmers' Society joined a

1993 boycott by farmers from eleven other factories in delivering their coffee to the Kenya Planter's Cooperative Union demanding the society be dissolved (*Daily Nation* 1993). The farmers' behavior is quite rational, considering the failure of the parastatal to make payments as scheduled and the large percentage that it consumes directly. Yet the response of opposition politicians to the structural causes of the agrarian crisis in Kenya has been quite disappointing.

Grassroots Ecology Movements

The postindependence development experience not only has widened inequalities but has undermined the resource base that sustains life. The emphasis on export-led strategy, ranging from cattle ranching to timber exporting, has intensified the competition for essential resources. Peasants and pastoralists are dislocated by more powerful social coalitions to marginal lands to make way for export plantations. Rivers and water sources that have long sustained pastoralists and small farmers are rerouted considerable distances to serve agribusiness, leaving local people to fend for themselves.

In a struggle for survival, ecology movements, peasant groups, and women's organizations in Africa are at a political crossroads and are challenging structures that have long kept them marginalized (During 1989). A case in point is Wangari Maathai and the Green Belt movement, which assist Kenyan women to plant trees in their homesteads. President Daniel arap Moi was shocked to discover the muscle of the Green Belt movement when foreign funding committed for the construction of a skyscraper in a popular Nairobi park was withdrawn after protest led by Maathai. The overall consensus among popular organizations and environmental groups is that the process of poverty alleviation must go hand in hand with instituting far-reaching political changes (Korten 1990). Even the World Bank, which for so long has tried to separate economics from politics, now advocates democracy and the merits of popular participation in the development process.

Ecology movements now think locally and act globally, for they see the usefulness of international support and publicity for their local struggles (McCormick 1989). In addition, social movements have become sophisticated in that they try to understand the interrelatedness of issues previously handled as if they were separate, and they build coalitions around these issues. They now undertake multifaceted concerns, such as the relationships between debt and the environment, trade and sustainable development, and democracy and sustainable development.

The Human Rights Movement

Given the predominance of military governments in many parts of Africa, the human rights movement remained underdeveloped until very recently. In fact, much of the human rights work regarding political prisoners and refugees has been conducted by northern NGOs and church groups. Since 1989, however, we have witnessed a proliferation of local human rights groups with a much expanded agenda far beyond the traditional focus on political prisoners. While some groups focus on shelter or development as a human right, others deal primarily with the rights of internally displaced persons, street children, displaced pastoral communities that have lost their entitlement, and ethnic and religious minorities. In close collaboration with Northern NGOs and human rights organizations, African human rights organizations have been able to bring to international forums the complicity of national governments and donor agencies who support development strategies that often conflict with peoples' rights for development and self-management.

This brief review of social movements confirms that ordinary people do not allow their frustration with state policies and programs to get in the way of bettering themselves and maintaining their self-reliance. In the process, such groups have become politically conscious and are educating themselves in organizational dynamics and self-government at the local level. In short, social movements are redefining issues in terms that address more fundamental questions of resource distribution and access and political rights and processes. In democratic parlance, this is self-government.

New social movements must come to terms with the fact that revolution is no longer an option. Even the most radical groups have to accept this if they are to play a crucial role in bringing change in Africa. For example, after many years of war and destruction, Ethiopians and Mozambicans are not prepared to die for empty socialist ideals. The only realistic option for reducing corruption, making political systems more responsive, and bettering the lot of the poor is to democratize both democracy and capitalism.

Dilemma of Agenda Mix

A comprehensive development alternative cannot go far enough without a basic change in political structures. Until this happens the popular sector can only pressure government for some policy changes and accumulate little victories here and there. This implies that the popular sector must have another political agenda over and above its main business of disempowering centralized structures. In other words, it has to come up with a state agenda of its own. This suggests entering the terrain of the nation-state—national politics.

Here lies precisely the dilemma of nongovernmental and people's organizations. By nature their main concern is social politics—in other words, self-governance whose success is measured mainly in terms of the circles or poles of popular power that they create at the base. In this context, state politics is of a different world. And yet civil society has to grapple with the unavoidable agenda mix. It will have to find the appropriate combination of strategies to effectively handle the contradictory trajectories of state politics, which is integrative or centralizing, and social politics, which is horizontal or centrifugal.

In their efforts to cope with the dilemma, NGOs and people's organizations (POs) face problems that tend to confuse their identity and undermine their core values, such as autonomy, pluralism, diversity, volunteerism, and closeness to the grassroots, bottom-up perspective.

One problem is state substitution. Some NGOs and popular organizations set up layers of bureaucratic structures and end up behaving like state institutions. Then some self- appointed leaders represent the loosely defined entity called NGO/PO community (like politicians), and bureaucrats lay claim to jurisdiction over citizens and territories.

A related problem is parallelism. In their frustration with state policies, NGOs tend to do things on their own as though government does not exist. Because they have set up substitute structures, they think they could make an impact on the overall situation in spite of the government. One cannot equate the spread of NGOs with democracy. In some cases, NGOs are spreading clientelism, thus undermining the collective action. These tensions have to be worked out. Our vision should not distract us from what is and what exists. Should civil society always be in confrontation with the state? Or should civil society be viewed as one stage in the development of community on the way to becoming a state? Or should it be viewed in terms of the relationship of the state to people—as an interface between people and the state?

Back to the Drawing Board

Contrary to the Eurocentric view arguing that Africans are strangers to democracy, democratic ethos and practices are ingrained in Africa at subnational levels, the locales that mean most for individual Africans. Since the colonial era and the advent of the nation-state, however, Africans have been deprived of democratic involvement. Fear and mistrust of central authorities have been widespread, and this has made it difficult to sustain democratic values and commitment. Compounding the problem has been decades of economic decline and resource competition, which have produced zero-sum mentalities and a tendency to resort to ethnic nationalism to get ahead in the competition for scarce resources. Because of these reasons, until recently people have been passive recipients of policies.

What is billed as Africa's second liberation has little chance of success if it cannot revive Africans' economic fortunes. The growing demand for democratization is a response to declining living standards in the face of widespread corruption and mismanagement by the political elites. Therefore, people do not just want multiparty democracy—they want fundamental economic changes as well. Therefore, the way out of the current political impasse lies with ordinary people reacquiring power control of their natural and human resources and strengthening their capacities to define development in their own terms. This fundamental process can be achieved only on the basis of people's participation in organization and decisionmaking at all levels. Only when African farmers have a political voice will their needs be properly addressed by governments.

Recognizing Peasants' Knowledge.   One of the biggest obstacles in forging institutional ties between urban-based movements and rural people is a serious communication gap. Although most urban Africans keep their family ties to the rural areas from which they originate, communication is one-sided and minimal. The authorities regard peasants as backward and ignorant. The new urban democrats, polished in pro-peasant rhetoric, behave much the same way as the authorities in power. They take their Western educational credentials as a license to decide what is good for peasants; what the peasants know and what they might need is no concern to them. Without mobilizing peasant support and active cooperation, the democratization and development projects will hardly succeed. But if peasants are supposed to engage their initiatives and enthusiasm, they must have reason to be convinced that they will be in control of their situation themselves, that their knowledge and initiatives matter, and that they will not once again be at the mercy of other groups' greed.

Acknowledging That Nothing Grows from the Top Down.   The only way to ensure democracy in Africa is to allow rural people to build on the indigenous. According to Ake, this refers to whatever the people consider important in their lives, whatever they regard as an authentic expression of themselves (Ake 1988: 19–23). For the peasant, the conditions for democratic participation are very much present at the community level. This will help determine the form and content of the development strategy and social institutions that are important in people's lives. People at all levels must be given the right to establish and manage their own cooperatives and organizations of women, youth, workers, and consumers. These local-level organizations must be given greater control over the allocation of resources, the disbursement of funds intended to benefit them, and the appointment and control of officials meant to serve them.

Strong popular organizations enable different sectors of the society to assert and fight for their particular social rights. These local organizations must also find ways to mobilize their constituencies for the purpose of gaining influence on the national level, opening channels of communication and representation of peasant interests up to the top level.

Making the First Step Toward Liberation.   We cannot talk about participation in a vacuum. Participation requires grassroots education to create far more active and competent citizens. Only by enlarging visions and raising consciousness can peasants undermine the vicious circle of mass exclusion and marginalization. While peasants, by and large, are aware of their situation at the local level, they have neither the capacity nor the resources required to influence events in the world beyond their villages. Heightened consciousness makes peasants aware of the range of value choices open to them and their social and political implications. This is of course a cumbersome, slow, and time-consuming job. It is not as easy as political speech making. As Hollnsteiner observed in the Philippines, it takes a long time for peasants living on the margin to move from simple, concrete, and short-term personal issues to more complex, abstract, long-term, and systemic issues (Hollnsteiner 1979).

Building Capacity in Peasant Institutions.   It is no use talking about peasant participation if the basic elements required for the instrumentalization of participation are not present at the village level. Capacity building entails leadership training for both men and women, establishing locally based research capacity, disseminating information, networking, and lobbying. Institution building would also involve improving communication flows between communities and different sets of rural institutions, thus helping peasants become catalysts for change. Democracy cannot work without a high level of information and knowledge. This is a crucial area often forgotten when one talks about mobilizing peasants and involving grassroots organizations.

Establishing the Rule of Law.   Because policy needs to be formulated into legal norms and requires the creation of structures and the definition of relations, the law has a very essential and active role in renewing and restoring democracy. However, declaring a law is one thing; living the law is another. Thirty years of experience in Africa have shown that public officials usually circumvent or violate the law when it is not expedient for them. For democracy to take root in Africa, ordinary citizens must be persuaded that the government sincerely believes in, and is willing to use its executive powers and prerogatives to ensure the rule of law, equality before the law, and due process of law.

The judiciary has been the weakest in Africa. One way to ensure democracy is to make the judiciary an effective institution and a true guardian of civil liberties and other rights of the private sector. But promulgating laws is not enough. We need to make sure that peasants acquire the minimum level of legal competency. Peasants must know their rights and understand what the law actually means to them, both individually and collectively. In this way, the lives and property of individuals do not rest in the hands of public officials. Victims should have recourse to the law.

Promoting Pro-Peasant Economic Policy.   Since subsistence agriculture is the mainstay of many African countries, the state must develop a supportive environment for economic growth to stimulate agricultural production. The biggest challenge in Africa has always been how to make the public sector more responsive to the needs of small farmers who need government support in the area of credit, inputs, markets, and fair prices to succeed.

Besides advocating radical changes in the above mentioned policy areas, the contentious issues of land ownership and tenure have to be addressed head on. Although *agrarian reform* has become a dirty term in international circles (because it smacks of leftism or revolution), real democracy cannot be established without fundamental land redistribution and a reorientation of agricultural policy in Africa. Opposition leaders cannot afford to hold back their punches on the land issue if they ever hope to attract significant support from rural people.

Instilling the Virtues of Self-reliance. The greatest assurance for peasants' security in Africa would be for political leaders to emphasize the kinds of economic relations that involve self-reliance rather than charity. According to Galtung, self-reliance implies selective resistance and the use of local resources effectively. By necessity, self-reliance demands mass participation (Galtung et al. 1980). Through participation, peasants become aware of the range of options open to them and of their own capacity to transform their communities. Therefore, self-reliance reinforces the democratic ethos at the subnational level, the level that means most to peasants. In contrast, IMF stabilization programs reinforce dependence and undermine the drive for mass participation by rewarding one group and penalizing others.

Recognizing the Role of Women. In Africa, women make up the majority of the rural poor. They produce the bulk of food and constitute 60–80 percent of the agricultural work force. Yet their contribution to the household as well as to the society is rarely recognized. Women are the first to be victims of famine, debt, and regional conflicts. Despite the weight of the crisis that is shouldered by women, they play only a minimal role in decision-making in national and local politics. For democracy to succeed, there must be a firm commitment to full constitutional guarantee of women to ascertain the rights of access to land and control of resources and opportunities for leadership training. This could lead to cessation of women's abuse, manipulation, and anonymity.

Promoting Transnational Civil Society. Democratization and social reform in the Third World is contingent upon the degree of internal change in the core countries. It is essential to link grassroots groups and NGOs generally (as well as local governments) across national borders and to address common concerns through joint action (Falk 1992a; Ekins 1992). Experience from the antiapartheid movement to the UNCED process has proven that this is not only possible but indispensable. Despite the ascendance of right-wing forces in the United States and Western Europe in the 1980s, Third World solidarity movements flourished and even scored some victories against great odds. These social movements are credited for helping to end apartheid and for raising awareness of the links between ecology and development, culminating in the Earth Summit. In the present world order, where corporate power and the state depress the welfare of ordinary people, solidarity movements based in churches and environmental NGOs offer real hope for the great mass of people.

Peasants constitute the single dominant social group in Africa. Yet they are the least represented and the most oppressed group. For democracy to take root in Africa, strong and independent peasant groups must be encouraged to check the excesses of state power. Until opposition leaders and urban elites respect the knowledge of peasants and acknowledge the fact that nothing grows from the top down, their efforts at building a democratic society will be an exercise in futility. Participation of peasants cannot simply be ordered from above. It has to be demanded and carried out from below. This is the cardinal rule of democracy. As it stands, opposition leaders have put the cart before the horse. It is not too late to set things right.

CONCLUSION

The fundamental political conflict in the coming decades will be between the forces of globalization and the various forms of locally based social movements in both the North and the South seeking to redefine a just, democratic, and sustainable new world order. It is therefore important to identify potential agents of transformation in diverse contexts and to build a durable transnational civil society movement to check the excesses of the forces of globalization. In the African context, however, more hard work is required for social movements to be able to develop a formidable counterproject. Organizing around daily subsistence increasingly consumes too much of people's energy and meager resources, thus making the task of developing a counterproject exceptionally difficult and slow.

June Nash
Christine Kovic **8**

The Reconstitution of Hegemony: The Free Trade Act and the Transformation of Rural Mexico

Global integration has often been achieved at the cost of undermining democratic institutions within newly industrializing countries. A favorable climate for investment in the 1970s and 1980s meant the assurance of low labor costs achieved by repressive governments prohibiting trade unions and other mass organizations that addressed the issues of the new labor force. Mittelman (Chapter 1) has pointed to the limits of this kind of international competition as the demands for democratic institutions have grown in new areas of development. Understanding how consensus is gained in the context of global integration of the society and polity requires an awareness of local political processes.

In this chapter we will consider the attempt by Mexican president Carlos Salinas de Gortari to reconstitute hegemonic accord in the neoliberal restructuring of the economy brought about by global trade and financial integration and the way this was challenged by the Zapatista National Liberation Army uprising on New Year's Eve 1994. Although José López Portillo and Miguel de la Madrid had relaxed many of the restrictive trade provisions and nationalistic investment priorities, Salinas made more dramatic changes than any of his predecessors in undercutting the old basis for hegemony with campesinos (rural cultivators) and national entrepreneurs. His government pursued policies of industry privatization that alienated sectors of organized labor, a reform of the Agrarian Reform Law that ended the paternalistic relationship with campesinos, and elimination of heavy import duties that threatened national industries. In the massive redistribution of income that occurred during his presidency, he reduced the political and economic base of the middle class, and as its consumption and political power was reduced he vigorously promoted export-oriented production in the world market.

These challenges to the traditional basis of hegemonic accord maintained by the ruling Institutional Revolutionary Party (PRI) during the first four years of Salinas's presidency were opposed by campesinos in peaceful demonstrations that were met by increasingly repressive military force, especially in the southernmost state of Chiapas. Protest came to a head with the Zapatista New year's uprising, on the very day that the Free Trade Act (known as the North American Free Trade Agreement [NAFTA] in the United States) was to go into effect. The Democratic National Convention called by the Zapatistas in August 1994 was a tentative step in charting an alternative course for entering global economic exchange.

The Zapatista uprising contradicted the image of modernity and democracy that Salinas had tried to forge in his commitment to international exchange and an export-oriented economy. This commitment followed upon a decade during which the country restructured its economy toward the export-oriented, privatized goals imposed by the International Monetary Fund (IMF) in 1982 as conditions for incorporation in the global economy. The restructuring of the Mexican economy in response to global integration reversed the postrevolutionary course of development that emphasized communal landholdings maintaining a semisubsistence economy in the rural areas and syndicalist organizations of urban workers and professionals. In contrast to U.S. democracy, whereby each person is the unit of individual rights and duties, Mexico incorporated campesinos, urban proletariats, commercial agents, and professionals through member organizations that were responsible for delivering the vote to the PRI. Founded in 1929, years after the revolutionary goals were crystallized in the constitution, the PRI reveals the paradoxical basis for power relations in an institutional nexus that asserts the memory of violent upheaval of a social structure. Contradictions were resolved through compromises with and co-optation of the leadership of the Confederation of Mexican Workers (CTM), the National Confederation of Campesinos (CNC), the National Confederation of Popular Organizations (CNOP), and many other organizations that brought their constituents into line. Indigenous villages became part of this corporatist structure through their caciques (native leaders co-opted within government spending programs), who delivered the vote to the PRI. Through these organizations, paternalistic relationships developed with state bureaucracies that were co-optive and opportunistic in practice.

The corporatist structure began to crumble in the debt crisis of the 1980s when the adjustment policies launched by the IMF in 1982 forced austerity measures. The decreased services to the most vulnerable—women, children, and the aged—along with wage and price freezes, which reduced spending power and inflation from 200 percent in 1987 to about 20 percent in 1988 (Beneria 1989), polarized the sectors that made up the PRI constituency. Cuahtemoc Cárdenas (the son of Lázaro Cárdenas, who had fathered the institutional framework for realizing the goals of the revolution during his term of office from 1934 to 1940) demonstrated the fragmentation of hegemonic control by the PRI with the strength of his Democratic Revolutionary Party (PRD) in the 1988 elections. Many read this as a rejection of neoliberal policies that had shifted the burden of the debt to the lower-income sectors in the rural and urban economy as the government increasingly withdrew from its responsibilities toward those very sectors.

In the political crisis caused by charges of electoral fraud and the assassination of PRD members following Salinas's election in 1988, Salinas attempted to integrate Mexico into the global economy by promoting private enterprise in both the agricultural and industrial sectors. In the fourth year of his six-year term, he unleashed his strongest attack on the corporatist structure of the state with Article 27, Reform of the Agrarian Reform Law. This reform allowed privatization of collectively held *ejido* lands that were the key to agrarian policies of the postrevolutionary government. It opened the door for private sales of land, particularly that of the colonizers who were already indebted by breakdowns in the marketing of cash crops. The minimal assistance in the form of marketing and credit given to rural smallholders lured into cultivation of coffee and fruit was abruptly withdrawn after 1992, leaving many with rotting harvests and debts that made it impossible to undertake renewed cultivation.

This rejection of the old politics of paternalism and co-optation combined with the failure to address the rising problems of commercial cultivation contributed to the discontent in the Chiapas rural population. On New Year's Eve 1994 the eight hundred men and women who joined the rebels forcibly entered the municipal headquarters of San Cristobal de Las Casas, Ocosingo, Las Margaritas, and Altamirano. The leaders specifically attacked the Free Trade Act for its failure to take the needs of indigenous people into account. They called for a democratic process to ensure free elections and greater participation of small-plot farmers and agricultural laborers who were left out of the development process in Chiapas. In the process of negotiating with the populist former mayor of Mexico City, Manuel Camacho, the Zapatistas extended their support among Lacandón jungle colonizers who had long-pending land claims and bore deep-seated resentment for the failure of the government to address their demands. Their call for reform echoed in some traditional highland towns as the indigenous people threw out the corrupt PRI officials in Zinacantan, threatened the autocratic rule of caciques in San Juan Chamula, and prompted the takeover of the Teopisca town hall by poor campesinos. These supporters' long-standing land claims were ignored, for the government favored large-scale capitalist enterprises that were taking advantage of the oil, hydroelectric, and lumber resources in Chiapas. Protests against the large cattle owners who took over land cleared by colonizers were consistently met by military repression, with arbitrary arrests, torture, and killing attested by the Fray Bartolome de las Casas Human Rights Center denied by the PRI government. Unlike in armed guer-

rilla movements of the past, the Zapatistas made it clear that they were trying not to seize power by force but to open the political arena for marginalized people.

In this chapter we will analyze Salinas's attempt to restructure hegemonic control in the context of integrating Mexico's economy in world market and financial structures while destroying the corporate base of the old
order during 1993. We will describe the process in which the Salinas government tried to retain cultural identification with the revolutionary tradition
of the early decades of this century while promoting new links between
regional power blocs and the center of power in Mexico City. The Zapatista
National Liberation Army rudely shattered Salinas's attempt to forge "a
shared sense of reality," which is central to hegemonic order among disparate interests (Gramsci 1973). The break between the new international
order and the paternalistic political structure challenged the moral economy
of the communal indigenous population and the rising militancy of the
uprooted peasants whose demands were consistently ignored.

Because of the predominantly indigenous ethnic identification of highland Chiapas communities, hegemonic control requires management of corporate politics among local elites and state as well as national governments
(Lomnitz 1992: 27 et seq.). The massive dislocations of semisubsistence
farmers in southeastern Mexico during the 1960s and 1970s resulted in
major changes in land use and labor mobilization that upset this control
(Collier, Mountjoy, and Nigh 1994). Yet state officials in Chiapas limited
themselves to forging a new social contract between modernizing sectors of
the economy and the elites of corporate indigenous communities. But the
masses of impoverished campesinos as well as expelled indigenes forced to
migrate to the city have been left outside the co-optive programs of the government. We will describe the emergent agrarian power bloc in Chiapas
wherein the old conflict between indigenes and ladinos (nonindigenous
bearers of European culture) is being replaced by a class-divided indigenous
bloc, with elites supporting the PRI and the disinherited turning to the PRD
or the Zapatista National Liberation Army.

FORGING A NEW AGRARIAN POWER BLOC

Salinas responded to the crisis of legitimacy in his party after charges of
fraud in his 1988 election with adroit management of the contesting forces.
In the events leading up to and following the passage of the Reform of the
Agrarian Reform Law, we can decipher his strategy of neutralizing a
campesino bloc that became increasingly opposed to the privatization and
commercialization policies contingent on the opening up of opportunities by
global capitalist investment.

To overcome the opposition of vested interests in the old paternalism and to engage vital new sectors of the agrarian economy, President Salinas initiated two major stratagems from 1991, when the proposed changes to the Agrarian Reform Law were announced, to 1992, when it was implemented. The first involved the ideological engagement of diverse interests threatened by the new phase of capitalist accumulation. The second involved the restructuring of agencies dealing with agrarian conflict and welfare programs; it required a shoring up of patronage through combined public and private initiatives. Concomitant with these goals, the Salinas administration targeted areas of opposition to the dissolution of state paternalism that had operated within corporatist power blocs. It channeled conflict cases into the new Agrarian Solicitors Office and deployed welfare funds in the new Solidarity program, PRONASOL, to co-opt leaders that objected to the changes. These stratagems will be described as we observed them played out in the spring and summer of 1993.

The Rhetoric of Reform Without Privatization

The linkage with the revolutionary victories of the early decades of the nineteenth century is maintained as the government mounts its campaign against corrupt paternalistic policies identified with the old order, using the rhetoric of popular organizations. In the foreword to the "New Agrarian Legislation" (1992), the brochure put together by Solidarity, changes in Article 27 of the constitution allowing the private sale and development of agrarian lands are presented as a reform of the Agrarian Reform Law:

> Under the principle of bringing greater liberty and justice to the Mexican countryside, the reform to Article 27 of the Constitution and the expedition of the Agrarian Law represents a change of great importance to overcome the low growth that the rural sector has had for 25 years in comparison with the rest of the economy. The recuperation of agriculture and the increase of the welfare of the campesino are a basic condition to modernize the region begun by the government of President Carlos Salinas de Gortari.

Clearly there was a need for reform in the Agrarian Reform Law corresponding to the changed conditions in the half-century since it went into effect. From the early decades of land redistribution in the 1930s, cattle interests in the north were excluded by Pres. Lázaro Cárdenas, and large landowners were able to evade expropriation in the south. In the first place, since there are no national lands available for redistribution, the needs of the growing agrarian smallholder population could not be met within the context of the old Agrarian Reform Laws without confronting the agroindustrial interests that were built up during the past four administrations. The 3.5 million solicitations for land pending, 7.6 million hectares in litigation, and two hundred resolutions responding to demands in limbo revealed the depth of the quagmire in 1991. Fifteen million campesinos received less than the minimal salary of 15 new pesos (about U.S. $5) a day, and only five million received the minimum. The solution of the Echeverría and Madrid administrations to send colonizers into the jungle areas has been countered by ecological concerns for the global impact of deforestation. Moreover, the existing bureaucracy of the Secretariat of the Agrarian Reform perpetuated the triple threat of *caciquismo,* arbitrary rule of the indigenous and mestizo intermediaries who justified acts of political repression and theft in the name of tradition and local autonomy. A social division of work corresponding to the social ownership of property that might have permitted technological advances in the *ejido* lands was rarely implemented by agencies that proliferated in the various administrations. Many of the small producers were forced to out-migrate because of the stagnation in the *ejido* sector and government policies controlling the price of subsistence crops while favoring global and national agroindustrial interests with large-scale development. Mexico has become dependent on food imports, with 30 percent of the basic food crop, corn, being imported in 1991. Campesinos complained that they were "corralled like sheep" between the limitations of the old corporatist interests and the threat of expropriations by the new capitalized sector. Rural migrants to the cities were nearly excluded from the process of adjustment required by the new conditions of land tenure and cultivation.

The rhetoric of reform of the land reform act masks the new relations of production while suppressing the opposition of disinherited power blocs. This has involved a realignment of the rural sector under reconstituted organizations claiming to represent the diverse elements in the countryside confronted with the privatization of the communal landholdings. The National Confederation of Campesinos, which had constituted the major voice of rural interests within the PRI, tried to mobilize support for the new law under the slogan of modernization without loss of the *ejido,* but it could no longer pretend to represent the campesinos who rejected their conformity to PRI policies that had resulted in the decapitalization of the rural sector throughout the 1970s and 1980s. As a result, there was a proliferation of new organizational structures that set about to construct consensus. The National Confederation of Small Propertyholders provided a voice for groups that sought title to land as independent owners. The Permanent Agrarian Congress (CAP) called for greater flexibility and modification of the agrarian law to permit free association between campesinos and private investors.

Opposed to these centrist interests modifying the act to make it more acceptable were new populist interests demanding representation in the negotiations. These included the Mexican Commission of 500 Years of Indian and Popular Resistance, the Democratic Campesino Union, the Independent Center of Agricultural Workers and Campesinos, and the Union of *Ejido* Unions and Campesino Solidarity Groups of Chiapas (UU) (*La Jornada,* 12 April 1991). The leader of the UU, Margarito Montes Parra, called for a new offensive to restructure the statist corporatist ideology eliminating the bureaucracies of Banrural, the Secretariat of the Agrarian Reform (SRA), and the Secretariat of Agriculture and Hydraulic Resources (SARH), whose powers would be transferred to the *ejidatarios*, giving them control over the transfers of land (*La Jornada*, 15 October 1991). He called for "modernization without privatization," which increasingly became the rhetoric of the official party.

In Chiapas the growing dissent in the 1970s and 1980s was channeled in the UU and in the Organization of Campesinos Emiliano Zapata (OCEZ), which has been the focus of discontent in Venustiano Carranza since 1975 when a peasant leader was assassinated. They protested the failure to compensate campesinos who were forcibly removed from their lands to make way for the Angostura hydroelectric dam in the township. In 1992 they staged a hunger strike to gain the release of members of their organization who were jailed because of the protest over unsettled land claims.

The discourse that emanated from the campesino organizations established in the 1970s and 1980s became a testing ground for framing the law in its final form. The framers of the law were thus able to assess the support or rejection for crucial clauses. They discovered the potential for opposition and neutralized it by addressing specific concerns. Concomitant with these goals, the Salinas administration targeted areas of opposition that surfaced in the elections deploying solidarity funds to co-opt leaders. But what was left out of account in both corporatist and opposition groups—the colonizers of the Chiapas and Oaxaca rainforest—became the leaders in the new mobilizations following the January 1st uprising. However, Salinas repressed or ignored the rising demands for land titles of dissident groups in the colonizing territories. Because of the geographic isolation, campesinos of this region were considered negligible opponents and hence were not accorded funds to deliver votes to the PRI.

Thus President Salinas appeared to have won a degree of consensus unmatched by his predecessors by introducing modifications of the law in accord with criticisms voiced by the campesino organizations. The key points were the following: the elevation to a constitutional rank of the *ejido* and community; the recognition of greater freedom and autonomy of the campesinos in regulating the sale and purchase of plots; the initiation of a new level of organization for production in commercial associations; the creation of agrarian tribunals in the Agrarian Solicitors Office; the attack on political favoritism and control (Gustavo Gordillo, *La Jornada*, 21 November 1991); the declaration of the latifundia as illegal and the reduction in the time allowed for breaking up these holdings; and the establishment of limits to ownership of land of the societies and the curbs on foreign acquisition of land. But falling outside of the organizations that constituted the hegemonic core were regional organizations of militant opponents mobilized in the OCEZ, the Rural Association of Collective Interest of the General Union (ARIC), and the UU. By far the greatest discontent has been registered in the colonizing areas of the Lacandón jungle. The government's failure to give title to lands farmed for over twenty years by colonizers, along with the dislocation of thousands of colonizers in the Montes Azul reserve, has been the core issue in the uprising.

The apparent success in the first year of restructuring of the agrarian sector was due to an adroit management of opposed interests from 1991 to 1992, combined with repression of dissidence. The official government document addresses the issues raised by rural constituents during the proposal and passage of the bill, and this is distributed free of charge throughout the country. To maximize stability during the transition, the document reiterates the continuity with the past: no one is required to change their present situation, and the decisions are made by the commissions and the advisory groups that dealt with *ejido* affairs in individual cases. These bodies, along with the Agrarian Reform offices in capital cities, are to be kept intact at least during the transition period. In response to the protests of the Tarahumara, Tepehuanos, Yaqui, Mayos, and indigenous groups of Chiapas, the new Article 27 assures them that the cultural integrity of their communities will continue to be recognized as the law distinguishes rulings regarding their "language, cultures, practices, custom, resources, and specific forms of social organization" from those applying to "agrarian communities." Accordingly, the new law passed in February 1992 "simply cancels the paternalistic guardianship of the state over ejidos and communities giving them an opportunity to make their own decisions in greater liberty through their own assemblies" according to the Solidarity pamphlet. The document reasserts the responsibility of the state to community development of the agrarian sector, a point that was much disputed in the discussion over the vote in the congress. It even asserts that the law rectifies the male bias in the previous agrarian regulations by guaranteeing women equality with men in gaining title to land.

The overwhelming vote of 50 to 1 in favor of the legislation in the senate was a tribute not only to the continued monopoly of the PRI in the senate but also to the astute management of consensus in the governing sector. On 6 December 1991 CNC campesinos were bused to the capital to demonstrate their approval in classic PRI style, but what carried the day was a consolidation of support by campesinos disenchanted with the old bureaucracy and seeking stability within a market economy in which they were enmeshed.

Dissent in Chiapas at the local level was managed by military force, with arrests, torture, and violence committed against campesinos. Visible signs of the growing repression included the increase in military installations throughout the country, particularly the buildup of the military regiment in Rancho Nuevo (just outside of San Cristobal de Las Casas), and the deployment of troops within indigenous communities, notably Tenejapa, a town that registered a high vote against the PRI and where there was strong protest because of the debacle to government-promoted coffee cultivation. The violence came to a head in 1993 when the army in Chiapas was charged with the arbitrary arrest, torture, and abuse of thirteen Tzotzil indigenes in the communities of San Isidro el Ocotal and Mitziton following the disappearance of two army officers (Minnesota Lawyers Advocate 1993; Center for Human Rights Fray Bartolome de Las Casas 1993).

New Administrative Agencies

The second stratagem, echoing the very corporatist policies that President Salinas attacked in rhetoric, was to institute a series of new agencies that have usurped the role of preexisting entities. Conflict denied in rhetoric but admitted in institutional practice bypassed the old SRA office into the new Agrarian Solicitors Office. Fortifying the rhetoric of national unity, the administration created the overarching institution called the National Solidarity Program, PRONASOL, in 1990, with member agencies that allocate funds for programs solicited by local governments and coordinate the resources made available. The principal unifying theme is that of solidarity between rural and urban sectors and in Chiapas between indigenous and ladino populations.

The Agrarian Solicitors Office.   With its decentralized offices throughout the country, the Agrarian Solicitors Office has become the chief agency adjudicating conflicts that might arise in the transformation from public to private ownership. The first director of this new agency, Arturo Warman, has in the past defended the *ejido* in his anthropological polemics against those like Roger Bartra who had for more than twenty years proposed the modernization of the rural sector with the disentailment of *ejido* property. Yet in the disentailment of communal property from a collective base, the Agrarian Solicitors Office hopes to regenerate the collective organization of rural campesinos in economic development projects for the countryside. The first annual report of the office (1993) points to the number of requests stemming from the communal *ejido* commissions, 94 percent of their total caseload, as an index to the increased revitalization of the *ejido*. Certainly the changes in law regulating communal holdings heightened the awareness of the threat to community control leading to a dialogue that has reinforced the defenses of local commissions.

When we interviewed members of the Amatenango del Valle *ejido* commission, they asserted that no one would sell his share to outsiders, and their record of homicide and expulsions of "nontraditional" members (Nash 1994) is fair warning to anyone who fails to heed their claims. It is not the "corporate" communities that will experience an erosion of their lands so much as the colonizers in the Lacandón and Oaxaca forests who arrive indebted before their first harvests and are more vulnerable to forced sales made possible by the new law. Land tenure is particularly precarious in the jungle region, where colonizers searching for lands compete with commercial, oil, lumber, and cattle interests. Hundreds of campesinos in this region have been forcibly displaced from their lands by state and local police, in several recent cases with the use of violence, illegal arrests, and intimidation. Lacking political representation, they were left out of the process of accommodation to the new law, and it is more than likely that many of them have joined the armed opposition.

The processing of claims under the new agrarian law has undergone a thorough renovation, including the establishment of new headquarters. The office of the Secretariat of the Agrarian Reform occupied an old building on the outskirts of San Cristobal de Las Casas. When we visited the agency, twenty or more Indians from Zinacantan and Chamula lounged around the dry fountain in the weed-covered patio. Inside the crumbling stucco walls an expansive ladino presided at a desk laden with files and surrounded by another group of Indians from Oxchuc and Huistan. A young woman in stiletto-heeled shoes tripped over the rough tile floor as she brought lengthy legal documents with many signatures and some thumb prints to the director. When we explained that we were studying the impact of the new Agrarian Reform Law on indigenous villages, she gave us the official document, "The New Agrarian Legislation," and referred us to the office of the Agrarian Solicitors. Other sources confirmed that this was the key office mediating disputes that rose in the new law.

We found the Agrarian Solicitors Office in a newly renovated building near the center of the city. Rosebushes lined the brick walk to the bright interior of the two-story building. We were ushered into the office of a young lawyer, who was settled uneasily at the polished, uncluttered desk. The office had no file cases, and there were no Indians. In response to questions about the background of the new law and why it was needed, the young lawyer had no response, not even the usual bureaucratic evasions. He referred one of our questions to another clerk, who also lacked an answer. Finally he stated, "You see, we are all young here and we do not know anything about the past."

This was the beginning of our initiation into the changes transforming Mexican agrarian legislation. We eventually were led to an *ejido* colony high in the western hills of the township of Villa La Rosas and to old, established communities that were part of the colonial *reducción,* or concentrated settlements that won back communal lands alienated during the Porfiriato after the implementation of the Agrarian Reform Law in the 1930s. The new law regarding corporate landholdings leaves the decisionmaking regarding the sale or contracting of lands with private enterprises up to the *ejido* commissions within the community. It is already clear, one year after the passage of the New Agrarian Law, that established communities in which the communal tradition is well founded and where the inhabitants have greater resources will not be likely to yield land to outsiders. In contrast, the colonies of new settlers, often pushed out of their homes and indebted in their attempts to clear and sow their new lands, have already been forced to sell their *ejido* lots.

We accompanied the lawyer from the Agrarian Solicitor's office on his trip to settle a dispute in San Mateo, an *ejido* of three hundred inhabitants carved out of rocky mountain land in Villa La Rosas. After waiting in vain for our guide, we climbed three hours up a path through the secondary growth of scrub oak and pine trees, frequently losing our way in a myriad of trails.

Upon our arrival, over twenty men, who had been lounging around the basketball court, gathered in the schoolhouse to hear what the lawyer had to say. The schoolhouse, a clinic, and the basketball court were all constructed by the Integral Family Development agency (DIF), whose logo was prominently displayed on all the public buildings along with that of Solidarity. Family, rather than community personified in the *ejido* in the decades since the revolution, is the minimal unit of social cohesion cultivated by the state in the late twentieth century.

The lawyer waited for a half-hour or more for the appearance of the *ejido* member who was at the center of the conflict that had led to the request for intervention by the Agrarian Solicitors Office. This man wanted to farm his share of the land separately from the other *ejido* shareholders. When he failed to appear, the lawyer explained the structural changes in government agencies related to agriculture and the services that his agency offered. Using charts and a bureaucratic language that the men, most of whom could not read or write, could hardly comprehend, he described the objectives of the Agrarian Solicitors Office to "promote agrarian justice and guarantee the legal security of the land," explaining that the agency would defend the interests of the *ejido* owners, communities, and other groups. He also went through a list of the benefits of the New Agrarian Legislation, which emphasized self-determination of the communities and the regulation of land tenancy. The men listened intently, and later, two of the *ejido* members asked questions about how the new laws would affect their village. The only woman we saw in the schoolhouse or among those who peered through the windows arrived after the discussion was over, bearing plates of scrambled eggs and cold tortillas for our group.

In many ways, the visit by the lawyer demonstrated the cunning strategy with which the Salinas administration is implementing the new "reforms." Although the conflict that had led to the request for the intervention of the solicitor was tabled because the defendant did not appear, and the lawyer's presentation was limited to bureaucratic jargon, the people seemed to appreciate that a government agent had taken the time to visit such a remote area. The lawyer had been in the village earlier in the month and while we were there made an appointment to go back within two weeks. Like Solidarity, the Agrarian Solicitors Office creates a visible government presence in rural communities. This new agency stresses contact with the people in their own environment, rejecting the in-office settlements by local officials apart from community scrutiny that characterized the old bureaucracies. Their training programs for young rural workers who will then extend knowledge of the law to other campesinos will broaden the base for government intervention in the agricultural sector (Procuraduria Agraria 1993: 31). Their explicit concern for the sectors disprivileged under the old paternalistic system—women, youths, wage workers, and urban migrants—could change the character of the populist support if the projected goals of the Agrarian Solicitors Office are realized (Procuraduria Agraria 1993: 8, 13). These include growth and development of the small landholders addressing the decapitalization and growing impoverishment of this sector. But this transformation depends on democratic participation of the rural smallholders, as the Zapatista National Liberation Army contends.

Given the limits on available national lands, it is questionable whether the government can sustain its promises to the groups most affected by the reforms to the agrarian law. Anticipating the expulsion of more than two million campesinos from communal lands and the growing polarization of wealth, opposition to the new policies has persisted within the PRD, the Socialist Party of Mexico, and independent campesino organizations, including the National Movement of Resistance and Campesino Struggle; the Independent Center of Agricultural and Campesino Workers; the General Union of Workers, Campesinos and Popular Interests; and the UU. They have continued to reject the Salinas proposal on the basis that the capitalization of the countryside is indeed linked to privatization.

National Solidarity Program. To diffuse the continuing opposition to the proposed changes, President Salinas reinforced the redistributive policies of the state under the new program of Solidarity (PRONASOL). Solidarity programs have excelled past efforts in addressing local needs in short order while giving less power to local *cacicazgos.* Bypassing the institutions of the state, whose corruption was well-known, they deliver direct remedies on demand of local officials who supervise the production and control financing along with national agents. As Christopher Wood pointed out (*The Economist,* 13 February 1993: 14), the personality of the president was salient in the attention President Salinas gave to petitions from local officials, receiving each one personally and appearing in the village when the project was delivered, thus bestowing credit on himself rather than the PRI as a party. Salinas wrote his doctoral thesis on the correlation between public spending and political support for the system and concluded that there was none (Wood 1993: 12). Yet in his policies he updated the old co-optive political system in a streamlined bureaucracy that carried out projects formerly dispersed in the National Indian Institute (INI), organized in 1951 to hasten the incorporation of the indigenous population in the nation, and the

SARH, organized to promote the agricultural sector. Already weakened by charges of misappropriation of funds and loss of key programs to the DIF, INI was reduced to a shambles of agencies that lacked coordination and funding, while SARH competed with several parallel development agencies. Both had been reduced in budget and personnel throughout the 1970s and 1980s as new agencies relieved them of strategic projects.

The new agencies operate differently from their predecessors. The principal agency disbursing national and international funds from 1972 to 1982 was the Program for the Economic and Social Development of the Highlands of Chiapas (PRODESCH). Charged with improvements in education, health, agriculture, communication, electrification, and community organization, most of its funds actually went into constructing 2,000 kilometers of roads. Often these were built using the free labor of Indians while their leaders appropriated the funds for themselves (Deverre 1978). This encouraged the development of an indigenous bourgeoisie of truckowners owned individually or organized in transport cooperatives. Some of these leaders acquired monopolies of the sale of Coca Cola and Pepsi Cola, which were quickly incorporated into official ceremonies replacing the locally distilled "posh," or cane liquor. Caciques also appropriated the fruit trees, chickens, and fish stock that PRODESCH donated to the highland communities. The agency discredited government and party policies, as well as the officials charged with carrying them out.

In contrast with these old agencies, refuted for promoting favoritism and co-optation of local leaders, Solidarity exemplified the streamlined approach of the Salinas administration. Unlike earlier projects under INI, which were directed exclusively toward the indigenous population, Solidarity is set up to assist all campesinos, as well as those living in marginalized sectors of urban areas. The young director with whom we spoke in Tuxtla Gutierrez emphasized that their approach differs from earlier programs in overcoming the paternalism that characterized past relations with government agencies. Under Solidarity, a community is able to select the project that will serve its needs. Also different from earlier programs is the highly public manner in which Solidarity operates, giving the PRI the greatest visibility for spending money in communities. Solidarity funds projects such as the construction and rehabilitation of mills, roads, bridges, irrigation projects, potable water, population control projects, health centers, and school classrooms. Communities that desire funds from Solidarity must form an assembly that selects the project. Once the request is signed by the municipal president, it will be sent to the Planning Committee for Development (COPLADER) for approval. A very competent and knowledgeable agent of COPLADER whom we interviewed explained that Solidarity has been more successful in carrying out public works than in the past, since projects are completed quickly. In fact, according to its regulations, Solidarity will only fund projects that can be completed within a year.

Agents processed requests from communities directly, assessing the proposals in a short period of time and cutting through the bureaucratic red tape that caused delays and misappropriation of funds from the national, state, and local administrators. Further, the maximum cost per project was 100 million pesos (roughly U.S. $33,000). The Solidarity projects were visible public works that benefited many members of the community. Completed projects bore a sign announcing the project with the president's and governor's names, the number of people the project would benefit, and a Mexican flag. Hence, the school buildings, health clinics, municipal installations, and basketball courts served as monuments to the national concern for remote areas of the nation. Even though the programs were often funded by international agencies such as the World Bank, Solidarity had effectively drawn them into a redistributive network that garnered support for the PRI.

Solidarity promoted itself as making a break from the overly bureaucratic and corrupt institutions of the past. The literature on Solidarity described its programs as honest, efficient, and clear, emphasizing that they strengthen the government's responsibility to society and promote community participation in all stages of the project. To overcome the corruption characteristic of government spending by previous administrations, Solidarity contained three dependencies, which have tightened up control over the disbursement of funds: the Federal Secretariat of General Control, the Secretariat of Programming and Budget, and the State Board of Inspection. The irony is that while Solidarity supposedly represented a break from the corrupt bureaucracies of the past, the National Solidarity Program itself was yet another bureaucracy.

Solidarity has been effectively used by the PRI in numerous cases to diffuse conflict. First, communities that are supportive of the PRI at the onset are the most likely to reap the benefits of Solidarity. Although an employee of COPLADER informed us that Solidarity will assist all pueblos whether they are supporters of the PRI, PAN, or PRD, the fact that the municipal president has to approve the plan can cause problems since these officials are in most cases PRI incumbents. We were informed of a case of a barrio of San Cristobal de Las Casas making a request for potable water from Solidarity that was never filled because the municipal president did not complete the proper papers. The municipal president was from the PRI and the barrio was PAN-dominated; this failure in communication demonstrates the control that the PRI held over who would benefit from Solidarity funds.

Redistribution of public funds in areas undergoing rapid development or posing conflict continues to be a key element in the hegemonic control exercised by the government through the PRI and the constituent agencies. In October 1991, Solidarity gave 400 million pesos to Venustiano Carranza to pay for crops that were lost because of drought. It is more than coincidence that this township has been an area of unrest over landholdings for centuries. Lands that were promised to Indians in 1767 were still in dispute in 1991, and the smallholders pushed out of the lands flooded by the hydro-electric dam in Socoltenango have not been compensated (Guzman 1977; Nash and Sullivan 1992).

These dispersals were sometimes highlighted by the appearance of the governor or president as the PRI mended its fences in preparation for the 1994 elections. Punctuating the conflictual as well as high growth potential of the southern frontier, President Salinas made two trips to Chiapas in the spring of 1993, the first to Oxchuc and Ocosingo and the second to Tuxtla Gutierrez in April. In Oxchuc, a Tzeltal-speaking township in the highlands, every detail of the visit was well orchestrated, from the arrival of the helicopter 15 minutes before the ceremony to the flag raising drill. Thousands of Indians from nearby villages had been bused in at government expense to watch the ceremony, announced as the *abandaramiento* (salute to the flag). In his speech, the president announced that Solidarity was giving 1 billion pesos for the economic and social development of the area, emphasizing specific projects such as providing potable water to overcome pressing health problems. During the speech, a group of Indians calling themselves Abuxu (the Ants) who had marched on foot were detained outside Oxchuc. The marchers protested that none of the Solidarity funds were going to the northern part of Chiapas, claiming that over 50 percent of the Indians living in the northern part of the state had "never seen the famous resources of the National Program of Solidarity so celebrated by the authorities" (Lievano 1993). Because they were not allowed to enter, Salinas's visit went smoothly, with no visible dissent.[1]

Later in the day, Salinas lunched at the Lion's Club in Ocosingo, the ladino-dominated center of a township that includes Tzeltal villages, where he announced that funds were to be given to develop tourism on this main route to Palenque. His visit later that week to the Lacandón jungle, where colonists had been protesting both the lack of government services and the corruption of forestry agents (Nash and Sullivan 1992) for years prior to the uprising on New Year's Eve, was a further demonstration of his attention to potential areas of dissension. Shortly after the visit, the state governor announced the allocation of 3,800 new pesos (approximately U.S. $1,200) for the paving of the highway to Palenque and 800,000 new pesos (about $266,000) for potable water in Pakal Na, a jungle colony (*El Tiempo*, 4 May 1993). Given that this is where the uprising occurred, Salinas's visit was indicative of the PRI's awareness of conflict and a desire to co-opt leaders, but clearly it was a question of too little, too late to stem the tide of rebellion.

While some projects (such as potable water) are essential to the people living in the villages, others (such as the construction of elegant municipal buildings) demonstrate that the bureaucrats are often divorced from the needs of the people. The window-dressing projects failed to address the rising demands for land titles and cash crop assistance among dissident groups in the colonized territories of the Lacandón jungle. The infrastructural improvements in road building and establishing power lines served the agroindustrial development sector, while most local communities in the colonizing area were left without electricity or subsidies to assist them in marketing their cash crops.

DISSENT, HUMAN RIGHTS VIOLATION, AND HEGEMONY

As Mittelman points out (Chapter 1), there is increasing international pressure for democracy. The Zapatista National Liberation Army put this at the head of its agenda to the team negotiating the peace agreement in March 1994, and it has been consistent in asserting that it wants participation in certain decisions but has no desire to take over power. Since the outbreak of the rebellion, the Mexican government has been crafty in its approach to the negotiation table, hoping to diffuse the impact of the uprising, which was broadcast throughout the world. This increased visibility of Mexican politics is itself due in large part to the passage of NAFTA and the globalization process in which the political protest is enmeshed.

In the highlands of Chiapas, as well as in other parts of Mexico, the national government often lets the local caciques perform the dirty work of controlling or eliminating dissenters. These are the very people co-opted within the hegemonic core. Perhaps the most evident example of this is the expulsion of over twenty thousands Indians from their villages during the past decade (Nash and Sullivan 1992; Sullivan 1992; Tickell 1991). The Periferico, a group of neighborhoods on the outskirts of San Cristobal de Las Casas, is inhabited by thousands of Indians who have been expelled from neighboring villages, including Chamula, Mitontic, Zinacantan, and Oxchuc. The Periferico is dotted with churches, including those of Presbyterian Evangelicals, Pentecostals, Seventh Day Adventists, and Jehovah's Witnesses. On Sundays the area is filled with the sounds of sermons and singing from the church loudspeakers. Shortly after the uprising, government troops bombed one of the neighborhoods in the area called "El Cerrito."

Local caciques justified the expulsions on the basis of preserving the integrity of traditions by eliminating Protestants. However, as the Fray Bartolome de Las Casas Center for Human Rights points out, the expulsions have as much to do with money and politics as with religion. For example, in Chamula in 1973, a candidate of the PAN won the local election. In November of the next year, a PRI candidate, Augustin López Hernandez, was involved in expelling over two thousand people from the village under the pretext that a group of evangelicals, who were also PAN supporters, wanted to burn down the Chamulan church. In the following years, similar incidents followed in other villages. While the pretext for the expulsions is almost always religion, those forced to leave commonly belong to the PAN or PRD. In March 1993, 150 members of the PRI detained a group of evangelicals belonging to the PRD in the town of Teopisca. The San Cristobal newspaper *El Tiempo,* noted for its work in exposing abuses of human rights, pointed out that villages could tolerate evangelicals but not PRD members.

Expelling people for religious reasons is unconstitutional; those who are expelled lose their land and thus their only means of livelihood. In San Cristobal de Las Casas and other areas, the expelled survive however they can, selling artisan products in the streets and market and working in construction or transportation. In spite of the illegality of the expulsions, the Mexican government has yet to take significant action against the caciques who are responsible or to facilitate the return of the expelled. Lopez Moreno, the interim governor of Chiapas following the uprising until the inauguration, heard the complaints of a group of 584 Chamulans expelled in October 1993 for the first time, but he did not provide the security forces many felt were necessary when the expelled returned to their homes in August. Three were later killed by villagers. The failure to take action in the courts against the offenders is not surprising given that many of the expelled belong to the two dominant opposition parties, the PAN or the PRD. The fact that the expulsions are cloaked in an appeal to tradition makes them appear less opportunistic. Some anthropologists accept these claims, asserting that the expelled are a threat to Indian communities because the Protestants do not contribute to or participate in the festivals so important to community solidarity. Yet it is clear that conflicts over the allocation of *ejido* plots and rights to communal resources expressed in opposition to political leaders result in internal forms of oppression comparable to those experienced under colonial domination. This opposition, rising from the growing class differentiation within communities, lies behind the expulsions.

Women's access to land has always been mediated through communal and familial patriarchal structures that have marginalized those who do not have husbands or grown sons. Their exploitation within their own communities is rarely given expression, bound as they are to loyalty in these most intimate networks (Toleda Tello 1985). Women constitute the majority of the expelled, reflecting their predominance among the ranks of Protestants.

The conflict between the expelled indigenes and the communities of origin remains at explosive levels. The caciques of San Juan Chamula forced all household heads to join a demonstration in San Cristobal against the CRIACH mobilization calling for recognition of the human rights of the expelled in 1992. There was stone-throwing by the ten thousand Chamulans, and the exiled populations experienced many wounded. With the current buildup in arms in the area, the settlers have now procured weapons. Rumors to this effect were confirmed in July 1994 when expelled Protestants living in the offices of Asuntos Indigenes fired at Chamula traditionals who approached the premises with an Uzi automatic rifle, killing two.

Local caciques will likely play a role in the privatization of the *ejido* lands. Just as in the case of the expulsions, this will place the burden of the negative effects of privatization on caciques rather than the national government. While the Reform of the Agrarian Reform is cloaked in the language of giving more autonomy and self-determination to the Indians by allowing them to make the decision to sell *ejido* land, it may actually give more power to the caciques in some areas since it eschews a central authority. At a conference on human rights in the state of Oaxaca in 1992, indigenous organizers expressed concern that caciques could pressure the poorest members of communities to sell their land to local leaders since they would not have recourse to a higher authority.

Further, many have tied the privatization of the *ejido* with the passage of NAFTA, noting that the combination will allow the development of both domestic and foreign enterprises, such as petroleum exploration, on what had been communal land (De Villar 1991). If the powerful caciques are bought off, they will be able to pressure members to sell *ejido* land to outsiders. Again, the Mexican government will leave with its hands seemingly clean.

The attack by the Zapatista National Liberation Army exposed the limited hegemonic maneuver to Mexicans and to an international public that raised questions about the human rights record of the government and the legitimacy of its rule. Those who were left out of Salinas's reforms—poor farmers and especially indigenous colonizers of the jungle region—were most active in the uprising. Much attention has been focused on the central role taken by women in the movement. Two women were present among the group of Zapatistas for negotiations with the Mexican government in February 1994 in San Cristobal. Women also played an important although less visible role in the armed movement. According to a female infantry major in the EZLN, approximately 30 percent of the Zapatista combatants are women who have renounced forming a family to take part in the armed struggles. When the Zapatistas broke into the jail near San Cristobal to set free the prisoners, it was women who entered to open the doors (*La Jornada*, 7 March 1994.)

Among the thirty-four points of the Zapatistas' "Commitments for Peace" are several specifically dedicated to the concerns of women. These include the demand for childbirth and gynecological care; public programs ensuring sufficient food for their children; child care centers; the development of projects for farming, baking, and crafting; technical training schools for women; and improved transportation for bringing products to markets. The nature of the demands reveal how women have been affected by the economic crisis of the 1980s and the neoliberal reforms that followed. Although some Solidarity programs are specifically directed to assist women and children, their real concerns were never addressed—most of the money has been allocated to the construction of town halls or the purchase of trucks, which do not help women in their daily responsibility for feeding their families. With rising population in rural areas, lack of fertile land, limited credit, and high interest rates, indigenous women have turned to artisan production to assist in meeting their family's basic needs (Nash 1993; Eber and Rosenbaum 1993). The Zapatistas have demanded artisan workshops for women, with machinery and primary materials; markets for the sale of artisan products at fair prices; and transport for taking the products to markets. Although land is a central issue in the Zapatista demands in the "Commitments for Peace," the women do not demand the right to possess land. One woman notes that the problem of land involves everyone; therefore they do not demand the right for widows or single women to inherit land (*La Jornada,* 7 March 1994). The participation of women in the uprising is symptomatic of the crisis they face in ensuring survival.

The Zapatista uprising exposed the limitations of Salinas's hegemonic strategies to Mexicans and an international public. The repressive control over campesino organizations and the failure to address the need for land and social programs finally exceeded the power of co-opted indigenous leaders to contain.

Negotiations between the government representative and the subcommandant were broken off in March 1994. There have been important concessions, however, such as the rejection of former Chiapas governor Gonzalez Garrido, who had left office to serve as minister of government in Mexico City, and his replacement, Elmar Setzer, who had served as interim governor. There have also been restrictions on election expenditures to ensure fair elections. The August elections did not resolve the issue of whether the ruling party is capable of extending its hegemonic control to include the people marginalized by the liberal economic policies. The Zapatistas rejected the legitimacy of the elections, and Amado Avendaño, the candidate of Civil Society, supported by the PRD, has vowed to run a parallel government outside the governing palace. Whether the ruling party is capable of maintaining hegemonic control given the still active insurrection by the people marginalized in the liberal economic policies is the issue clouding the presidency of Ernesto Zedillo. Mexican indigenous people, especially at the southern frontier, have initiated a wide-ranging reform policy that is transforming the political culture of the country.

CONCLUSION

The Mexican state is the product of revolution, and much of its authority rests on its fulfillment of social and economic obligations. Thus careful management has been required to implement neoliberal reforms promoting Mexico's entry into global markets while cutting social programs and increasing privatization of land and industry. President Salinas bypassed the corrupt bureaucracy of PRI while maintaining the principles of co-optation inherent in public spending. His particular skill was the adroit management of limited funding of locally desired projects, often packaging internationally funded projects with national programs and tying them to local initiatives that strengthened his presidency. But the limitations of his government in restricting the co-optation to favored segments of both indigenous and the ladino populations left out many people who were neither part of the corporate communities nor had found representation in the new urban barrios to which they were forced to migrate. Women, who represent one-third of the Zapatista National Liberation Army, are important in the mobilization of the populations left out of these centers of power (the urban poor and the colonizers in the Lacandón and Oaxaca jungle territory). Whether they participate directly in the uprising or not, these opponents now have a voice in the Zapatista national mobilization of civil society.

While some indigenous sectors of the country are seeking entry into mainstream political channels, others are appealing directly to international groups to regain a collective base that will allow their distinctive cultures and productive systems to survive. Those who have internalized the struggle for land within the parameters of populist co-optive forms have gained entry to the new technocratic state at the expense of their own solidarity as a group. As the "politics of class" supersedes the "politics of rank" (Collier 1994) in indigenous communities, differences in wealth are flaunted rather than concealed or redistributed in ceremonial expenditures. The new politics of the state endorses the competitive distinctions that were masked in traditional communities in past decades. At the local level the new brokers of state-funded projects and credit facilities have already emerged as the Agrarian Solicitor and Solidarity agents extend their activities into what were called "refuge regions." In contrast with the tactics of the past decade, buying the loyalty of local officials with state-funded projects will no longer be feasible with the new austerity imposed by limited state and federal funding. Instead, the new hegemonic alliances will draw upon entrepreneurial activities combining community and private initiatives to further private and individual gains. Even with this major reorientation in state and local relations, community service and the support of traditions will probably still validate leadership—and the redistribution of public resources—at the local level. The linkages now being forged with the private sector have already generated the new rhetoric of democracy, progress, and modernization at the national level.

Mexico's attempt to move from outright suppression of protest to a reconstruction of hegemonic control is now in jeopardy. The political future of the PRI itself is questioned, as President Zedilla attempts to rally supporters in a country demoralized by assassinations and charges of electoral fraud. Whatever internal restructuring occurs, it is clear that the government can no longer ignore the cry for democracy among people who have been ignored too long. The Zapatistas demand to be heard and are asking for not just government assistance but structural change: "We are not asking for charity or handouts, we are asking for the right to live with human dignity, with equality and justice as did our parents and grandparents" (Commitments for Peace, 1 March 1994; *La Jornada,* 3 March 1994).

The Chiapas rebellion may yet break the hegemonic control of the PRI. As the shots fired resound in a growing reaction against control exercised by international banks and transnational corporations, the uprising may succeed in igniting the drive for democracy in the new world order. The very process of globalization against which those in Chiapas are protesting provides greater visibility for their protest.

NOTE

1. Wood (1993) cites cases where Solidarity funds "tend to be spent where the PRI feels most threatened electorally," in Michoacan, where $135 million was spent in recognition of the strong presence of the PRD.

Mustapha Kamal Pasha
Ahmed I. Samatar

9

The Resurgence of Islam

The global economy perspective sees the Third World as a residual, marginal factor, a non-entity. —Robert Cox (1993: 286)

When men [and women] fail to see reason in human institutions, and much more if they set it opposed, they take refuge in the inscrutable counsels hidden in the abyss of divine providence.
—Giambattista Vico (1744: 347)

After the failure of all other ideologies of the region, a Muslim people want to be ruled by Islam. —Ibrahim Massoud (1992)

The insertion of a new Islamic consciousness into the daily political life of many Muslim societies is increasingly becoming an incontestable fact. In countries like Iran, Sudan, and Afghanistan, state power has been captured by Islamic movements. For others, such as Algeria, Egypt, Tunisia, and Turkey, there is deadly intensity with high stakes as numerous civil associations define themselves as Islamic and, as a result, violently challenge the legitimacy of political authority. Even in less contested countries (e.g., Morocco, Pakistan, Indonesia), Islamic consciousness assumes a more prominent place in the articulation and making of political life. Islam's cultural expression and the presence of Muslim immigrants in several Western countries highlight the influence of Islam beyond its established physical boundaries. It is no wonder that the appearance of an Islamic wakefulness and movements bearing the idiom of piety present a disconcerting challenge to the broad and universalist mission of modernity and globalization. Islamic resurgence suggests deep fissures in the globalization process.[1]

How can Islam, with its stamp of assumed particularity, be reconciled with an emerging world culture? What are the internal connections between the two processes? Is the Islamic awakening a countervailing tendency in the transition toward a global society? Or does Islam offer an alternative path to modernity, unhooked from its presumed center in the West? This chapter explores these questions by focusing on the relationship between globalization and the rise of new social movements bearing the parlance of Islam.

Eschewing a strictly descriptive historical account, we seek a new angle here. First, we situate "globality," as a feature of modernity, in a more interactive framework—as the product of a long historical exchange between different cultures, including elements that draw their inspiration from the Islamic civilization.[2] Second, we treat Islamic piety as an integral part of an alternative vision of modernity. Given the problematic and the cluster of questions, we suggest as a basic and working thesis that the rise of Islam in its myriad forms is a response to a double alienation. The first is a feeling of being subjected to the logic of the modern world system but not being of modernity. In other words, many Muslims see themselves as objects rather than active subjects in the constitution and appropriation of modernism. The second alienation is located in the domestic context where both civil associations and the state are in some form of decomposition. Confronted by inexorable material deprivations, repressive and inept politics, and demeaning cultural dislocation, many in the Muslim world feel compelled to take a stand—including participation in drastic rethinking and dramatic acts. In our estimation, the phenomenon of globalization closely ties these two sources of acute estrangement while bestowing on the situation a sense of uncommon transparency and immediacy. Globalization underscores change, perhaps of a revolutionary kind, in the texture and modalities of international reality.

To explore these points more earnestly, our discussion is divided into three sections. The first explores globalization and its most current interface with Islam and its resurgence.[3] The purpose here is to escape from some of the limitations of existing notions of globalization by bringing in a cultural dimension embedded in the idea of civilizational dialogue, notable between Islam and the West. This permits us to historicize globalization but also to treat it as a process of more universalistic proportions. The second section takes on the relation between globalization and some of the principal new social movements in many parts of the Islamic world. An underlying theme in this section is an appreciation of Islamic piety as more than simply a reaction to (Western) modernity. The third section builds upon this theme and introduces the lineaments of an alternative (Islamic) notion of international life.

The motivation for undertaking this assignment is based on two intellectual concerns. First, the vast majority of conventional writers in international political economy, as well as the practitioners of the craft, have very little, if any, understanding of Islam—and particularly this moment. Those who give any attention usually relegate anything that smacks of Islamic thinking or activism as fundamentalist. Second, while some critical thinkers make references here and there that do not dismiss all distempers as unthinking religiosity, they too rarely make any mention of, let alone offer a dissertation on, Islam's real or potential contribution to much needed intersubjectivity and suprasubjectivity—both necessary for counterhegemonic efforts as well as the construction of a different world order. (Here, Cox's exemplary article on Ibn Khaldun's ideas is the exception.)[4]

GLOBALIZATION AND ISLAM

Notions of globality find currency in extant accounts on world culture and global civil society (Robertson 1992). A common theme in these accounts is the emergence of a global consciousness, superimposed on a compression of time–space processes of global political economy. Elements that are often seen as part of a new architecture of global politics include newer forms of transnational economic organization and interaction, global networking made feasible by a technological and communications revolution, and the rise of global nonstate institutions with a whole set of political and cultural agendas.

Many scholars tend to see globalization either as a variant on Westernization or as a moment of late/postcapitalism. Recent pronouncements of the end of history (Fukuyama 1992), the movement toward convergence (Pye 1990), and the triumph of liberal values, though with imminent opposition from civilizations organized on different principles (Huntington 1993), stress the Westernizing character of globalization. Others speak of the heralding of a global civil society, made possible by new technological advances in cybernetics and information networks (Frederic 1992) and the expansion of a realm of global public space (Falk 1992b).[5] Those of a critical persuasion tie globalization to world capitalism, as a materialist product of its dictates and compulsions (Cox 1993) (notably, the dialectic of capital and labor on a global scale [Mittelman, Chapter 1]) or as its cultural logic (Jameson 1991).

Cox sees two main aspects of globalization: (1) global organization of production and (2) global finance (Cox 1993). The first entails the rise of complex transnational networks of production, which secure profitability through the most advantageous labor procurement, combining dimensions of political security and predictability. Global finance, according to Cox, is "a very largely unregulated system of transactions in money, credit, and equities" (Cox 1993: 260). He notices two major consequences of globalization: the "internationalization of the state" and the "restructuring of national societies and the emergence of a global social structure." Internationalization of the state means that states become "transmission belts" from the global to the national economies; they are "instruments for adjusting national economic activities to the exigencies of the global economy."[6] The latter connotes the arrival of a post-Fordist, decentralized system of flexible production.

In addition to the spatial reorganization of production and global finance, Mittelman includes the homogenizing of consumer goods across boundaries, massive inter- and intracountry transfers of population, and a quest for democracy among the multiple manifestations of globalization (Mittelman, Chapter 1). Central, however, to his analysis of globalization is the notion of a new "global division of labor," the dispersion of economic and political power, growing polarization between and among nations, and marginalization of vast sectors of the human population.

Falk's distinction between two types of globalization allows us a useful framework to identify the aggressive and reactive dimensions of globalization, both interacting with one another as they condition the life situations of individuals and collectivities. The first type, globalization-from-above, reflects "the collaboration between leading states and the main agents of capital formation" (Falk 1992b). The key feature of this type of globalization is a relentless drive for accumulation undergirded by a consumerist ethos; its chief actors are transnational capital and (transnational) political elites. Combined, they create a powerful momentum that leaves behind a high degree of seemingly functional integration and, at face value, homogenizing habits that make all other cultures submit to the pervasiveness of the West's perception of the world and its conception of lived reality. By contrast, globalization-from-below indicts the dysfunctional and degenerative consequences of the phenomenon by pointing to a corrosion of autonomy, individual and group efficacy, a weakening of the local bases of material sustenance, and the diminution of ecological values and breakdown of cultural foundations.[7] All of this, in Falk's thinking, is associated with the deterritorialization of politics, economies, and culture and the preponderance of time over space. In response, globalization-from-below foregrounds and stresses the rise of a global civic alertness concerning ecology, liberty, and human rights—perspectives, according to Falk, that originated in Western societies but whose institutionalization and practices are now acquiring a transnational appeal.

At the center of globalization, the argument goes, is a new global political economy. The principles that undergird this spatial arrangement appear more uniform: market rationality and the drive for profit, reliance on secondary associations as vehicles for self-expression and self-realization rather than primary ties (of either kinship or community), and a convergence of lifestyles. Finally, the lateness of capitalism and its cultural logic can also be seen as a moment of globalization: the conquest of cultures by capitalism, a process most palpable in its reconstitution of identities (Jameson 1991). Flexible accumulation, a postindustrial and disorganized capitalism, correlates with newer cultural forms, including the incidence of yuppie culture, postmodernism, and the spectacle society (David Harvey 1989; Swyngedouw 1986). Although globalization processes of capital/labor reorganization may lurk in the background, the experience of decentralization (of individuals and groups) defines this condition.

While elements of Westernization and capitalism are both important to globality, the notion critical to our present analysis is an appreciation of globality as the product of an intercivilizational encounter and dialogue. Within this larger compass, we see Islamic piety not simply as antimodernist, though it may yield antimodernist signs, but as an alternative construction of modernity, cognizant of nonmaterialist dimensions of progress and their place in an ethical (Islamic) social formation. No doubt, an emphasis on the recent reorganization of time–space via changes in transnational production and exchange is quite integral to any notion of globalization. However, from an Islamic (cultural) perspective, the phenomenon is to be seen comprehensively in historical terms. This presupposes a longer view of civilizational exchange.

For the many who are heralding the twilight of sovereignty while celebrating the makings of a shared universal culture, globality underscores, in essence, the realization of enlightenment's great promises: the triumph of reason over natural determination, the ascendancy of Western liberalism over totalitarianism, the worldwide democratic revolution, and the passing of tradition and history's progressive march toward modernity. All that remains, the message reads, are the atavistic residues of a decaying order, the last gasps of an old world, the limp protestations of particularistic cultures unwilling and unable to contest the flowering of universalism. The onward march toward this civilization is irresistible, a historical necessity now having acquired the character of an objective law.

Yet, on the eve of a new millennium, non-Western frames of consciousness and habits of being seem ever so persistent, even more durable, impervious to the totalizing imprint of Western cultural hegemony. Triumphalism, registered as either the end of history (Fukuyama) or the rise of a universal civilization (Naipaul), faces the distress of a world ridden with growing contradictions, sometimes dismissed as a clash of civilizations between universal Western values and Third World particularism (Huntington) but often as the dead weight of tradition to be soon swept away by the forward march of globalization. From this top-down perspective, Islam appears as one of the last great challenges to the sweeping momentum of liberalism, as either a cultural logic standing outside the general flow of historical evolution or a civilization dragging its feet. Echoing former modernization themes, top-down globalization, with the West serving as the reference point, views Islam within the familiar matrix of tradition–modernity, with Islam's assumed resistances to rationality and progress. In this mode, Islamic social movements represent a retreat or return to primordialism, with obscurantism and societal regression as the necessary correlates of this logic. From this angle, the reversion to the idiom of piety is a reactive sentiment with hardly any prospect for an alternative vision of modernity and the establishing of a different world order.

Yet globality yields antinomies, actualizing the self-consciousness of non- or counterhegemonic social movements. Often, the boundaries of these movements become more recognizable as globalization processes seek to deprive or deny these movements their raison d'être. In appearance, the Islamic resurgence is a reverse movement against the hegemonizing pro-clivities of West-centered globality, resisting a universalism defined in the historical specificity of Eurocentrism (Amin 1989). But this is only part of the story. Islamic piety has been and is a purveyor of an alternative image of modernity, a point obscured both in orientalist renderings of Islam (Said 1978) and in fundamentalist discourse. A key supposition in realizing this other vision is the dynamic notion of seeing Islam as an integral cocon-struction of globality. By introducing this view of Islam into an analysis of the epoch and an emerging global culture, the constrictions of Eurocentrism can be recognized and transcended. Silenced in the current discourse on globalization are the lineages of a process of coconstruction. Monotonic sounds of top-down globality entertain the charitable view that non-Western forms of social consciousness are best seen as localism or a recycling of autochthonous sensibilities.

To move beyond the globalism–localism dualism, the initial step is to problematize globality in more historical terms. Recognizing the making of globality in intercivilizational dialogue furnishes the possibility of seeing Islamic consciousness as something quite apart from a sign of local or parochial sentiments. Extant descriptions of globalization often situate its determinants in the life and times of capitalism and rise to the status of a global Leviathan. On this view, there is a penchant for what Hodgson calls (in another context) "presentist" readings of modernity (Hodgson 1993). Supplanting the idea of globalization as the progeny of a budding world market economy (Wallerstein 1974), an emphasis on intercivilizational dia-logue and struggles, spread over several centuries, lends an alternative lens to our understanding of the process. As such, globality does not emanate from the North and work its way toward the South but, given its early roots in cultural, commercial, and political exchange, especially between Christendom and Islam, acquires a more horizontal dimension. The interac-tive nature of globalization vitiates the view that sees it vertically.

Phases of Globalization

For Muslims, the first phase of globalization has its roots in the early encounter between Christendom and Islam, when opposing principles for organizing social life and cosmologies to situate that life within a larger (spiritual) totality become recognizable. In this exchange, mutual misgiving rivaled mutual appreciation; the lines that divided the two communities of conscience and faith also provided the basis for an intercivilizational dialogue. Commerce and trade intermixed with scientific and cultural borrowing. For more than five centuries Islam played the tutor to both eastern and western Christendom (Hodgson). The highest achievements of Islam, seen by many as "the most brilliant civilization in the Old World," (Braudel 1994: 73) were witnessed in the incredible age between the eighth and twelfth centuries. It was a time of scientific, philosophical, literary, and economic flourishing. Distinctive is the often overlooked but successful conjoining of Islamic faith and piety with a relentless pursuit of *Falsafa*—a brand of Islamic humanism that was dedicated to the retrieval of classical philosophy. In this period of high and hybrid culture, some of the greatest thinkers of the Islamic world appeared—men like Al-Kindi, Al-Farabi, Ibn-Sina, and Ibn-Rushd. Their works became critical for the revival and development of European intellectual renaissance. The high point of this intercivilizational exchange was in Muslim Spain, which furnished Europe with the cultural resources to escape the seemingly unending horror of the Dark Ages (David Harvey 1990). Ironically, this debt was paid by the Inquisition in the Reconquista through forced expulsion of (both Jews and) Muslims from Spain toward the end of the fifteenth century.[8]

The great intercivilizational dialogue is regularly punctuated by holy and not-so-holy wars, a confrontation of cultures, a shifting of territorial frontiers dividing the two civilizations, and the crystallization of a sense of difference and uniqueness. Claims over the spiritual body lend the territorial conflicts an intensity readily serviceable in demonizing the Other. Yet it took a later historical encounter to reduce Islamic civilization to cultural subordination and its characterization as an unchanging repository of incivility, barbarism, decadence, and traditionalism (Said 1978). During this phase, the distinctive feature of this dialogue remains, if grudgingly, the principle of peaceful coexistence. Violations of that principle must be perceived in conjunction with the West's acceptance of Muslim contributions to Western philosophy, mathematics, geography, and the human and physical sciences (Watt). Only the political decay and decline of Islamic civilization ushers in a stinginess in mutual recognition and respect.

Colonialism, in its Western and Eastern variants, provides the setting for the second major historical encounter. During this period, Islamic societies came under severe strain and experienced a deep sense of internal weakness, frustration, and alienation. Self-doubt superseded an unshakable faith in the intrinsic superiority of Islam. Western technology and ideology undermined Muslim self-confidence. Subjection of vast areas of Muslim empires, either through direct European control or through politico-economic arrangements humiliated and parceled the *ummah* (i.e., community of the faithful). Newer forms of identification, mainly through ideas of nationalism and liberalism, led to the breakup of the Islamic community. Muslim elites, educated and socialized in European intellectual discourse, sought non-Islamic avenues of cultural and political self-expression, while the masses either turned inward to sustain their cultural universe and/or in concert with Islamicists joined with resistance movements against spiritual contamination. This twofold political and cultural rupture in the Muslim heartland and its growth is the backdrop for many of the new Islamic social movements in the nineteenth and twentieth centuries.

Anticolonial resistance in the Islamic world appears in a variety of forms. Puritanical religious reformism during the eighteenth and nineteenth centuries sought *ijtihad* (individual judgment) and a renewal of Islam from within (Fischer 1982). Often, its protagonists find no principle in Western civilization worthy of imitating or borrowing. The movements of the early twentieth century are fresh attempts to construct a bridge to modernity. Modernist reformism underlines learning at the root of Islamic renewal (Fischer). One may only rehearse the names of Jamal-ud-din Afghani, Muhammad Abduh, Sayyid Ahmed Khan, and Allama Iqbal to signify the richness of this line of thinking. Aware of the strengths and weaknesses of both Western and Islamic civilizations, these and myriad other Muslim modernist reformers invented a new language and structure of thought to meet the Western challenge. Clearly, they found opposition in the ranks of the *ummah* itself, obscurantists who would see modernity as an inherently stray path for the faithful.

Paradoxically, the third phase of globalization, from an Islamic standpoint, is the period when the Western project of modernity appears to have exhausted its possibilities internally, yet having increased its appeal worldwide. The antinomies of this phenomenon lie at the root of Islam's current dialectic with globalization. On the one hand, the bankrupt Westernized Muslim elites—with their sheer ineptness in presiding over societal development and their aping of Western consumerism, combined with a growing global divide between the haves and the have-nots—tend to delegitimize Western modernity. Yet Western capabilities to penetrate Muslim societies through technology, information, and entertainment have never been greater. Their hospitable reception by privileged groups in those societies gives top-down globality the appearance of incontestability. While sharing deep fears of these capacities, members of the new social movements in the Islamic world are not as reluctant to absorb the trappings of instrumental rationality. But the anxieties that cultural penetration pose for Muslim society and the growing privation of many of its people remain the basis of rejecting the West and its project of modernity. Usually, this rejection becomes the emblem of several of the new Islamic social movements. Their core, in most cases, is a renunciation of the antiseptically secularizing tendencies of modern social, political, and cultural life that are lacking in ethical or moral content.

GLOBALIZATION AND PIETY

There is much in resurgent Islam of a reactive nature—the myth of return to a City of God and a restorative sentiment; a repudiation of certain forms of progress, particularly those that stress materialism; a propensity for intellectual closure and the acceptance of literal interpretations of divine law—in a word, a generalized opposition to modernity. Yet this reactive shell conceals the complexity of an alternative vision and the role of Islamic piety in its dialectic with modernity. First, the singular emphasis, as well as partial interpretation, of the revivalist tendency in Islam obscures the workings of an internal principle that is not simply fixated on opposition but entails renewal (*tajdid*) and affirmation. Second, the dynamics of an intercivilizational dialogue, so central for situating the role of Islamic piety in global politics, is overlooked.

Extant accounts of the "return of Islam" (Lewis 1988) essentialize Islam's hostility to (Western) modernity while reducing Islam's alternative vision to a mere reaction. In this context, Islam is placed on the periphery of a modernist discourse, serving no real purpose in the transition to a universalizing global culture. In this dualist cultural universe, Islam, then, necessarily seems an adversary to a modernist telos. In large part, these tendencies are reinforced by the self-descriptions of those who see themselves culturally and socially marginalized in the thrust toward a globalizing culture. A reactive image replaces a more dynamic view of the historical underpinnings of Islamic piety. Globalization appears from the bottom up, more an alignment of global privilege than the establishment of a global civil society. The Islamic resurgence becomes a cry against a cultural and economic divide, pitting the few against the many, the North against the South, and, within each domain, zones of plenty and poverty, wealth and squalor. Marginalized by a West-driven movement toward cultural homogenization, the topography of the global village contains massive cracks: irreconcilable objectifications and subjectivities. Often, the latter take the form of a resistance to the excesses of a consumerist ethic. From this perspective, the Islamic resurgence does appear as an antithesis to modernity. The self-descriptions of the protagonists of the Islamic social movements give Islam the appearance of a bulwark against the liberalizing force of globalization. Notwithstanding these self-descriptions, however, the third phase of globalization crystallizes the deepening of unbridgeable, dichotomous cultural spheres.

But Islamic piety operates at a number of levels. In the first place, as in other faiths, piety in Islam lies at the heart of religion. As a pure feeling of dependence upon God (Merklinger 1993), piety in Islam articulates a definitive model for structuring a relationship with Allah. The concept of *tauhid* (unity), of God's singular preeminence, while subordinating will to Allah, liberates humans from its materialist cage. Submission to Allah, as sanctified in the Quran, the hadith, and the sunna, lends order to human affairs by giving men and women the certainty of God's presence in the world and of the limitations of worldly existence. In the context of a disorienting materialist world, faith becomes the last bastion of solace and strength, particularly for communities under stress, as has been historically the case with the Islamic *ummah*. The importance of this essential quality of Islam to its adherents is mistakenly seen as a denial of modernity, in that the latter (in its secularized and instrumental version) places faith in reason, rationality, science, or technology. Islam-as-faith places materialism within a wider context of divine purpose; it also shows the ephemeral nature of a civilization devoid of spiritual content.

At the social level, Islamic piety has often assumed the form of a covenant (Khaldun 1958; Vico 1984; Walzer 1979), specifying the ethical boundaries of a community but also serving as its regulating principle. Reposed in a state, this is the legitimation principle. Notions of just and unjust rule, so critical to Islamic societies, derive from this principle. Adherence to the covenant, even in an imperfect state, lends accountability to governance. In the absence of democracy, the covenant separates merely bad rule from tyranny. For the *ummah,* it establishes a sense of solidarity. Citizenship for the members of this community, which combines political and religious elements, no longer emanates from juridical or contractual arrangements but from a more durable and sacrosanct source. European domination of Muslim lands or present attempts to subordinate the *ummah* through newer instruments, therefore, appear more menacing; they undermine the *ummah*'s capacity to uphold the covenant and ensure an ethical life for its members. From an Islamic perspective, neither civic liberties nor property rights, the centerpiece of modern political life, can in themselves restore the *ummah* to its rightful place, which lies precisely in its capability to order political life as an aspect of divine purpose.

Outside the state, Islamic piety regulates social relations—in the family, community, and civilized society. Again, divine purpose in Islam suffuses societal intercourse. The notion that social relations ought to be conducted in accordance with a covenant imposes grave responsibilities that otherwise assume the character of exchange in a secular society. Giving social obligations the element of sacrosanctity links the individual to the collective and both to divinity. As an ideal, this aspect of Islamic piety bridges the political and social parts of the *ummah*—hence the need to recognize the source of Islam's resistance to secular attempts that are aimed to delink the two.

Even during the breakdown of political and social institutions under Western impact, the abstract notion of the covenant has often been the difference between the annihilation of the *ummah* and its durability. More often than not, recent endeavors to rebuild institutions on Islamic principles, though not often so clearly discernible, can be regarded primarily as an attempt to reconstruct the critical link between the political and social aspects of the *ummah* rather than a return to a mythical Islamic state.

Finally, Islamic piety appears as a social movement, ranging from monastic (apolitical) Islam, to its zealous expressions, to an Islam that seems pragmatic and willing to engage with modernity. In contrast to piety as faith or covenant, Islam as a social movement registers a mobilizing tendency to move large populations to seek a better world, to put materialism in its proper place, and/or to negotiate a new relationship with modernity. This is a wide spectrum of alternatives. The domain of choice, however, is based on Islam's capacity to simultaneously provide cultural identification, psychic and emotional resources, and boundaries. Islam's appeal also lies in being able to connect the faith, the covenant, and the mobilizing elements to produce powerful resistance to foreign intrusion. In times of extreme stress, Islam's capacity to synthesize the above elements has often produced definitive outcomes, as the recent Algerian case demonstrates.

The growing cultural divide between Islamicists and secularists in many Muslim societies (like Algeria) underscores how historically generated divisions have acquired a life of their own. Algeria's cultural bifurcation under colonialism is now intensified in the era of declining welfarism and the systemic failure of the state to provide social protection to the disadvantaged. Social grievances were congealed in the Black October riots in 1988, propelled by unemployment, declining living standards, and political corruption. Ironically, the cultural divide made its most recent political appearance with the introduction of a variant of Western multiparty parliamentary democracy in Algeria, after over two decades of secularist, one-party rule. Elections, designed to give legitimacy to the ruling party, only produced an opposite outcome. In the local and regional elections in 1990, and in the first national multiparty elections the following year, the FIS (Front Islamique du Salut) emerged as a clear winner. Representing mostly the urban poor and an ideological alternative to the ruling FLN (Front de Liberation Nationale) and privileged sectors of Algerian society, the FIS quickly found itself confronting the military. Martial law was declared, the election results were summarily annulled, and the top FIS leadership and hundreds of its rank-and-file supporters were put behind bars, tortured, or sentenced to death. Against the collective memory of unsuccessful earlier Muslim attempts to curb Western military, political, and cultural excesses, Western support for an authoritarian regime against Islamicists could only heighten their distrust of the West. Active backing of the military action against the FIS was provided by Western powers, with exhortations of not allowing this party to come to power through democratic channels. After three years of ruthless repression of the FIS, the civil war in Algeria shows no signs of abatement. Scores of FIS supporters, members of security forces, and innocent civilians have been brutally killed in this former French colony. Political and economic power, though entrenched in a Westernized elite, faces a massive grassroots challenge from those who share an alternative conception of social and political life.

In popular media representations, the FIS neatly fits the description of an anti-Western fundamentalist party, committed to illiberal politics and a retrograde social policy. The FIS's self-description gives these images certitude. Closer scrutiny will reveal its status as a party that escapes the narrower definition either of a fundamentalist party or merely of a protest movement. Against the imperviousness of the privileged few and the inability of the state to deliver the social good in times of economic liberalization, Islamic networks, centered on mosques, have furnished the security net to the many. From providing education, to collecting garbage, to giving timely economic help to those who have been abandoned by the rich and the state, the Islamicists have demonstrated genuine concern for the populace. Yet the crucial dimension is not economic but social.

The Islamicists offer cultural sustenance to those who have been thoroughly marginalized by West-centered economic liberalization, whose defining feature is not the strengthening of liberal values but consumerism. If the social world that Islamicists in Algeria or elsewhere inhabit is regressive and their tactics illiberal, it is due mainly to constraints of globalization, which has collapsed real possibilities of dialogue and tolerance in culturally divided societies by accentuating social stratification.

Both monastic (apolitical) Islam and zealotry are dead-end streets; they provide no viable bridge to modernity. Concerned with salvation of the soul, monastic Islam ably captures the dissonances of the human condition but offers no guide to political action. Remedial action to reconstitute the *ummah* and prepare it to face up to the challenges of modern (and postmodern) life is completely subordinated to a quest for the soul's journey into immortality. Against the backdrop of growing marginalization of Muslim populations, both globally and within Islamic countries, this route seems least promising. And yet, monastic Islam has shown considerable resilience and following among the *mustashieen* (have-nots), alienated from and exhausted by politics or disinterested in uniting worldly with otherworldly pursuits.

Zealotry begins with a deep sense of deference to God and manages well to capture the letter of Islamic principles. Yet in its enthusiasm for exegetical purity it often reduces those principles to a set of slogans. In practice, rituals displace the content and straitjacket a complex tradition into a narrow reading of Islamic texts. Offering no generosity of interpretation, zealotry constructs a Manichaean world of good and bad Muslims, while proposing closure toward non-Islamic influences. Usually, the totalitarian propensity dispensed toward the texts extends to notions of public and everyday life. Undemocratic and illiberal, this type of Islam combines all the ingredients of obscurantism with a thoughtless antimodernism. Too often, its deeds are registered as the representations of Islam as a whole. Ironically, as

Western responses to zealotry often fail to discriminate among the different types of Islam, they usually end up provoking reactions from less zealous Muslims as well, who perceive blanket Western condemnations as an assault to Islam as a faith.

Pragmatic Islam, appreciative of its limitations and the need for a creative approach to modernity, offers a more viable possibility for Muslim societies. If the first path disconnects Muslims from modernity, the second option suggests even greater perils of cultural and scientific involution (Hoodbuoy 1990); by contrast, pragmatic Islam, akin to the practices of an earlier era, is constitutive of critical and synthetic principles. But pragmatic Islam is not secularism, as in the case of Turkey. Secularism shares no organic links to the Islamic stream, and its limitations in organizing Muslim society have become quite pronounced. The rise of Islamicists in secular Turkey illustrates the shortcomings of positivist social engineering.

In contrast to secularism, pragmatic Islam seeks a dynamic interpretation of the Islamic *shariah* (sacred law), willing to privilege spiritual intent above textual rigidity (Fazlur Rahman 1982). This process includes a proclivity toward historicizing the reach of the canon, separating contingency from law, and acknowledging the cultural specificity of diverse Islamic lands. Pragmatic Islam takes modernity as a strategic problem that requires a total reorientation but establishes the rules of engagement within Islamic philosophy itself. Traditions of intercultural communication and rationalist tendencies in Islamic history provide signposts. Significantly, it is Islam's own commitment to betterment that serves as the chief nexus to modernity. The objective of building a viable *ummah* is inseparable from material progress, constitutional and democratic politics, and the accoutrements of development. Pragmatic Islam reclaims a crucial principle. Moreover, with piety as the point of departure, material progress loses its bestial quality. Both the critical and synthetic dimensions of pragmatic Islam make it appear as a more viable path for Muslims in their attempts to come to grips with the contradictory effects of globalization.

ISLAM AND INTERNATIONAL LIFE

In both modern and postmodern discourse, the notion of metaphysical or ontological dislocation (Lyotard 1984) as the sign of the times is quite pronounced. Whether in the human sciences, ecology, or international relations, the foundations appear to be fairly tenuous. For some, the rationalist and commodity-defined civilization is reaching its apogee. However, without a spiritual content, as many in the Islamic world would argue, modernity is a dehydrated project, capable of swiftly disintegrating into barbarism. Hedonism, consumerism, and narcissism become its natural supports. To rehabilitate human civilization, modernity must be reformulated. This requires, from an Islamic perspective, a shift away from anthropomorphism to the rekindling of a more purposeful relation to the divine. Accepting God's suzerainty involves acknowledging the importance of other life-forms and retreating from the imperial project of control and exploitation of nature for human self-achievement and desire. A disavowal of Cartesian dualism, which allows for a separation of nature and humanity, is the first step toward a restoration of humanity to its possibility.

In human affairs, this means the reactivation of an ethical principle, not simply the quest for an endless self-realization where the self is unbounded, untamed. The purpose of a covenant is precisely to regulate the self and selves by placing action in a structure of objective morality.

The role of Islamic piety in providing an alternative vision of the future cannot be dismissed on the mere basis that its use in fundamentalist discourse resurrects antimodernist sentiments. In stressing the pitfalls of materialism, piety compels a language of propriety and pushes toward a humanization of the world. It qualifies the arrogance of reason with a gentle reminder that ultimately the content of any civilization rests on its capacity to organize social life on the foundations of justice and equality—above all, on humility. Islam does not propose an antirationalism but emphasizes taming rationalism to serve human need and dignity.

In the context of the widening global rift between and among societies, the Islamic injunction to humanize the relations between those in positions of power and privilege and the vast millions who have neither, in accordance with a covenant, squares well with the imperative of rethinking global society. Too often, it is said, objective historical laws or natural necessity constitutes the determining process of human relations. Human agency, though invoked in these matters, is usually absent. Recognizing human efficacy involves, first, the awareness that any modernist project that lacks an intersubjective dialogue between cultures and civilizations is shallow and, in the end, dangerously chauvinistic. Pragmatic Islam, accepting of the Other, faces up to this challenge by reminding us of the eternal, but Herculean, task of balancing utility with responsibility and justice.

The challenge for Muslims is how to capture the massive dissonances of these times by retrieving the depth of faith without slipping into monasticism or zealotry. A democratizing and synthesizing Islam, reflecting influences from the bottom, is better placed to respond to globalization. For the non-Islamic world, particularly the West, the task is to recover memory and history, acknowledge the diversity of the Islamic *ummah,* and strive toward a solidarity based on mutual recognition and respect. The existence of these conditions can remove the civilizational impasse that seems to lock the West and Islam into a preventable but protracting suspicion and belligerence. An appreciation of the context by those who are situated at the top of globalization-from-above is a sine qua non of reconciliation. Only then can the bitterness left by earlier faces of globalization be forgiven while a mutual strat-

egy is set forth to deal successfully with globalization's current malignan-
cies. To visualize a posthegemonic world demands the creation of supraintersubjectivity (Cox 1992b). But the initial steps toward that goal involve a
recognition and knowledge of cultural diversity and the exigencies of reci-
procity.

NOTES

We thank Şerif Mardin and James H. Mittelman for their invaluable comments.
Mustapha Kamal Pasha also acknowledges the Wilma and Roswell Messing Jr.
Faculty Award (1992–1993), which provided generous support to complete the first
phase of this project.

1. Even in the non-Islamic societies (e.g., the UK, France, Germany, the United
States) where a noticeable diaspora is emerging, there are loud enough rumblings of
Islamic revivalism.

2. *Civilization,* in this context, means a way of being in this world that encompasses collective mentality, material underpinnings, and social institutions. Societies
that belong to the same civilization, while they could manifest some peculiarities to
each, have the central tenets of the way of life engraved in all and passed on from
one generation to the next. In this formulation, we echo the thinking of Braudel, who
writes, "Civilizations are made of people, and hence of their behavior, their achievements, their enthusiasms, their commitments to various causes, and also their sudden
changes" (Braudel 1994: 26).

3. No normative bias is intended in the use of the terms *resurgence, rebirth,* and
renaissance as they apply to the phenomenon of the growing political role of Islam
in global life. Nevertheless, we reject the assumption that this phenomenon is a
return to some primordial roots, à la Lewis (1976, 1988).

4. See *Production, Power, and World Order: Social Forces in the Making of
History* (New York: Columbia University Press, 1987), and "Toward a Post-
Hegemonic Conceptualization of World Order: Reflections on the Relevance of Ibn
Khaldun," in James N. Rosenau and Ernst-Otto Czempiel (eds.), *Governance
Without Government: Order and Change in World Politics* (Cambridge: Cambridge
University Press, 1992).

5. The idea of a global civil society is quite problematic. For one alternative
usage, see Falk (1992b).

6. The global economy, which is constituted by these developments, is to be
distinguished from an international economy, which refers to mostly regulated inter-
country transactions.

7. Falk (1992b: 40) writes, "Globalization-from-below is, in its essence, an
expression of the spirit of 'democracy without frontiers,' mounting a challenge to the
homogenizing tendencies of globalization-from-above. At the very least, the construction of global civil society is seeking to extend ideas of moral, legal, and environmental accountability to those now acting on behalf of state, market, and media."

8. For an excellent account of the ravages of Christian intolerance on Muslim
Spain, see the novel by Tariq Ali, *Shadows of the Pomegranate Tree* (London:
Verso,1993).

Part 3

The Potential and Limits
of Neoliberal Globalization

Globalization, Democratization, and the Politics of Indifference

Alexander Solzhenitsyn, Russia's most famous living writer and symbol of resistance to communism, recently hurled a bolt of moral outrage at Russia's political leadership, accusing it of indifference to suffering, incompetence, betrayal of the state and gross corruption. The people, he said, "have lost heart . . . they do not believe the reforms undertaken by this government are in their interests. . . . Russia is not a democracy but an oligarchy." People at the grassroots had been practically excluded from public life. "[The people] have only one miserable choice—to drag out a lowly and humble existence or to cheat on the state and each other." He said that the sale of land was tantamount to "selling Russia." On privatization he said that the process had taught seventy million people a very hard lesson—"never believe the state and never work honestly."[1]

> Indifference is actually the mainspring of history. But in a negative sense. What comes to pass, either the evil that afflicts everyone, or the possible good brought about by an act of general valour, is due not so much to the initiative of the active few, as to the indifference, the absenteeism of the many. What comes to pass does so not much because a few people want it to happen, as because the mass of citizens abdicate their responsibility and let things be. . . . The fatality that seems to dominate history is precisely the illusory appearance of this indifference, of this absenteeism. (Gramsci, 1977: 17)

The question of globalization raises the issue of globalization for whom and for what purposes. In this chapter, I attempt to probe the quality, limits, and contradictions of the primary form of contemporary globalization: that driven by transnational capital and associated neoliberal social forces—a form of globalization that tends to expand social inequality and strengthens the strong at the expense of the weak. I query the claims to progress and criticize the myopic and economistic logic of this form of globalization. I argue for a stronger countermovement of global politics, which would involve a "double democratization"—of government and of political life, at both local and global levels. Efforts need to be intensified to substantially democratize more internationalized forms of state and an embryonic global civil society. In this sense, the neoliberal globalization tendency will continue to be countervailed politically—it is neither inevitable nor an "end of history," as some of its advocates and apologists seek to claim.

WORLD ORDER AND THE "DOUBLE MOVEMENT"

It has become common to observe that postwar world order structures associated with the metastability of the Cold War have begun to break down and to be transformed. Seen in a longer time frame (albeit differently than the age of Nazism, fascism, and Stalinism), perhaps the world is experiencing yet another phase of a deep civilizational crisis characteristic of much of the late nineteenth and twentieth centuries. In the current crisis, the power of capital and the scope and depth of global market forces are being reasserted substantially. This crisis is compounded by not only the accelerating material capacities and creative destruction of capitalism, the effects and consequences of war, the potential use of nuclear weapons, and the proliferation of violent social conflicts but also, for many people, a sense of political indifference, government incompetence, and a decay of public and private responsibility and accountability.

Governments seem unable to cope effectively with the challenges of the times. In the absence of alternative strategies for dealing with the repercussions of fiscal crisis and intensified economic competition, substantial insecurity and social dislocation has been caused by unreflective and socially irresponsible application of neoliberal policies (e.g., the structural adjustment programs supervised by the International Monetary Fund [IMF] and the World Bank in Latin America and Africa).

In the 1990s, as to a degree in the 1930s, atavism, fatalism, nihilism, and violence figure in many human relations, and there is increasing dissatisfaction with and alienation from politics as usual. This phenomenon is manifest not only in postcommunist Russia and Poland but also in wealthy countries such as Italy, Japan, and Germany. Especially in Italy and to a lesser extent in Japan, the old corrupt order is being challenged and perhaps swept away, and a new form of post–Cold War politics is emerging. These developments are part of a broad, widespread process of political transformation, realignment, and constitutional revision while apparently contradictory trends develop in world politics. Many of the larger capitalist countries are turning inward politically (e.g., postunification Germany, Japan, the United States) while their economies and polities become ever more attuned to an economy of planetary reach. The broader economic context for these developments is, for many parts of the planet, a second great depression of the twentieth century (China and parts of East Asia are significant exceptions here) at the very moment when global market integration is extending and deepening.

The emerging world order involves a contradiction between globalization and democratization, one that is perhaps more intense today than in 1900 given the broad processes of proletarianization and political emancipation that have occurred in this century. The state was "internationalized" in the age of imperialism, in part because of the institutions of the balance of power and the international gold standard and because of the role of *haute finance,* which was crucial to the development of both constitutionalism and imperialist colonialism. In the 1990s we are witnessing a similar but in some ways rather different process, involving both the internal restructuring of the state and its globalization; these elements are interrelated with and are responses to the restructuring of the global political economy. Both the state and capital are reconfigured by neoliberal forms of restructuring, as post-Fordist economies of flexibility begin to replace economies of scale and as financial capital becomes more mobile in an era of market liberalization. Forms of state are either mutating or collapsing; there has been a general shift from redistributive forms of state to more internationally competitive forms.

Regarding this process, Van der Pijl (1989) argues that the "Lockeian" state-civil society form has begun to spread and to supplant the more state-capitalist, centralized, and regulated, or "Hobbesian," political economies. To a degree, politically centralized forms of capital accumulation are superseded by indirect, economic forms as the global political economy is restructured along neoliberal lines. A global civil society, organized along Anglo-American Lockeian self-regulating principles, increasingly becomes the model for emulation on a worldwide basis. Seen in another way, as just noted, the enlargement of the scope of the Lockeian state-civil society form implies a worldwide shift toward what Polanyi (1957b) termed the construction of a self-regulating market form of society.

As Polanyi noted, in the case of nineteenth-century Britain the creation of a market society was an unprecedented and revolutionary development, insofar as it implied the subordination of all other social and political processes to the creation and maintenance of the capitalist market system. It was also premised in particular upon a strong state able to implement and enforce the measures that created the market society: "*Laissez faire* itself was enforced by the state [and involved] an enormous increase in the administrative functions of the state, which was now endowed with a central bureaucracy able to fulfill the tasks set by the adherents of liberalism" (Polanyi 1957b: 139). Today the trend (or at least the announced aim of liberal policy) is toward downsizing this bureaucracy and making its operations more "economical" or efficient and imbued with market values (Mather 1993). In fact, the role of the state has so expanded that, at best, neoliberal reforms have prevented further growth in the scale of its operations. Also, state apparatuses have been restructured internally to make them more responsive to the extension of market society.[2]

This may or may not imply a corresponding constitutional form, premised upon the separation of powers, the sanctity of private property, and religious toleration (see Locke 1965). Seventeenth- and eighteenth-century societies were in large part configured by religious metaphysics, monarchy, mercantilism, and moral economy. Now the order of the day involves a metaphysics of the market, with its microchips, consumerist materialism, and rationalization of social life. Moreover, in recent history the deification of Mammon—the Biblical allusion is that riches or material wealth can be an influence for evil or immorality—has come increasingly to supplant other gods. The "self-regulating" market society, with its associated processes of commodification, has tended to encompass larger fractions of the world's population.

In my view, such tendencies will not continue unchallenged. As noted, perhaps one historical analogy could be drawn by reference to Polanyi's *The Great Transformation*. Polanyi wrote of a "double movement" of history. On the one hand were social forces that served to create, and then to extend, the laissez-faire "market society" in England from the 1790s onward (and to a lesser extent in continental Europe). On the other hand were forces that opposed the commodification of not only land but also labor; these forces ranged from the early trade unions to utopian socialists like Owen and conservative reformers like Bismarck and Disraeli, as well as businesses seeking protection from the rigors of international competition.

The latter forces developed unevenly and, according to Polanyi, crystallized in the creation of new forms of state in the 1930s in response to the crisis of global capitalism. Despite clear differences between the two periods, the contradictions of globalization in the 1990s are giving rise to countermovements as in the 1930s to reassert social control over apparently natural and eternal economic forces. In the 1920s, attempts had been made to restore the old, pre-1914 order, where gunboat diplomacy, imperial prerogatives, and capitalist internationalism of the financier ruled the waves. The workers of the world did not unite. In the 1930s they did in some places but rallied round the flag in rejection of the old order, which had been dominated by the cosmopolitanism of rentier capital. The countermobilization took a variety of political forms—from the New Deal in the United States to Nazism in Germany.

This historical process, with the struggles and forms of collective action it entails, continues. This means that there can never be an "end of history" in the sense of Fukuyama's much publicized dystopia. I would suggest that a more appropriate way to describe the nature of our times is with reference to Gramsci's (1971) celebrated remark, "The old is dying, the new is being born, and in the interregnum there are many morbid symptoms." In this interregnum, as in others, a sense of indifference prevails, but one tempered increasingly by a willingness to question and challenge the logic of globalization and its socially disintegrative consequences. However, whereas some of today's countermovements involve attempts to reassert democratization as a reaction to growing inequalities, others are more ethnonationalist, or fascist and reactionary; some have gone with a rise in intercommunal violence. This context informs our analysis of the dominant concepts of globalization; the question of democracy, equality, and justice in the emerging world order; and the conditions under which countermobilization is developing.

"BUSINESS CIVILIZATION" AND NEOLIBERALISM

As noted, globalization is not a new phenomenon. As a process of structural change it has a long lineage, which coincides with the development of modern capitalism: In particular, as British capitalist industrialization correlated with a policy of free-trade imperialism and the international gold standard in the nineteenth century. This phase of globalization was also characterized by the rival imperialism of the other great powers, notably by the social mercantilism of Germany and, later in the century, of the United States, with its combination of protectionism and a free-enterprise system.

Of course there are substantial differences between the world orders of the nineteenth and twentieth centuries. Today's globalized capitalism is hugely more productive than its nineteenth-century counterpart, and its development is intimately related to a third scientific-industrial revolution, as new technologies (e.g., at the interface between computing, biology, and communications) help to automate tasks and link them together over vast distances. Accumulation has become more knowledge-based and increasingly dematerialized and deterritorialized—especially in the post-1945 era of transnational capitalism and the so-called information revolution. There have been enormous increases in global population over the last century, indeed, a greater proportion of that population is affected by contemporary processes of globalization. We can perhaps make the general point that a key difference between nineteenth- and twentieth-century forms of globalization is that the latter is greater in scope, reach, and intensity than its precursor. Nevertheless, both forms can be viewed as part of a single, uneven, and contradictory process of historical transformation.

For those who are integrated economically into the production and consumption structures of a more globalized capitalism, the reaction time for political and economic survival has shortened, as time and space become more compressed in economic terms. The political content of globalization also differs. Alternative forms of social organization to capitalism have risen and fallen. Nevertheless, the twentieth century has also involved not only the growth in the size and scope of state activity but also proletarianization, mass-party politics, and the construction, destruction, and reconstruction of nation-states (and now macroregional and microregional political communities). In what we might call the early history of capitalist globalization (i.e., prior to the nineteenth century), most international economic activity was related to trade, raw material extraction, or plunder rather than to integrated production or direct investment. At the same time, the bulk of economic activity and the focus of political and social life continue to be primarily "national" or local, although the globalizing trend appears to be strengthening. Indeed, it may be a condition of our times that political life and political identities are becoming simultaneously more localized and fragmented, as well as more globalized and integrated as we enter the next millennium.

Thus, twentieth-century capitalist globalization is perhaps best understood as part of a wider historical pattern of structural change that helps to give shape and meaning to a given type of world order. It is not a complete or fully realized social and political transformation. Although the social and economic processes associated with capitalist globalization (with its characteristic forms of rationality and social rationalization) have extended and deepened since World War II (in the sense of the spread of bureaucratic state structures, market forces, possessive individualism, and mass consumer culture), we are still a long way from an approximation of a pervasively neoliberal world order where market discipline is virtually automatic, where state forms have become more fully "marketized" and commodified in outlook, and where social identities and interests have become reduced to the formula: self equals rational economic person. Indeed, as I will show, a fully neoliberal world order is not just a contradiction in terms but a logical impossibility in a world of many civilizations.

In recent years the term *globalization* has come to be used with increasing frequency by scholars, politicians, businesspeople, and the media. Although the term means different things to different people, in this chapter I am particularly interested in aspects of the process of globalization associated with transnationalization, or the dominance of internationally mobile capital. The growth in the power of such capital—relative to labor and in the way it reconstitutes certain ideas, identities, interests, and forms of state— is the primary social content of the process of globalization. In the latest phase of globalization, neoliberal economics and conservative political forces have been ascendant. If we use the term to refer to the most recent phase in the social and geographic extension of the power of capital (a process that perhaps can be traced back to the Glorious Revolution in England in 1688), globalization in the 1990s developed initially within and between the major capitalist powers. It has spread—in quite different social conditions and circumstances—to the Third World and to the formerly communist states. Thus the form of globalization I analyze in this chapter is neoliberal in character, up to a point.

In the discourse of what Strange (1990) has called "business civiliza-tion," business is held to perform, albeit perhaps unintentionally, a civiliz-ing mission through the operation of the "unseen hand" of market competi-tion and the ceaseless search for profit. Quintessentially, in this liberal view of the world, economic forces are represented as having potentially plane-tary reach and are akin to forces of nature; they are represented as beyond or above politics and form the basic structures of an interdependent world. The concept of business civilization, one of whose key notions is that of global-ization, is part of a wider neoliberal discourse suggesting that through the growth of an "enterprise culture" and through "market discipline" the virtues of prudence, responsibility, good governance, and social progress will arise, in partly spontaneous fashion, giving shape and direction to a "new" world order in the so-called post–Cold War era.[3]

This use of the term globalization and of the associated concept of busi-ness civilization is ideological in the sense of a set of ideas that justify and legitimate forms of class domination (i.e., of capital); it is abstract insofar as it reifies complex social processes and institutions such as the market. Proponents of this school of thought often seek to identify a broad and some-times wrenching reconfiguration of social and spatial patterns of world order with ideas of social progress. Such concepts of globalization may act as a discursive supplement to the discipline of international market forces and the power of capital and the ideological hegemony of neoliberal political economy. Moreover, the phrase *business civilization* has to be seen as an oxymoron, insofar as its spread is associated with the destruction or restruc-turing of other civilizational forms and possibilities. To be civilized involves a respect for and tolerance of other ways of living and ways of organizing society. Although one clearly has to appreciate the gains to society that have stemmed from greater productive power, treasured aspects of earlier or con-temporary civilizations are more fundamentally appropriated and commod-ified in capitalist societies.[4]

Globalization is broadly represented in conventional political discourse in the OECD countries as inevitable, if not desirable. Indeed, this discourse is reflected and reinforced worldwide by the global spread of transnational media corporations, which are often controlled by politically conservative neoliberals (e.g., Rupert Murdoch's News International). The message is reinforced by increasingly pervasive advertising and sponsorship, which stress the virtues of individualism and consumption associated with cultural and sporting events, such as the World Cup soccer tournament. In this sense, the discourse of globalization is ideologically convenient for transnational capital, although some transnational firms (e.g., in military industries) may fear the advent of increasing competition and the loss of state subsidies and forms of protection that underpin their profitability.

The globalization trend is occurring in a situation of military unipolari-ty and political-economic multipolarity. Interstate politics are characterized by an oligarchic (e.g., G7) and hierarchical power structure, although recently Russia has been admitted to this powerful club, in what has been called the Group of Eight "political"—Russia does not sit at the "economic" high table. The G7 countries, led by the United States, have begun to reconfigure their military capacities and alliance structures in the aftermath of the collapse of communist states and the Gulf War (Gill 1991). While the former Red Army has begun to disintegrate and the post-Soviet militaries are in substantial disarray, the United States and some of its allies have moved to extend their capacities for flexible response and rapid deployment in other parts of the world. Changes are slowly taking place to draw Germany and Japan into collective military exercises, sometimes under the guise of UN peacekeeping efforts. This type of policing of what former U.S. president George Bush called the "new world order" is paralleled by an apparent strengthening of G7 leverage over economic and political reforms in many countries, especially as political alternatives to capitalism have collapsed. The peoples of the Third World and the former Soviet bloc now experience a new form of economic subordination, this time administered by the institutions of a neocolonialist capitalism: the "economic" G7, the World Trade Organization (WTO), the IMF, and the World Bank.

Nevertheless, one might argue that the very contradictions engendered by neoliberal forms of globalization are now prompting a range of political alternatives. Some of these challenges entail different conceptions of globalization, based on democratization of an emerging global civil society and a renovated form of authority and governance at the global level. Indeed, the very mass media that reify the culture of consumption for the world's televisual masses also show the suffering of millions in Africa—amid the bewildering gyrations of the financial and exchange markets, waves of bankruptcies and rising unemployment, and neoliberal politicians charged with corruption, all in the name of free enterprise.

The principle of action that most seems to drive the political economies of the OECD countries is the attempt to provide the greatest happiness for the greatest number of politically influential consumers, citizens who are an affluent and politically central minority. These people are crucial to the constituencies that sustain oligarchies of power in a range of countries. While many such citizens—and their leaders—often show indifference to the fate of others (see the quotations from Gramsci and Solzhenitsyn at the start of this chapter), this is not to suggest that these people are existentially happier than many others. I suggest merely that their material situation is more comfortable and better protected than that of the vast majority of world society. However, threats to their own sense of security—and sense of the pervasiveness of social, financial, and ecological risks—have mounted in recent years (reflected, for example, in the worldwide increase in suicides and stress levels associated with fear of crime, fear of illness, unemployment, or personal bankruptcy). Nonetheless, this situation, especially in countries like the United States, increasingly rests on the political "absenteeism of the many"—that is, on the political apathy and acquiescence of the subordinate classes; it is an absenteeism that may not continue for very much longer. In the United States, for example, the members of what Galbraith (1992) calls the "culture of contentment" tenaciously defend their financial privileges (e.g., government insurance for an individual's bank deposits up to $100,000 per account—the poor and most of the middle classes do not have such large savings). In so doing the privileged often abdicate any generalized sense of social responsibility. Many of these people live in enclave housing—that is, complexes that resemble medieval fortresses, with their own private guards and electronic surveillance systems (Davis 1990). Galbraith suggests that these people have a "laager" mentality when it comes to the rest of society. Thus, despite the near universal professed belief in God in the United States, many members of the culture of contentment press not for charity and social investment in the bleak inner cities but for a punitive regime of workfare for the poor. This type of attitude has parallels with debates about the Poor Law Reform in nineteenth-century Britain.

This political situation, however, may be changing, although not necessarily in progressive ways. Opposition to the status quo is manifested as a disgust with traditional mainstream political parties (e.g., Ross Perot in the United States) or as a much more reactionary mobilization. Protest is coupled with a clamor for order, stability, and clean government, and it is exemplified to a degree by the rise of far-right and neofascist groups in Europe. Indeed, the situation has moved beyond right-wing forms of resistance and protest since, for example, the neofascist MSI (Italian Social Movement) became part of the Berlusconi government in Italy in 1994. The neofascist Liberal Democratic Party led by Zhirinovsky in Russia may also be a harbinger for future trends in the politics of some of the former communist countries.

DEMOCRATIZATION AND GLOBALIZATION

The globalization trend has been associated with a paradox: the spread of commodification and market forces have had socially polarizing consequences but they have apparently been linked to the spread of democratization, which implies greater political equality throughout the world. However, this paradox is not as real as it may seem. In the past thirty years we have seen the spread of liberal democratic political forms in varied circumstances (e.g., in southern Europe in the 1970s, in Latin America and Africa in the 1980s, and in parts of eastern and central Europe in the late 1980s and 1990s). There has been a spread of formal aspects of liberal democracy (free elections, freedom of speech and association, a plurality of parties, constitutional guarantees of other rights and responsibilities, etc.).

However, in the same period there has been enormous growth in social inequality and the erosion of public social provisions (e.g., education and public health) and forms of economic redistribution (e.g., social welfare and unemployment insurance systems). This has meant that the very social and material basis for greater political equality—central to the very idea of democracy—has been undermined in many countries. Formal democratization has also gone with significant changes in power relations (e.g., the weakening of organized labor).

Neoliberal discourse tends to understand democratization in a certain way. Direct democracy along the lines of the Athenian polis, with an involved and public-minded citizenry (women and slaves were not citizens) acting as both legislators and public administrators (selected by drawing lots), is normally understood as impossible in a mass-based society. Political democracy is understood by neoliberals as an elite form of democracy and competition for votes. Thus, following Schumpeter (1976), democracy becomes an indirect mechanism for (periodically) electing leaders (representatives) who then govern. The author of *Capitalism, Socialism and Democracy* felt that such leaders needed to be drawn from "a social stratum, itself a product of a severely selective process, that takes to politics as a matter of course . . . [with leaders the] products of stocks that have successfully passed the test in other fields—served, as it were, an apprenticeship in private affairs" (Schumpeter 1976: 291). Democracy in this sense is indirect and tends to rest upon the activism of the few for the governance of the many. Thus liberal democratization is not direct democracy (either of the polis or of the grassroots); it is an indirect, and therefore attenuated, form of the attempt to institutionalize political equality. It involves, as a result, limited conceptions of participation, accountability, and political responsibility. The following is a list of the requirements of popular rule (or direct democracy) as outlined by Lively (1977: 30), from the strongest to the weakest. (Schumpeter's definition would perhaps satisfy only points 4–7 or, more likely, 6 and 7.)

1. All should govern and be involved in legislating, deciding on general policy, applying laws and in public administration.
2. All should be personally involved in crucial decisionmaking—i.e., making general laws and policies.
3. Rulers should be accountable to the ruled and be obliged to justify their actions to the ruled and be removable by the ruled.
4. Rulers should be accountable to the representatives of the ruled.
5. Rulers should be chosen by the ruled.
6. Rulers should be chosen by the representatives of the ruled.
7. Rulers should act in the interests of the ruled.

"Politics," for many neoliberals, is therefore a sphere of activity to be constructed to give disproportionate (unequal) weight to the enlightened and/or the propertied proportion of the citizenry—a view consistent with the ideas of Locke (1965). On the other hand, in the sphere of "economics," a democracy of consumers voting in markets is viewed as much more feasible. Indeed, some prominent neoliberals suggest that because of advances in technology and information processing the financial marketplace behaves in ways analogous to the polis, making ongoing judgments or referenda on the credibility and performance of governments. Bad government will tend to drive capital away; good government will attract capital flows. Often, therefore, we hear the refrain (e.g., from the business Hegelian flank of neoliberalism, typified by the banker Walter Wriston [1992]) of the inevitability and desirability of a "new information standard." Wriston claims, with some overstatement, that this standard "disciplines" governments more automatically than did the nineteenth-century international gold standard. He suggests that the market, especially the financial market, is an ongoing referendum on the policies and credibility of a particular government and, indeed, its political orientation. In this example, institutional investors and bond dealers play roles analogous to political parties and agents in the "global democracy" of the marketplace.

Since the 1960s there has been dramatic growth in social inequality within and among nations. Indeed, the already massive gap in income and wealth among the richest 10 percent and the poorest 10 percent of people worldwide increased almost tenfold during the 1980s, according to UN statistics:

> Between 1960 and 1989, the share of global income held by the richest fifth of the world population increased from 70 to 83 percent, while the share of the poorest fifth dropped from 2.3 to 1.4 percent. Statistics on changes in the distribution of income within specific countries paint similar pictures of increasing inequality. This noteworthy process can also be observed among regions. While growth in some areas of Asia has been remarkable over the past two decades, most African countries lag further behind in the sharpening competition to capture a portion of the world's wealth. Between 1970 and 1989, the participation of sub-Saharan Africa in global trade dropped from 3.8 percent to 1 percent, and foreign investment in that continent declined markedly. (Ghai and Hewitt de Alcantara 1994: 9)

These statistics would indicate that the participation in the daily market referendum on government policies in the financial markets is highly uneven and unequal—since by definition the poor have little disposable capital to invest and are thus, in Wriston's world, economically disenfranchised. Other studies indicate that a disproportionate burden of adjustment to harsh circumstances has fallen on the shoulders of women, children, and the weaker members of society (the old and the disabled) as social and educational provisions have been reduced, partly because of pressures to cut government budgets and balance the books exerted by the financial markets and the "new information standard." Despite the setbacks to their situation that have occurred since the mid-1970s, the subordinated classes—including the marginalized of the global political economy—are neither indifferent nor inactive in the face of their oppression. Indeed, these people have the capacity to undermine and disrupt the privileged circuits of production and consumption and the sense of security of the "contented" majority of world society, especially in a global political economy that is organized primarily around and from a number of heavily populated urbanized regions containing rich and poor alike.

Neoliberal constitutional proposals at the global level form a counterpart to the Schumpeterian elitist theory of democracy at the domestic level, with the exception that the form of governance involved is even more indirect and selective in terms of participation than at the domestic level in liberal democracies. Rules and constitutional mandates are being redesigned to sustain neoliberal arrangements so as, for example, to give greater veto power to the minority interests of capital and to make certain kinds of political change in the future more difficult. Innovations in constitutional provisions mean new constraints that circumscribe the maneuvering room of (future) politicians to manipulate monetary and fiscal policy or trade protectionism (e.g., to provide social protection from world market forces). Examples of the types of "economic constitutionalism" I have in mind are the North American Free Trade Agreement (NAFTA), the Maastricht Treaty, and the latest GATT Uruguay agreements. These arrangements are designed to supplement market discipline with binding constraints or "rules" in ways that might prevent elected politicians from using a wide range of policies to defend national or local interests. These innovations, which I have called "the new constitutionalism," are direct political counterparts to the growth in the structural power of internationally mobile capital—that is, to the reconstitution of capital on a world scale (see Gill 1992a, b).

In contrast to the early or mid-1970s, ideas and proposals of a neoliberal type have come to represent the orthodoxy for the reshaping of institutional and policymaking frameworks in economic matters. Indeed, some of the most dedicated converts of neoliberal policies are former communists in Eastern Europe, who have come to criticize the welfare states in Western Europe for cosseting workers and protecting inefficient firms. Other, more theologically strident, economic neoliberals are found in the Third World.[5] As David Law has noted, in the 1970s many of the ideas associated with this discourse did not really seem all that new. For example, monetarism was based upon the quantity theory of money, and the reliance on more market forces and less state planning is an old idea associated with Adam Smith's critique of mercantilism. Even privatization was not really an original idea.

What may be more novel, however, is innovation with regard to the international constitutional constraints noted earlier, the reconfiguration of international organizations, and the orientation of government institutions. Neoliberal innovations are designed to be compatible with business civilization (e.g., the attempts in the UK and in the former communist countries to engender an "enterprise culture" within the state through the application of new systems of incentives and surveillance), as well as with market forms of discipline. State agencies are made to compete with the private sector in, for example, service provision and to behave as if they were marketplace animals.

Such developments have tremendous implications for our experience in and understanding of society and for our sense of the future. This is particularly the case since neoliberal globalization has coincided with a general economic stagnation or depression in much of the capitalist world (and a catastrophic economic collapse in the former communist countries), although there has been rapid economic growth in East Asia and, until the early 1990s, Japan. The winners and losers in the process of global restructuring are becoming easier to identify both nationally and globally.

At the same time, the democratic gains in many countries are real, although they may be fragile and brittle—in Gramsci's famous phrase they may not be embedded deeply in "the fortresses and earthworks" of a developed, participatory, and democratic civil society. Thus the democratization trend, if it deepens, may prove to be the central element in the reshaping of capitalist globalization. The threats to and destruction of the postwar social contract that existed in many countries from the 1950s to the 1970s have helped to cause a renewed self-organization of people to protect themselves from the atomizing consequences of market and other reforms. While there is an apparent powerlessness among the powerful (e.g., the inability of G7 leaders to sustain domestic legitimacy and effective management of the global economy), there has been growth in the power of the apparently powerless (Sakamoto 1994). Even the poorest members of world society are combining politically to oppose their oppression. For example, and without romanticizing the phenomena, the 1980s and 1990s have witnessed an enormous flourishing of grassroots organizations, a proliferation of nongovernmental organizations (NGOs), and growth in informal, quasi-spontaneous networks of resistance. Such politicization "from below" may constitute a major, although not necessarily revolutionary, change in the condition of the emerging world order, and perhaps in a more democratic direction.

In this context it is crucial to emphasize that the neoliberal vision of a globalized market utopia (associated with the ideology of business civilization) is both theoretically and in practice unachievable—and not only because certain types of business enterprise (e.g., large-scale, monopolistic, or oligopolistic firms) seek systematically to restrict market competition rather than to promote it. The pure commodification of society that this type of globalization implies is fundamentally contradictory; it implies the atomization and perhaps annihilation of the social and cultural basis upon which the entire edifice of market institutions stands and depends upon for its existence (Hirsch 1976). It is politically unachievable because its very mobilization, over time, gives rise to countermovements and forces expressed in political struggle, which combines elements of an old order and a new "emerging" world order. Thus the term *emerging* in this sense is meant to convey something protean but not inchoate, since, to paraphrase Marx, people make history, although not always under conditions of their own choosing.

Moving from the often very local to the national, regional, and global dimensions of change, reregulation and a longer-term perspective, with internationally coordinated planning, are also needed to democratize and constrain some of the socially disintegrative tendencies associated with the latest phase of globalization and to create an ethic of responsibility in global politics. The criterion of democratization (including the substance and quality of democracy understood as a real capacity to exercise social choice) can be used to assess whether the dominant forces of globalization are to be perceived as equitable and sustainable or perhaps unjust and socially disintegrative trends in the emerging world order. This criterion can also be attached to an emerging counterhegemonic politics. The goal of the new social movement of world politics should be to initiate a broad process of human empowerment that can promote a more substantive democratization of both state structures and civil society. This double democratization must be both local and global and intended to forge authentic alternatives for all people on an inclusive basis. It might be seen as a central and a hopeful part of a second "double movement" of politics and society in the twentieth century against the socially polarizing logic of unfettered global market forces.

THE SOCIAL PATHOLOGY OF
A GLOBALIZED WORLD ORDER

With the democratic question still in mind, we might observe that the global political economy—the social infrastructure of globalization—is dominated by, concentrated in, and organized from a number of what Braudel (1981) called "world cities." These include New York, London, and Tokyo, the principal financial centers, with Frankfurt, Paris, Los Angeles, Toronto, São Paulo, Sydney, Singapore, and Hong Kong in the second tier with tax havens in Luxembourg, Switzerland, and the Caribbean crucial to the existing global structure of finance (and the ability of mobile corporations and wealthy individuals to evade taxes). Washington, D.C., and to a lesser extent New York, Paris, Geneva, and Vienna represent the key administrative control centers for the processes of international organization and for the disciplinary capacities of the U.S. state apparatus and military-intelligence establishment.[6] The interchange of personnel in the U.S. system and the presence of the international financial institutions (the IMF and the World Bank) means a steady circulation of key members of what I have called the globalizing elites of transnational capitalism into and from Washington, D.C. (Gill 1994b).

More broadly, the interrelation among the world cities gives a degree of both hierarchy and coordination to the global political economy. A limited number of cities and urbanized regions (and their contiguous hinterlands) form the major centers of production and consumption and house the vast bulk of corporate headquarters or their subsidiaries. However, the organizational control and research and development functions of transnational firms are generally located in North America, Western Europe, and Japan, the so-called triad of capitalist power and wealth, although there is a growing number of transnational firms with headquarters in countries outside these regions. In other words, what we might call the regions of privilege are themselves formed in a complex hierarchy, with finance and knowledge production being concentrated in a smaller number of centers than the patterns of the global division of labor might, on the surface, suggest.

The links between these centers are complex and cannot be discussed in detail here. Nevertheless, these links are not simply functional—they are social and political. They are consolidated not only by cross-cutting patterns of investment and trade, by information grids and communications facilities, but also by the political networks of fractions of the ruling classes of the triad and elsewhere. These networks are the prototype of an emerging transnational class formation, which incorporates some "privileged" workers in the corporate sector (those with job protection and higher wages) and others dependent on transnational production and finance for their livelihoods, to form a transnational historical bloc (Pijl 1984; Gill 1990). This bloc, despite its rivalries and conflicts, is committed to the strengthening of the patterns of neoliberal political economy associated with globalizing capitalism. (For example, German and Japanese capital appears less than wholehearted in its support for Anglo-American economic liberalism.)

As was the case during much of the nineteenth century, the ruling classes of the triad often have more in common with each other than with the mass of the population in their respective societies. However, in contrast to that period, the broad process of proletarianization has meant that accommodation of some of the interests of subordinate classes becomes a force majeure of political life. Thus these privileged islands of production and consumption are organized hierarchically and are both internally and externally policed (often by U.S. military power in concert with allied or coalition partners) and thus defended and protected from the encroachment of the marginalized people of world society—a pathological situation.

The islands of privilege are surrounded by vast seas of poverty, insecurity, and violence. In a world where approximately eight hundred million people live in affluence, a similar number are on the point of starvation. Notably in the Third World, social inequality is massively more pronounced than in the privileged regions of the OECD. In much of the Third World, Horsemen of the Apocalypse stalk the earth in the form of war, violence, disease and epidemics, and famine. For a large proportion of the world's population, conditions are often worse than those experienced by the urban and especially rural masses in the fifteenth to eighteenth centuries (Braudel 1981):

> Many governments fail today to enable their people to meet even their most basic needs. Over 1.3 billion lack access to safe drinking water; 880 million adults cannot read or write; 770 million have insufficient food for an active working life; and 800 million live in "absolute poverty," lacking even rudimentary necessities. Each year 14 million children — about 10 percent of the number born annually — die of hunger. (MacNeill et al. 1991: 6)

In 1990, over one hundred million people were afflicted by famine (*Guardian Supplement,* 29 May 1992). At the same time in Western Europe we witnessed phenomenal levels of overproduction of food, reflected in the European Union's "wine lakes" and "butter mountains." In North America, the principal form of malnutrition is caused by overeating by the world's most obese population.

Moreover, in much of the Third World child labor is widespread (and is also found in the European Union and the United States). A majority of the world's population is under the age of eighteen and lives in the Third World. Of these young people, the vast majority are denied the possibility of autonomy and the prospect of exercising social choice in their lives, both now and in the future. In the 1980s, the burdens of adjustment to socioeconomic restructuring have fallen particularly unequally, at least when compared with the 1950s and 1960s. The process of structural adjustment in the 1980s and 1990s meant that in the Third World burdens were increasingly thrust upon women and children (women do approximately two-thirds of all work in both the household and the "formal" and "informal" sectors of the economy in the Third World; see Feldman and Beneria 1992; Wallace and March 1991). This raises the issue of a global crisis not only of development but also of social reproduction, insofar as it can be argued that the household forms a key social institution. Today we are witnessing a crisis of development of global proportions — a true crisis of global civilization. It involves a counterrevolution of the powerful against the weak. In much of the Third World, the processes of urbanization and economic decline have gone with social chaos, anomie, and nihilism (Vieille 1988).

REFLECTIONS ON THE POLITICS OF INDIFFERENCE

At the very moment when the global political economy is accelerating in terms of the speed and geographic reach of capitalist restructuring, we see a bankruptcy of conventional political alternatives, a kind of historical regression where the changes are being linked to archaic notions of political economy and constitutionalism. New discourses of power seek to discipline the struggle in the streets, the villages, the cities—the points where the pressures, constraints, and contradictions of the process of globalization are localized and applied. Structural adjustment in Latin America and Africa, and now in the former Soviet Union, has helped to atomize many state capacities. Nevertheless, the complex processes discussed are also generating new social movements and political parties, which may in time come to challenge the thrust of neoliberal orthodoxy.

Not all of these parties and forces will represent beneficent trends in world politics. Some, such as the far right in Russia, will be malignant elements. In Eastern Europe, the reintroduction of neoliberal marketization is generating a combination of widespread disillusionment and resentment, sentiments that to a certain extent are reflected in the revival of populism, racism, fascism, and gangsterism. In Russia, for example, the concept of marketization is increasingly associated with desperation and a massive upsurge in crime and violence, as nuclear power stations begin to decay and collapse and as state arsenals are plundered of weapons by armed gangs. The market is being reintroduced in the context of a general collapse of law and order, and its reintroduction is part of a fundamental social crisis.[7]

Indeed, within the ranks of the privileged there is a struggle over the political and social aspects of the emerging world order. For example, different models of the appropriate state form for capitalism (including the social market model of Germany, Jacques Delors's European social democratic model, and the compensatory state mercantilism of Japan) are competitors to Anglo-American laissez faire neoliberalism (in the Western European case, the model of financial and free trade Europe) and its attendant vision of restructuring for the former communist states and the Third World. Part of the claim to superiority of the continental European and Japanese models is often couched in terms of the greater social solidarity and longer-term time frames they seek to promote. It may be no coincidence that the more that neoliberal forces win the struggle over the appropriate political form for capital accumulation, the more that social inequality—including gender inequality—tends to deepen and political conflict to intensify.

When this is related to the turmoil in the Third World it gives grounds for considering whether the neoliberal world order is socially and ethically sustainable. Yet the world is increasingly interdependent both economically and ecologically. Political turbulence and growing disparities in living conditions are driving unstoppable waves of migration. The governments defending the regions of privilege will be hard-pressed to cope with or to contain such pressures. To stem such migration requires a more just and egalitarian economic and political structure to the emerging world order.

Nevertheless, while there have been other signs of democratization (e.g., in some of the bureaucratic authoritarian capitalist countries, such as South Korea and to a lesser extent Taiwan), there has been worldwide growth in right-wing populism and a resurgence of fundamentalism of both metaphysical and social types (in this sense, the 1930s and the 1990s are in some ways comparable). There are already significant signs of reaction and authoritarianism in many of the former communist states, especially in the context of a resurgence of intercommunal violence and political chaos, often fueled by the descent into economic entropy. In China, of course, with its massive and rapid economic growth since the late 1970s, many of the contradictions associated with commodification and democratization have begun to surface, and its economic situation seems on the verge of spinning completely out of control.

Whereas the leaders not only of China but also of the G7 countries appear unable to contain the rise of new forces that challenge the status quo within their own territories and to reverse widespread disillusionment and alienation with "normal politics," many in the Third World are taking responsibility for their own survival and beginning to exercise social choices that reflect their own interests and sense of identity. Here we see movement where an initially defensive response becomes something more creative, participatory, and organic — a development that produces its own ethic of responsibility. In many parts of the Third World, new types of politics are developing (some relatively invisible and outside the traditional conception of political action), in silent revolution of the apparently powerless against the forces that oppress them (Cheru 1989; Scott 1985, 1993). Another indicator of the power of the apparently powerless is the new forms of local political organization and multilateralism that have begun to emerge among the poor and marginalized (e.g., the indigenous peoples of North and South America and parts of Asia). Moreover, in many countries there are myriad forms of local cooperatives, associations, and programs. Public opinion in the United States continues to be divided over the questions of foreign intervention (partly reflecting a strong peace interest), economic liberalization (e.g., as reflected in debates over NAFTA and GATT ratification), and environmental issues (U.S. NGOs have been at the forefront of pressures to make the World Bank more socially and environmentally responsive). It is important to link these local and transnational initiatives in a global political process and to relate them to labor organizations and other progressive elements of global civil society. This would help to create the basis for a "new multilateralism," a basis partly reflected at the Earth Summit in Rio in 1992, and perhaps at the World Social Summit in Copenhagen in 1995 (Gill 1994c).

These examples, especially from groups often considered to be the most marginalized or excluded, emphasize the human capacity to be able to create alternatives where the formation of a collective political will develops. In this sense it is important to apply the label of political indifference precisely and to those who actually display it.

What is also needed, however, is more help on the part of the left to create new political alliances and alternatives to neoliberalism and to reconstitute a more legitimate basis for the democratization of state and civil society and new forms for the internationalization of authority. This problem is extremely complex and involves not only the reconfiguration of material power but also the mobilization of resources and capabilities to develop new institutional structures and longer time frames. Central to this endeavor is an ethic of responsibility and the tolerance of differences, both within and across particular societies and civilizations. We need to move from a rather economistic sense of defensive alliances and coalitions against neoliberal forces to a new form of world society that goes beyond materialist consumption and relentless competition. There is a need to create a more cooperative, equitable, just, and sustainable pattern of world order. The idea of resistance is simply not enough. The vision of the left should be more supple, more creative, and thus more revolutionary, even if it is tempered by the need to work within the limits of the possible. The traditional left has often failed to take the initiative on the question of democracy during the past two decades—in part because many of the organizational and political structures of left-wing parties and governments are themselves elitist and centralist in nature. In this sense, the forces of the left need to renew and to take more seriously their commitment to the democratic principles they claim to represent. This is a precondition for going beyond a purely economistic, defensive, and rather one-dimensional vision of politics to a more complete and comprehensive notion of a possible and desirable world order—a form of democratic globalization.

This does not mean the search for impossible utopias, although it does mean a form of thinking that is not totally constrained by a defensive mentality. The limits of the possible are not constrained by the "iron law of oligarchy" and are not determined by the globalizing elites of transnational capital. Despite the belief of some of the key intellectuals of the globalizing elite that they are the trustees of the future of the planet and the "public good of sustainable growth" (e.g., Nye writing in 1991 for the Trilateral Commission; see Gill 1994b: 189), the masses they wish to rule are neither inert, apathetic, nor indifferent to their fate. Moreover, it is not only workers and peasants who have suffered in the recent restructuring of the global political economy—hundreds of thousands of businesses have gone to the wall during the 1989–1992 world recession. For example, at the economistic, or "corporate," level of analysis, some sections of business need protection not only from international competition but also from instability in the marketplace, in order to plan for longer-term and costly fixed investments and to allow for such things as the training of workers and the creation of supplier networks.

From a counterhegemonic viewpoint, then, one question to pose initially is which parts of business might be potential allies of certain workers' organizations and other progressive elements? And under what circumstances will they exist? In the 1930s the Swedish farmers and the small capitalist sector were crucial in combining with labor to create the Social Democratic ascendancy and the so-called Swedish model, which has been held up as an example of a successful, democratic, and inclusive form of accumulation. Some kinds of business might benefit from reregulation of the environment; others, from the reregulation of finance. The same might go for ethical standards in public life so as to break the link among political corruption, neoliberal government, and the politics of the rentier, which have spread like a plague in the 1980s and early 1990s. At issue here, in part, is the battle between financial (or rentier) and productivist viewpoints and the time frames they entail. Even within manufacturing there are important differences among industries (e.g., those that involve more high technology and are more capital-intensive and those that are more labor-intensive and thus vulnerable to cheap imports from Third World sites).

Thus in the absence of protectionist measures—prohibited under the latest GATT agreement—industrial forces would react to labor questions in very different ways. High-technology firms producing sophisticated software products would seek to attract and retain highly skilled workers and offer good benefits packages and might have a relatively tolerant view of labor organization. In the capital-intensive auto industry, labor costs amount to only about 10 percent of total costs, and workers receive, as a result, relatively good wages and (at least until the 1980s) a reasonable amount of job security, in part because of traditionally well-organized unions. Logically, attempts to destroy independent labor organizations and to press for the abolition of minimum wages and for little regulation of health and safety in the workplace would appeal more to industries most threatened by a liberalization of trade and thus by cheap imports, such as the garment trades.

Left-of-center parties need to weigh the situation carefully and maintain contacts with certain sectors of industry with a view to getting at least some support for reregulation. Also at issue is the growing anxiety among the middle classes in the OECD, including the highly paid, as a result of the disintegration of the social fabric and the sense of insecurity in their everyday lives. Youth unemployment in many OECD countries has become, it would appear, an intractable problem and even encompasses the offspring of the privileged. This means that the legitimization of neoliberal policies is proving to be ever more difficult. Neoliberalism in this sense is devouring its favorite children. A pervasive sense of social anxiety and insecurity is becoming more and more widespread and is cutting across the so-called

North-South divide. With this in mind, there has been a multiplication of community and grassroots organizations in many parts of the world, as well as other developments that show that real alternatives to neoliberalism and the politics of austerity are being forged—even though these conditions are also proving to be fertile for the revival of fascism.

Thus, one way to interpret the political changes of the 1990s is by comparing the social movement of world politics today to that of the 1930s. In the 1930s, "productivist" elements (not only industrial and agricultural workers but also business) pressed for social protection. In some countries this was due partly to the power or organization of labor. In others, the power of organized labor was quite weak, which explains the simultaneous development of fascism and Nazism (and their attempts to crush the left and destroy independent trade unions), as well as authoritarianism, in many countries. Thus, new forms of state emerged in the 1930s—some relatively democratic, others quite the opposite. The shift toward fascism occurred at the same time as more managed, interventionist, and cartelized forms of capitalism were consolidated. This occurred to a degree even in Britain, and these statist tendencies were consolidated in the OECD in varied welfare nationalist forms of state after World War II. Arrangements were made at Bretton Woods that sought to place constraints on a resurgence of rentier power at the international level (Helleiner 1994).

In conclusion, new concepts of collective power are required—ones that can be applied not just locally or nationally but also internationally. Much more important than countervailing power is the more constructive concept of power associated with the mobilization of people's abilities to create viable and practical sets of alternatives and capacities for social choice. This type of mobilization is essential to democratize the power of capital on a world scale. Such democratization of civil society and the state does not entail the abolition of markets, or indeed, the replacement of the market as an institution by a totalist vision of state planning. It does, however, mean that the constitution of society, and thus of markets, is not premised increasingly upon tendencies toward the pure commodification of human life and of nature. Consequently, there would need to be efforts to enlarge and localize control over common lands and facilities while recognizing and extending the idea of global commons. Although local control and accountability are vital, some form of international planning and cooperation is needed, in this example, with regard to the use of land and natural resources so that policies are developed in ways compatible with global environmental sustainability.

We may, then, be in the midst of a 1990s version of Polanyi's double movement as social movements are remobilized and new coalitions are formed. Some of these will seek to protect society from the unencumbered logic of neoliberal globalizing forces and to contest the restricted idea that human possibility and worth is defined primarily through the process of consumption. More constructively, this type of development (which by its very nature would be indeterminate and would not have a teleology, an end point, or a mobilizing myth about progress or human perfectibility) will involve the enlargement of human autonomy and the capacity for social choice for more and more people on the planet. For it to prevail would require not only ideas and networks but also institutional and material capabilities, access to resources, and the capacity to demonstrate in practical ways the ability to meet the broad needs of the people. At the heart of such possibilities lies an increased willingness on the part of citizens, including the intellectuals, to contest the indifference of the privileged few and to adopt an ethic of global responsibility. This would not produce a perfect, "ethical state" or a necessarily "good" society. It would provide minimum criteria for new models of global governance and for new principles and processes of political participation and accountability. Indifference would no longer be an attitude that the privileged few could opt to enjoy.

NOTES

I thank especially David Law and Jim Mittelman for detailed comments. I would also like to thank participants of the globalization conference organized by Jim Mittelman at American University in March 1994 for their comments. In particular I thank Nick Onuf, Mustapha Pasha, Magnus Ryner, and Christine Zacharia for their thoughtful remarks, although I am sure that this chapter will not satisfy their criticisms and may provoke even more.

1. Solzhenitsyn had just returned from a lengthy journey throughout Russia to meet ordinary people (Lloyd 1994).

2. The fiscal crisis of the state and the need to increase the effective rate of taxation to finance state programs when interest rates remain high (especially when direct taxes were cut in the 1980s) have created other pressures for the restructuring of the state. Increasingly in the OECD countries the police, security services, and tax and health and welfare administrations have integrated database systems that enhance surveillance capabilities (Gandy 1993).

3. Various forms of social "discipline" may be identified. One is the discipline of the family; another is that of custom, tradition, and ideas about good conduct and morality; another is that of political authority. A form particular to contemporary history is the systematic discipline of the market—for land, labor, and money. Market discipline is largely indirect and structural. For example, a pure market form of discipline would force all debtors out of business and into bankruptcy at the point where they were unable to repay their debts. Likewise, in a pure competitive capitalist economy a firm that cannot make sufficient profit to cover its costs is forced into bankruptcy, workers lose their jobs, and investors lose the value of their shares. However, the social costs of such a collapse (especially of a large firm or bank) may be such that a government comes to the rescue in a discretionary bailout. In doing so, or by providing loan guarantees, it socializes the risk associated with business and undercuts the market discipline. New classical economists have coined the term *moral hazard* to describe this process (perhaps implying that market forces have some intrinsic morality). This term suggests that individual economic agents (e.g.,

lenders and borrowers) will not behave according to the disciplines of the market because they anticipate that the government is likely to come to the rescue to avert a financial collapse or panic—that is, the government will act as lender of last resort. This example indicates that in the real world there is no such thing as "pure" market discipline.

Generally speaking, financial market discipline is weak in an inflationary situation where real interest rates are low or negative (as they were for periods in the 1970s, when many Third World countries borrowed abroad heavily in the Euromarkets). When rates are high, as they were from the early 1980s onward, repayments rise and access to new credit becomes both more difficult and more costly. Here, in general, we have a situation where financial discipline is substantial but not total; the bailouts associated with the debt crisis (and also in support of domestic banks) show the social and political limits to the acceptance of market discipline.

4. For example, the U.S. software giant Microsoft has launched a strategy to acquire the electronic rights to the catalogs of museums and art galleries worldwide. While this will provide income to care for museums and works of art, Microsoft is endeavoring to obtain global intellectual property rights over the creations of millions of artists, alive and dead. Multiple Mona Lisas would become accessible from new information highways. Of course, wider access to the wonders of Leonardo da Vinci is to be applauded as culturally enriching. However, instead of these artifacts being part of the common heritage of the people of the earth they will become commodities in an electronic marketplace.

5. I mention this because it is one way to emphasize to some readers that this chapter is not silent concerning the Third World, as was suggested by a commentator at the preparatory conference for this volume at American University in Washington, D.C. Many of the most ultraliberal economists and political leaders today are in and of the Third World, and the processes I am seeking to describe have their most profound social impact in Third World societies. Moreover, it is clear that neoliberal and authoritarian political leaders in many Third World countries oppose attempts by some Western governments to add environmental and labor standards to trade agreements. The standard response of these ultraliberals is that better global labor and environmental standards are really only disguised forms of protectionism by wealthy nations, with the intention of undermining Third World countries' comparative advantage in cheap labor and "tolerance" for pollution.

6. Washington is also, of course, the headquarters of the world's largest and most comprehensive military-security apparatus, from where the global activities of the Pentagon, the National Security Agency, and the CIA are planned and coordinated. The intelligence and planning agencies benefit from a worldwide network of military and intelligence bases and an exotic array of electronic eavesdropping and surveillance capabilities. These installations allow for not only a unique U.S. monitoring capacity but also foreign platforms for rapid deployment forces and military intervention. What this also reminds us is that even though there has been an official declaration of the end of the Cold War, much of the infrastructure and institutional arrangements associated with the postwar era persist. At the same time, the United States has become the unchallenged military superpower, as the post-Soviet military apparatuses have fallen into decay and disarray. The U.S. leadership recognized this change at the time of the Gulf War, which Secretary of State James Baker called the first post–Cold War international conflict involving the United States.

7. In 1993 the death rate in Russia jumped 20 percent, "according to official figures which have largely been kept hidden from public debate." The average age of male mortality has sunk to 59, "far below the average in the industrialised world and the lowest in Russia since the early 1960s," caused principally by a rapid increase in "killings, suicides and conflicts." This has coincided with a sharp

increase in infant mortality from 17.4 per 1,000 in 1990 to 19.1 per 1,000 in 1993. The report was produced by the Institute for Socio-Economic Studies of the Population, whose director attributed the developments to a "psycho-social crisis" in which "greatly rising insecurity . . . worry about crime, hardship and change" have caused the massive drop in the Russian population. All quotations are from J. Lloyd, "Russia Faces Population Crisis as Death Rate Soars," *Financial Times,* 14 February 1994.

11

How Does Globalization Really Work?

In the idiom of popular opinion, globalization means that instantaneous telecommunications and modern transportation overcome the barriers between states and increase the range of interaction across international limits. The cliché is that people are exposed to the same global media and consumer products, that such flows are making borders less relevant, and that with footloose capital leapfrogging from one locale to another, employment patterns are changing rapidly, drawing vast numbers of immigrants from one country to another.

This image is accurate but only as far as it goes. What is wanting are explanations for the way globalization really works and the directions in which it is headed. In this volume, the authors, especially Gary Gereffi and Saskia Sassen, reveal the modalities by which, since the 1960s, technological breakthroughs have accelerated global transfers of capital, labor, information, and knowledge. More than merely spreading or internationalizing, these shifts constitute an integration of economic activities. There exist a vastly increased mobility of capital, a changing hierarchy among national units, and the emergence of major regional actors—most notably the Asia Pacific zone, the European Union, and the North American Free Trade Agreement (NAFTA) countries—as varied sources of political strength and economic vitality. No longer is the world organized into a set of discrete sovereign states exercising a large (though never complete) degree of control over their domestic economies. Globalizing patterns add new complexity to what is quaintly called international relations; they transcend, blur, and even redefine territorial boundaries.

Yet the compression of time and space is limited because flows of capital and technology must eventually touch down in distinct places. Globalizing trends combined with national initiatives and informal networks have made new locations such as a handful of world cities (New York, London, Tokyo, etc.) and newly industrializing countries important nodes in the global political economy. Some of these locales are subject to a push toward democratization, which is partly an attempt to wrest control of the unaccountable forces of economic globalization. Also, there have been different responses to globalization—ranging from uncontested accommodation and strategies for managing its currents to outright resistance, often in the form of the invention and assertion of particularistic identities. States, international organizations, corporations, and social forces are all trying to take back control and convert the formidable challenges of globalization into unparalleled opportunities.

To probe the dilemmas presented by the new correlation of challenges and opportunities, I will first examine meanings and usages of the concept of globalization, exposing myths about it along the way. The next section explores key determinants and the processes that globalization comprises. Finally, I will turn to the pressure points inherent in globalization and the implications in terms of cooperation and conflict. The discussion of these strains builds on Polanyi's foundational analysis (1957b) of a "double movement"—a thrust of market forces followed by reactions to it in the form of demands for self-protection within domestic society—but pushes this framework to lay out a third phase of responses to changing global structures.

MEANINGS AND MYTHS

Both an objective and subjective phenomenon, globalization may be viewed from three observation points, each of which provides diverse shadings of the total picture. By no means an entirely novel process, globalization may be regarded as a phase in the history of capital, whose lineage has brought together many different societies into one system. Long-distance trade and the emergence of nation-states were important conditions for the development of this single configuration. A feature of the Westphalian interstate system has been the rise and decline of various hegemonic orders, the last one being the Pax Americana from the end of World War II to the early 1970s, marked by the breakdown of the Bretton Woods system. Although its institutions continue to be operative and play a major role concerning Third World debt, the abandonment of gold parity and fixed exchange rates allowed for changes in the international monetary order. With the weakening of the U.S. position in the world economy, Europe and Japan could challenge the hegemon's role (Cox 1987: 224). Inasmuch as military power cannot be infinitely sustained by external creditors, the United States, the largest debtor nation, lost a substantial measure of its strength. While the U.S. share of world output dropped from one-third in the 1950s and 1960s to one-fifth in the early 1990s (Bach 1993: 11–12), the U.S. domestic economy became increasingly enmeshed in international trade as well as host to foreign investment, heralding a new mode of global organization.

With the move toward a posthegemonic order, there emerged a series of structural changes in the global political economy, a period known as globalization. Understood historically, these shifts entail not only an intensification of previous patterns (e.g., from cross-national lending to the hypermobility of finance capital) but also a quantum transformation of a system lacking the staying power of effective means of regulation. In this sense, globalization constitutes a dialectic of continuities and discontinuities.

More than a set of historical benchmarks, globalization is also a movement of capital involving a deepening of commodified forms of political and social integration. But is this merely a continuation of "going multinational" and an extension of "global reach" (Barnet and Muller 1974), as it was called in past decades? One aspect of what is new is the sheer number of globalizing firms. In the richest fourteen countries over the last twenty-five years, the number of such companies has more than tripled, from seven thousand in 1969 to twenty-four thousand, according to the UN Conference on Trade and Development. Throughout the world, thirty-seven thousand transnational corporations generate sales of $5.5 trillion, and for countries such as the United States, revenues from manufacturing abroad far exceed their export earnings ("The Discreet Charm . . . " 1994: 65). It is not simply that more makes all the difference. Rather, as Sassen (Chapter 3) indicates, the centralizing tendencies of the most powerful corporations, lodged in select cities and equipped with the social and economic infrastructure to facilitate global control, are joined to a spatial dispersal of economic activity. In this sense, globalization comprises a particular constellation of economic concentrations and the denationalization of economic activities.

Another distinguishing feature of the current era of globalization is that production can be transferred overseas to drive out competitors, and its frequent spatial relocation reduces impediments to the free movement of people and ideas. To overcome the countervailing forces of nationalism and localism, globalization is inscribed with an ideology to promote neoliberalism. As both Cox (Chapter 2) and Gill (Chapter 10) observe, globalization is encoded with the values of economic liberalism—the inevitability of progress and ultimately a market utopia. It is a utopia in the sense of portraying ideal conditions that have never existed, certainly not without state intervention in the economy. As an ideology extolling the efficiency of free markets, globalization offers the prospect of an open world economy in which actors compete in a positive-sum game, wherein all players are supposed to be able to win. Panitch (Chapter 5) notes that this model of competitiveness ultimately asks how an appropriate corporate strategy can be crafted to maximize profits and market share to meet the requirements of globalization—the métier of such business gurus as Ohmae (1990) and Porter (1990).

All ideologies involve myths to justify a social and political order as well as to form consensus and thereby lessen the use of coercion. If so, and before delving into the inner workings of globalization itself, it is important to slay three dragons whose breath clouds its underlying dynamics.

One myth about globalization is that it embodies a teleology, or a pre-determined logic with an imputed final state of affairs—a global village, a worldwide economy, a world government, and so on. On the contrary, even if globalization involves a set of deep historical structures, and since history has no end, its course must be resolved through the intervention of human agency. It is a mistake to rigidify the structures of globalization and transform them into a form of structuralism, which banishes agency and severs historical moorings.

A closely related trap is to reify globalization as an ineluctable trend, a juggernaut rolling into a new millennium. Indeed, if it is agreed that globalization is something more than a reflex, then one must ask, who are the authors of this action? Joining structure and agency in a compelling manner, Cox offers a multilevel, historical perspective; Panitch stresses the state; Sassen emphasizes nonstate forces submerged in the economy; Adler, Nash and Kovic, Cheru, and Pasha and Samatar all focus on the disembeddedness of the economy from society and explore the role of social movements trying to write their own histories—labor unions seeking to reinvent their position vis-à-vis globalization, peasants organizing around subsistence, and resurgent Islamic forces attempting to maintain an ethical existence in the context of, or in opposition to, neoliberal globalization.

In light of these disparate tendencies, the conventional notion of globalization as an advancing force bulldozing the world around it is clearly at odds with the multiplicity of forms encountered or engendered in diverse contexts. Confusion occurs when one overlooks the way that the centralizing elements of globalization fuse with distinctive local and regional conditions, graphically portrayed in the fine-grained analysis in some of the preceding chapters. These conditions are brought into sharp relief in Nash's and Kovic's downstairs-upstairs, anthropological view from Chiapas, where peasants have confronted the rupture caused by globalization in a dual form—the state's privatizing reforms and NAFTA, whose stated goals incorporate the thrust of the global neoliberal project—only to mobilize and demand self-protection from its shattering effects.

In rural Mexico, the sense of growing social divisions and the rigid political hierarchy are perhaps no less relaxed than during Aztec times, unemployment is soaring to new heights, private enterprise has supplanted state structures, and whole communities have been depopulated as refugees head north to look for jobs in towns or lives across the border. As expressed in the voices and action of the Zapatistas, who perceive themselves as principal victims of neoliberal reforms, the enduring and unresolved issue is whether the underside of globalization will contribute to its transformation. Self-perceptions aside, their protest not only poses the long-range question of whether globalization is indefinitely sustainable but also is freighted with more immediate implications about changing global structures.

GLOBALIZING STRUCTURES

With globalization, new relationships among social strata are forming, manifest in stark differences between those who have moved onto the fast track and the laggards in liberal-economic restructuring, especially an entrenched underclass. The widening of social and economic disparities is apparent both within countries and between them. Though riven by an upsurge in poverty and unemployment in private sectors that cannot expand rapidly enough to absorb workers laid off by defunct or rump state industries, relatively few entrepreneurs within three countries of the former Warsaw Pact (Poland, Hungary, and the Czech Republic) show signs of affluence, whereas new opportunities in countries like Romania, Bulgaria, and Slovakia are hard to find. As numerous journalistic accounts document, despite a patina of neoliberal globalization (private retail stores, mass privatization plans, export promotion schemes, etc.), fledgling market economies have encountered resistance from entrenched strata and the *nomenklatura,* who do not merely impede their rivals but profitably use their access to what had been state capital to enter the market.

A large part of the debate concerns the role of the state in the globalization process. While the policy discourse concerns primarily who will guide the state and what size it should be, the more basic question asks whether the state is sidelined in the globalization trend. Notwithstanding their markedly different interpretations, the authors contributing to this volume generally agree that in the face of a growing concentration of unaccountable economic power at the world level, regulatory frameworks are still, if only partly, able to control global flows, and the state is engaged in internal restructuring, realigning the scope of and hierarchy among economic ministries, enhancing outward-oriented agencies whose portfolio is finance or trade, and diminishing welfare activities. But this proposition begs the question: is the state now a suboptimal unit for coping with the challenges of globalization? The elegantly argued debate in the preceding chapters probes whether the state is an interested observer, an active facilitator, or a motor force in the globalization process. Quite clearly, irrespective of its role as carrier or propellant of globalization, the state is adopting policies to adjust to and manage the process in diverse ways.

To globalize more, the state in Asia, for example, abets the process of labor migration. In labor-sending countries such as the Philippines, Sri Lanka, Pakistan, Bangladesh, and Indonesia, the state promotes the outmigration of able-bodied and productive nationals. The old-fashioned exercise of national development planning, based on the assumption that states are autonomous and that leaders can really determine their destinies, has, for all practical purposes, been abandoned and replaced by globalization projects. These include the types of alternative industrial and technological strategies mapped in Gereffi's penetrating chapter, as well as the growth triangles discussed in Chapter 1.

The loss of control is evident in various countries but, as Cheru shows, is most pronounced in parts of Africa where international financial institutions and international nongovernmental organizations substitute for the state in certain activities. Diminishing control, however, is not a unique feature of donor-driven development or underdevelopment, for even in the most advanced countries the politics of disillusionment is rife and reflects the brute fact that many global trends are beyond the purview of citizens and elected officials. Strikingly in the United States, voter turnout is well below the rates of participation in other Western countries. Polls show that when opposition candidates are elected to office, the public does not expect meaningful change. There appears to be a sense, a sophisticated understanding among the citizenry, that electoral politics cannot provide an antidote to the problems of globalization.

Global restructuring also involves a changing hierarchy among states. While finance has established a quasi-autonomous structure, substantially free of state regulation, the projection of power by large corporations shapes a global trading system and partially defines the division of labor at a global level. Not only is there rivalry among great powers, but as evidenced in the chapters on labor unions (Adler) and peasants who organize around both human rights and subsistence (Cheru; Nash and Kovic), there is sharp polarization between the rich and the poor. For the rich, international interests are coordinated by an oligarchy (the Group of Seven plus Russia on political but not economic issues); the poor no longer effectively espouse their aspirations through the Group of 77, seemingly a throwback to another era of North-South relations. Challenged by the dialectic of the force of globalization and the counterforce of opposition to its deleterious effects, citizens in diverse locales have sought to reconstitute civil societies, which may be analyzed through different modes of inquiry.

Methodologically, it is evident that there is tension between the upstairs-downstairs approach of observers such as Cox, Gill, and myself and that of others, especially Adler and Nash and Kovic, who study the balance of social forces on the ground and movements at the base as a means to grasp the big picture. Although it would be wrong to present a dichotomy between top-down and bottom-up perspectives, or between macro- and microlevels of analysis, one cannot simply posit that in work on globalization there is room for views from both above and below. Rather, the task is to determine how various aspects of globalization merge and interpenetrate under concrete and varied conditions. One way to do so is to examine a series of interactions that constitute the globalization process.

In the matrix of structural changes known as globalization, three linkages serve as important dimensions (illustrated in the discussion that follows), though others could also qualify. Whereas these three relationships are particularly closely interrelated, other tendencies are arguably more tenuous. There is a dearth of scholarly research on all of these parameters, understood not as discrete phenomena but as key aspects of globalization.

Elsewhere I have explored the global restructuring of production and migration, a crucial piece of the globalization mosaic (Mittelman 1994a). Although the extensive movement of peoples from their homelands to other areas of work and settlement has been an enduring feature of world history, the patterns and scope of migration have changed dramatically both in magnitude and direction. From fifty million immigrants in 1989, the world total doubled to one hundred million in 1992, the latter figure constituting two percent of the world's population (UN Population Fund 1993: 7). The global restructuring of production (explicated in Chapters 1, 3, and 4) has accentuated differences between receiving and sending countries, drawing massive imports of labor to the advanced capitalist countries. The transfers of population are primarily from the South to the North, although movements within each of these areas are significant. Migratory flows from the South are increasingly diverse, for they include new birds of passage, such as members of North Africa's middle strata fearing Islamic resurgence and environmental refugees propelled by natural disasters. Meanwhile, the global restructuring of power has brought an influx of migrants from Eastern Europe and the former Soviet Union to Western Europe, North America, Israel, Australia, and elsewhere. Competition between immigrants from the South and the East reflects the interrelationship of the restructuring of global production and global power relations.

Representing a vital globalizing tendency, the changes in migration patterns are not merely matters of individual choice but rather reveal structural factors beyond the control of individuals. The displacement of labor and the distribution of the world's refugees are best understood as a movement that both shapes and is constitutive of globalization. With increased competitiveness and the spatial reorganization of production, hypermobile capital seeks out receptive locales in the global economy, and labor follows the flow of capital. But there is more to the globalized production-migration link than analyzing the growth poles of competitive participation in the global division of labor. Although there are many types of voluntary and involuntary migrants (political refugees and asylum seekers, environmental refugees, professionals, legal workers, undocumented workers, etc.), the lines of demarcation are increasingly blurred. The proximate causes of migration are often combined—civil unrest, ethnic and racial strife, and economic conflicts accompanied by marked inequality. Further, the distinction between political and economic refugees, used by receiving countries as a screening mechanism, obscures the fact that both categories of migrants have as their origin the same globalizing of production relations.

In this radically altered environment, a global economy that has become freer spurs greater trade but often in harmful substances with little regulation. It seems that with new transitions in Eastern Europe and the Third World, there would be an opportunity to recover from the bureaucratic sclerosis of previous regimes by building railroads and fewer highways, licensing products that could be recycled, and legalizing only the chemicals that are safe. Accompanying the expansion of market economies in Eastern Europe, however, are a reduction in public transportation, the rush for the automobile along with its emissions, and heightened levels of pollution.

Globally, as barriers fall, ecological problems become more challenging. Newly porous borders have helped to create a world trading market in environmental waste. For entrepreneurs in waste, the opening of Eastern European markets and the growth of Asian economies offer new opportunities for disposal and processing in host countries. Closely related to soaring manufacturing in Asia and Latin America is the development of the global waste management market—worth more than $90 billion, about half the value of world trade in metals and ores (according to the Ecofin Ltd. consulting firm and reported in the *Washington Post,* "Free Market Intensifies Waste Problem," March 23, 1994).

Although the West is still the biggest polluter, the newly industrializing countries are gaining rapidly. With the cost of disposal mounting in the West, particularly with concern about hospital products and contaminated blood, traders have tendered lucrative contracts to such places as Croatia, Albania, the Philippines, and sub-Saharan Africa to build incinerators. Hence, some states and cities in the United States now send as much as two-thirds of the plastic collected from recyclers to Asia, where soda bottles and milk jugs are sorted by low-wage laborers, melted, reused, and burned or buried, often in violation of local law. When Asia's and Latin America's rising classes press the state for an effective international system of waste management and more stringent standards over low-technology and high-waste-producing companies, which frequently dump in the nearest river or sea, they encounter difficult trade-offs between economic growth, which still eludes a large portion of the population, and the environment. While the revenue and jobs from the international movement of the waste industry present a vista of opportunity, they also contradict efforts at environmental cleanup in receiving countries.

As markets expand, and with the fall of socialist regimes, a new echelon of crime bosses, often in collusion with government officials, is developing. The extension of the information economy makes protecting intellectual property more challenging, as evident in China, projected to be the world's largest market by 2010. Piracy of CDs, laser discs, books, and computer software spurs the export of black market products back to the United States and Canada, the loss of many thousands of jobs in the West, and conflict between the governments concerned over the issue of the enforcement of Western copyright in a country where the basic protection of intellectual property does not exist. Elsewhere in the postcommunist world, pro-democracy groups in Russia voice concern about opposition from an alliance of the Mafia and entrenched politicians, profitably engaged in activities such as privatization, military conversion, currency reserves, natural resource use, and the weapons industry.

Meanwhile, a major aspect of globalization is drug trafficking, which accounts for about one-half of the revenue from international organized crime. But transnational criminal groups are also heavily involved in car theft, trade in nuclear materials, smuggling of migrants, arms deals, money laundering, and sales of human organs. The UN estimates that major crime syndicates have combined annual sales of $750 billion, aided by the use of modern management, strategic transnational alliances, computer technology, and investment in research and technology (National Public Radio 1994). Global crime fighters have sought to strangle criminal groups' financial networks, but with other trends such as those noted above (e.g., the semiautonomy of finance and the hypermobility of capital), there are many escape hatches and safe havens for funds. While the interstate system seeks new means of coordination and cooperation, distrust among rival actors, variations in criminal codes, and insistence on protecting national sovereignty are obstacles to fighting the globalization of organized crime.

PRESSURE POINTS AND RESPONSES

To a very large extent, then, globalization is about opportunities arising from reorganizing governance, the economy, and culture throughout the world. As we have seen, the pressures of globalization threaten, but do not dissolve, the Westphalian interstate system, opening up possibilities for more vigorous political participation at nonstate levels. The globalization process can liberate people (say, women drawn out from seclusion in the home and into the industrial workforce) as well as displace the constraining albeit solidary values in their lives. The types of technological patterns mapped by Gereffi can release people from arduous, repetitive jobs and present opportunities for new paths of career advancement and cultural discovery.

At the same time, globalization is about challenges that emerge from the loss of control over economic and technological flows that circumvent the globe and easily escape regulatory frameworks. There is not only a reconstitution of the role and purpose of the state but also, to varied degrees and in different forms, a revitalization of the independent organs of civil society. In the face of contestation over redefining the myriad institutions that constitutionalize the international system and attempt to manage the global economy at the world and regional levels (e.g., the UN, Group of Seven, World Bank, etc.), new centers and subcenters of control have appeared through the globalization process. As Sassen argues, global governance is every bit a matter of agglomeration in select places (some of them nonstate institutions), resulting from concentrations of infrastructure and the properties of new technologies, as it is a challenge of refurbishing state or interstate forms of authority.

In this sense, globalization is about trying to resolve a number of problems or, one might say, the conflict between different logics operative at the turn of the millennium. This contest of logics constitutes the two major pressure points, or contradictions, within the globalization process.

First, and to repeat a crucial point, a new logic of agglomeration suggests an expansion of centralizing activities in territorially dispersed locales (Chapter 3). A globalizing economy increasingly free of territorial bounds coexists with a territorial mode of political organization, a system of governance inaugurated in the seventeenth century. What drives many policy debates is the fundamental asymmetry between a horizontal system of economic relations, speeded by state-of-the-art technologies that elude regulatory regimes, and the Westphalian framework of vertical units, or nation-states. The economic and political axes of globalization turn unevenly, for there are fundamental differences between the components of this vehicle and the ones used as its accessories and spare parts. (Efforts to rewrite this script are documented in the chapters on Africa, Mexico, and Islam.)

Second, against this backdrop, pressures are mounting for increased democratization at the national level. Those seeking to effect democratic transitions regard civic power as a means to limit state power, curbing abuses and corruption and ensuring accountability. Yet global concentrations of economic power are remote and difficult to rein in, whether by domestic society or by constellations of entities that claim to be sovereign. Matters of appearance aside, the structures of central forces are proving impervious to the challenge of democratization, a chasm regarded by some as evidence of the need for institutional mending and by others as unbridgeable.

These dilemmas are greeted by four types of reactions. One response is an uncontested acceptance of globalization. In some cases, the most vulnerable actors — say, very poor states, notwithstanding their rhetorical flourishes — have adopted a policy of blanket acquiescence on the ground that there is no alternative. In fact, some impoverished countries first tried to renegotiate their positions in the global division of labor and were rebuffed. Mozambique, for example, was severely disciplined by a complex of internal opponents, apartheid South Africa's destabilization campaign, pressure from the United States against the liberation movement, and the conditions of structural adjustment required by international monetary institutions (see Mittelman 1991).

Many other developing countries, including ones not subject to structural adjustment programs, have gladly embraced liberal-economic globalization, seeking to navigate its currents and ride the crests to national advantage. Singapore's experience, for instance, buttresses Panitch's thesis that the state is not only a facilitator of globalization but also an author of this process. Having rejected the antiquated exercise of national development planning, Singapore officials now formulate what they call a "globalization plan," coordinating activities in industry, science and technology, finance, communications and transportation, and so on. Following suit, in 1995 President Kim Young Sam announced that Korea would adopt a policy of globalization. He immediately reorganized the cabinet to achieve his globalization aims, giving greater emphasis to sharpening the competitive edge of the economy, encouraging ministers to improve their English, and attempting to translate the credo of his policy pronouncements into concrete actions. As in Singapore and South Korea, the statist response is to fashion a favorable accommodation with the global market under the umbrella of an ideology of competitiveness.

In light of the challenges to sovereignty posed by cross-border flows, states may of course pool their efforts and offer a multilateral reply to globalization. In this regard, the UN is a defense against globalization inasmuch as it enshrines the principle of sovereignty. However imperfectly, it constitutionalizes, harmonizes, and stabilizes the international system. The UN also reflects the notion that a world of states is desirable and that its affiliates, international financial institutions, are charged with the task of managing the global market. Proposals for institutional reform have as their purpose the smooth execution of the neoliberal project.

Third, corporate responses to globalization may go hand in hand with state initiatives. As complex organizations, businesses react by attempting to define their niche, shift to new production methods, upgrade their technologies, and create competitive advantage. There is no lack of discussion of business strategies, and some of them have, by the firms' own criteria, succeeded brilliantly, turning adversity into advantage, as the following vignettes illustrate.

Despite India's grinding poverty, poor communications, and inferior transportation system, some of its firms have drawn on a low wage scale, highly skilled workforce, specialized universities in science and technology, and English-speaking population to become major exporters of computer software products. The country is now home to its own Silicon Valley, about five hundred miles south of Bombay and centered in Bangladore, where more than one hundred software companies and hardware industries produce state-of-the-art work. Today, only the United States and perhaps Russia employ more software engineers than does India.

Further, industries in Zimbabwe have optimized their conditions—a climatic advantage, low labor costs, and freedom from state marketing controls in some sectors—to specialize in horticulture. Varieties of flowers grown nowhere else in the southern hemisphere are bred in Israel, cultivated within ten minutes of an airport in Zimbabwe, and sold directly to supermarkets in Europe or via Dutch auctions to countries such as Canada and Japan.

Fearing the power of the antismoking lobby in the West, white farmers decided to diversify from tobacco. They also faced the prospects of a government-mandated redistribution of white farmland to satisfy land hunger among black Zimbabweans, the major cause of the war of independence. Flower production has enabled white farmers to use small areas of land intensively and profitably. Expectations for high returns are linked to the projection that the Western European market for cut flowers will grow from $12.5 billion in 1990 to more than $19 billion at the turn of the century ("Zimbabwe's Flower Exports . . ." 1994).

While the stress points in globalization present new opportunities, they also prompt a willingness to question and challenge the logic of the current restructuring. Far from riding the high tides of globalization, the fourth response is to contest this process. Indeed, it is worth underlining Gill's (Chapter 10) point: must collectivities accept the remarkable idea that human potential and worth are defined primarily through the processes of consumption? Must large zones of humanity on the underside of globalization merely accept the consequences of market outcomes as the answer to their aspirations, or is there a way to appeal? As Cheru (Chapter 7) indicates, the poor in Africa register their protest against globalizing forces by exclaiming, "Please don't develop us!" But what are the alternatives for those who seek to protect themselves from a system not of their own choosing?

The right proposes fascism or hypernationalism, which are forms of identity-based politics rooted in civil society. Under present conditions, these are vestiges or variants of a type of nationalism from bygone decades, vehicles for protest against systemic injustice, as, for example, unfavorable international conjunctures and anticolonial struggles. Today's identities have become politicized in a way that balks at external processes and attempts to reconnect an idealized past with the vagaries of an uncertain present containing a mix of democratic and undemocratic tendencies. Other movements (e.g., "social unionism" in South Africa and peasant organizations in Mexico) have participated in promoting autonomous and strong civil societies. In response to the costs of globalization (notably, a sense of estrangement from society, including the old nationalist rhetoric and political leaders who appear to be relics of another era), resurgent Islamic movements project a vision of modernity that fuses an ethical dimension for establishing an alternative world order with a struggle for empowerment. These varied groups aim to construct an identity denied to them in a globalizing world.

The first three responses seek to accommodate globalization, whereas the fourth, mounting countermovements, highlights its chaos, questions whether it can be sustained, posits the malleability of this set of structures, and raises the prospect of its eventual downfall. Put differently, there is a clash emerging between two models: neoliberal globalization, which at present is the dominant force, and democratic globalization, a far less coherent counterforce. But these scenarios are not the only possibilities, for what if globalization doesn't really work?

Bibliography

Aboulmagd, A. Kamal. 1992. "Islam in the Postcommunist World." *Problems of Communism* 41 (January–April): 38–43.

Abu-Lughod, Janet Lippman. 1995. "Comparing Chicago, New York and Los Angeles: Testing Some World Cities Hypotheses." In Paul L. Knox and Peter J. Taylor (eds.), *World Cities in a World-System*, 171–191. Cambridge: Cambridge University Press.

Addleton, Jonathan S. 1992. *Undermining the Centre: The Gulf Migration and Pakistan*. Karachi: Oxford University Press.

Adelzadeh, Asghar and Vishnu Padayachee. 1994. "The RDP White Paper: Reconstruction of a Development Vision." *Transformation* 25.

Adler, Glenn. 1989. "Withdrawal Pains: General Motors and Ford Disinvest from South Africa." In Glenn Moss and Ingrid Obery (eds.), *South African Review 5*. Johannesburg: Ravan Press.

———. 1990. "African Workers Say 'Disinvest—On Our Terms.'" *Z Magazine* 3 (2).

———. 1994. "'The Factory Belongs to All Who Work in It': Race, Class, and Collective Action in the South African Motor Industry, 1967–1986." Ph.D. diss., Columbia University.

Adler, Glenn, and Eddie Webster. 1995. "Challenging Transition Theory: The Labor Movement, Radical Reform, and the Transition to Democracy in South Africa." *Politics and Society* 23: 1.

"After Stall, Koreans See Need for Economic Reform, Too." 1992. *New York Times*, 15 December.

Ake, Claude. 1988. "Building on the Indigenous." In Swedish Ministry for Foreign Affairs, *Recovery in Africa: A Challenge for Development Cooperation in the 1990s*, 19–23. Stockholm: Swedish Ministry for Foreign Affairs.

Aksen, Gerald. 1990. "Arbitration and Other Means of Dispute Settlement." In D. Goldsweig and R. Cummings (eds.), *International Joint Ventures: A Practical Approach to Working with Foreign Investors in the U.S. and Abroad*. Chicago: American Bar Association.

Albert, Michel. 1994. *Capitalism vs. Capitalism*. New York: Four Walls Eight Windows.

Albo, Greg. 1994. "'Competitive Austerity' and the Impasse of Capitalist Employment Policy." In R. Miliband and I. Panitch (eds.), *Between Globalism and Nationalism: The Socialist Register 1994*. London: Merlin Press; New York: Monthly Review.

Ali, Tariq. 1993. *Shadows of the Pomegranate Tree*. London: Verso.

Aman, Alfred C., Jr. 1995. "A Global Perspective on Current Regulatory Reform: Rejection, Relocation, or Reinvention?" *Indiana Journal of Global Legal Studies* 2: 429–464.

Amin, A. and N. Thrift. 1992. "Neo-Marshallian Nodes in Global Networks." *International Journal of Urban and Regional Research* 16 (4): 571–587.

Amin, Samir. 1989. *Eurocentrism*. Translated by Russell Moore. New York: Monthly Review Press.

Amsden, Alice H. 1989. *Asia's Next Giant: South Korea and Late Industrialization*. New York: Oxford University Press.

———. 1990. "Third World Industrialization: 'Global Fordism' or a New Model?" *New Left Review* 182 (July/August): 5–31.

Andrew Levy and Associates. 1993. *Annual Report*. Johannesburg.

Armstrong, Philip, Andrew Glyn, and John Harrison. 1991. *Capitalism Since 1945*. Oxford: Basil Blackwell.

Armstrong, W. and T. G. McGee. 1985. *Theatres of Accumulation: Studies in Latin American and Asian Urbanisation*. London: Methuen.

Arrighi, Giovanni and Jessica Drangel. 1986. "The Stratification of the World-Economy: An Exploration of the Semiperipheral Zone." *Review* 10 (1): 9–74.

Atik, Jeffrey. 1992. "Investment Contests and Subsidy Limitations in the EC." *Journal of International Law* 32: 837.

Ayubi, Nazih N. M. 1982–1983. "The Politics of Militant Islamic Movements in the Middle East." *Journal of International Affairs* 36 (Fall–Winter): 271–283.

Bach, Robert L. 1993. *Changing Relations: Newcomers and Established Residents in U.S. Communities: A Report to the Ford Foundation by the National Board of the Changing Relations Project*. New York: Ford Foundation.

Barnet, Richard and John Cavanagh. 1994. *Global Dreams: Imperial Corporations and the New World Order*. New York: Simon and Schuster.

Barnet, Richard J. and Ronald E. Muller. 1974. *Global Reach: The Power of the Multinational Corporations*. New York: Simon and Schuster.

Barraclough, Solon. 1991. *An End to Hunger: The Social Origins of Food Strategies*. London: Zed Press.

Baskin, Jeremy. 1991. *Striking Back: A History of COSATU*. Johannesburg: Ravan Press.

Bates, Robert. 1981. *Markets and States in Tropical Africa*. Berkeley: University of California.

Becker, David G. 1983. *The New Bourgeoisie and the Limits of Dependency: Mining, Class, and Power in "Revolutionary" Peru*. Princeton: Princeton University Press.

Beckman, Bjorn. 1992. "Empowerment or Repression? The World Bank and the Politics of African Adjustment." In Peter Gibbon, Yusuf Bangura, and Are Ofstad (eds.), *Authoritarianism, Democracy and Adjustment*, 83–105. Seminar Proceedings No. 26. Uppsala: The Scandinavian Institute of African Studies.

Beneria, Lourdes. 1989. "The Mexican Debt Crisis: Restructuring the Economy and the Household." Paper presented at the workshop "Labor Market Policies and Structural Adjustment," 29 November–1 December. Geneva, International Labor Organization.

Bentham, Jeremy. 1859. *The Works of Jeremy Bentham*. Published under the superintendence of his executor, John Bowring. Edinburgh: William Tait.

Berger, Peter L. and Hsin-Huang Michael Hsiao (eds.). 1988. *In Search of an East Asian Development Model*. New Brunswick, N.J.: Transaction Books.

Bergquist, Charles. 1986. *Labor in Latin America: Comparative Essays on Chile, Argentina, Venezuela, and Colombia*. Stanford: Stanford University Press.

Bergquist, Charles (ed.). 1984. *Labor in the Capitalist World-Economy*. Beverly Hills: Sage.

Bergson, Henri. 1889. *Essai sur les donnés immédiates de la conscience*.

Berry, Sara. 1994. *No Condition Is Permanent.* Madison: University of Wisconsin Press.

Birnie, Patricia W. and Alan E. Boyle. 1992. *International Law and Environment.* Oxford: Clarendon Press.

Bose, Christine E. and Edna Acosta-Belen (eds.). 1995. *Women in the Latin American Development Process.* Philadelphia: Temple University Press.

Boyd, Rosalind, Robin Cohen, and Peter C. W. Gutkind. 1987. *International Labour and the Third World: The Making of a New Working Class.* Aldershot: Averbury.

Bradford, Colin I., Jr. 1990. "Policy Interventions and Markets: Development Strategy Typologies and Policy Options." In Gary Gereffi and Donald L. Wyman (eds.), *Manufacturing Miracles: Paths of Industrialization in Latin America and East Asia,* 32–51. Princeton: Princeton University Press.

Bonacich, Edna, Lucie Cheng, Norma Chinchilla, Nora Hamilton, and Paul Ong (eds.). 1994. *Global Production: The Apparel Industry in the Pacific Rim.* Philadelphia: Temple University.

Braudel, Fernand. 1980a. *On History.* Translated by Sarah Matthews. Chicago: University of Chicago Press.

———. 1980b. "Unity and Diversity in the Human Sciences." In Fernand Braudel (ed.), *On History,* 55–63. Translated by Sarah Matthews. Chicago: University of Chicago Press.

———. 1981 [1979]. *The Structures of Everyday Life: the Limits of the Possible.* Vol. 1 of *Civilisation and Capitalism, 15th–18th Centuries.* Translated by Siân Reynolds. New York: Harper and Row.

———. 1994. *A History of Civilization.* Translated by Richard Mayne. New York: Penguin Press.

Brotchie, John, Mike Batty, Ed Blakely, Peter Hall, and Peter Newton (eds.). 1995. *Cities in Competition: Productive and Sustainable Cities for the 21st Century.* Melbourne: Longman Australia.

Buhlungu, Sakhela. 1994a. "COSATU and the Elections." *South African Labour Bulletin* 18 (2).

———. 1994b. "The Big Brain Drain: Union Officials in the 1990s." *South African Labour Bulletin* 18 (3).

Bulliet, Richard W. 1993. "The Future of the Islamic Movement." *Foreign Affairs* 72 (November–December): 38–44.

Burnham, Peter. 1991. "Neo-Gramscian Hegemony and the International Order." *Capital and Class* 45 (Autumn): 73–93.

Cammack, Paul. 1989. "Review Article: Bringing the State Back In?" *British Journal of Political Science* 19: 261–290.

———. 1990. "Statism, New Institutionalism, and Marxism." In R. Miliband and L. Panitch (eds.), *The Retreat of the Intellectuals: The Socialist Register 1990.* London: Merlin.

Campbell, Bruce (with Andrew Jackson). 1993. *"Free Trade": Destroyer of Jobs. An Examination of Canadian Job Loss Under the FTA and NAFTA.* Ottawa: Canadian Centre for Policy Alternatives.

Carbonneau, Thomas (ed.). 1990. *Lex Mercatoria and Arbitration.* Dobbs Ferry, N.Y.: Transnational Juris Publications.

Cargill, Jenny. 1993. "Debating COSATU's Reconstruction Programme: Where Does the Buck Stop?" *South African Labour Bulletin* 17 (4).

Carrez, Jean-François. 1991. *Le developpement des fonctions tertiares internationales a Paris et dans les metropoles regionales.* Report to the Prime Minister. Paris: La Documentation Française.

Carroll, Terrance G. 1984. "Secularization and States of Modernity." *World Politics* 36 (April): 362–382.

Castells, Manuel. 1989. *The Informational City*. Oxford: Blackwell.

Center for Human Rights "Fray Bartolome de Las Casas." 1993, 1994. Informe Semestral, January–June and July–December. San Cristobal de Las Casas, Chiapas.

Chalmers, Ian. 1991. "International and Regional Integration: The Political Economy of the Electronics Industry in ASEAN." *ASEAN Economic Bulletin* 8 (2): 194–209.

Chandler, Alfred D. 1989. "Technological and Organizational Underpinnings of Modern Industrial Multinational Enterprise: The Dynamics of Comparative Advantage." In Alice Teichova, Maurice Levy-Leboyer, and Helga Nussbaum (eds.), *Multinational Enterprise in Historical Perspective*. Cambridge: Cambridge University Press.

Charny, David. 1991. "Competition Among Jurisdictions in Formulating Corporate Law Rules: An American Perspective on the 'Race to the Bottom' in the European Communities." *Harvard International Law Journal* 32: 30–54.

Chazan, Naomi and Donald Rothchild (eds.). 1988. *The Precarious Balance: State and Society in Africa*. Boulder: Westview Press.

Cheadle, Halton. 1987. "Recognition at the Workplace: The Formulation of Strategy." Unpublished seminar paper, Southern Africa Research Program, Yale University.

Chen, Xiangming. 1994. "The New Spatial Division of Labor and Commodity Chains in the Greater South China Economic Region." In Gary Gereffi and Miguel Korzeniewicz (eds.), *Commodity Chains and Global Capitalism*, 165–186. Westport, Conn.: Praeger.

Cheng, Lucie and Gary Gerefffi. 1994. "U.S. Retailers and Asian Garment Production." In Edna Bonacich, Lucie Cheng, Norma Chinchilla, Nora Hamilton, and Paul Ong (eds.), *Global Production: The Apparel Industry in the Pacific Rim*, 63–80. Philadelphia: Temple University Press.

Cheru, Fantu. 1989. *The Silent Revolution in Africa: Debt, Development and Democracy*. Harare and London: Zed/Anvil Press.

———. 1992a. *The Not So Brave New World: Problems and Prospects of Regional Integration in Post-Apartheid Southern Africa*. South African Institute of International Relations, Bradlow Series No. 8. Johannesburg: SAIIA.

———. 1992b. "Structural Adjustment, Primary Resource Trade, and Sustainable Development in Sub-Saharan Africa." *World Development* 20 (4).

Cheru, Fantu, and Stephen Gill. 1993. *Democratization and Globalization: The G–7 "Nexus" and the Limits of Structural Adjustment in Africa, Eastern Europe and Russia*. Unpublished mimeo.

Cheru, Fantu and Winston Mathu. 1989. *Integrated Land Use and Rural Development Project: Fedis Awraja, Ethiopia*. Baseline survey conducted for the UN Sudano-Sahelian Office. Addis Ababa.

Choueiri, Y. M. 1993. "Theoretical Paradigms of Islamic Movements." *Political Studies* 51 (March): 108–116.

Clarkson, Stephen. 1991. "Disjunctions: Free Trade and the Paradox of Canadian Economic Development." In D. Drache and M. S. Gertler (eds.), *The New Era of Global Competition*. Montreal and Kingston: McGill-Queen's University Press.

Cohen, Robin. 1987. *The New Helots: Migrants in the New International Division of Labour*. Brookfield: Gower.

Cohen, Stephen S. and John Zysman. 1987. *Manufacturing Matters: The Myth of the Post-Industrial Economy*. New York: Basic Books.

Collier, George A. 1994. "Basta! Land and the Zapatista Rebellion in Chiapas." Oakland: Food First.

Collier, George A., Daniel C. Mountjoy, and Ronald B. Nigh. 1994. "Peasant Agriculture and Global Change: Effects of Mexican Oil Production on Peasant Agriculture." *BioScience* 44(June): 398 et seq.

Competition and Change. 1995. *The Journal of Global Business and Political Economy* 1 (1).

Coombe, Rosemary J. 1993. "The Properties of Culture and the Politics of Possessing Identity: Native Claims in the Cultural Appropriation Controversy." *Canadian Journal of Law and Jurisprudence* 4 (2): 249–285.

Corbridge, S. and J. Agnew. 1991. "The U.S. Trade and Budget Deficit in Global Perspective: An Essay in Geopolitical Economy." *Environment and Planning D: Society and Space* 9: 71–90.

Correspondents for Singapore newspapers. 1991. Interviews with the author, 15 December. Singapore.

Corrigan, Philip and Derek Sayer. 1985. *The Great Arch: English State Formation as Cultural Revolution*. Oxford: Basil Blackwell.

"Costs May Be Too High for All-American Chips." 1992. *New York Times*, 1 January.

Coulson, Andrew (ed.). 1980. *African Socialism in Practice—The Tanzanian Experience*. London: Spokesman Books.

Cox, Robert W. 1986. "Social Forces, States and World Orders: Beyond International Relations Theory." In R. O. Keohane (ed.), *Neorealism and Its Critics*. New York: Columbia University Press,.

———. 1987. *Production, Power, and World Order: Social Forces in the Making of History*. New York: Columbia University Press.

———. 1992a. "Global Perestroika." In R. Miliband and L. Panitch (eds.), *New World Order? The Socialist Register 1992*, 26–43. London: Merlin.

———. 1992b. "Toward a Post-Hegemonic Conceptualization of World Order: Reflections on the Relevance of Ibn Khaldun." In James N. Rosenau and Ernst-Otto Czempiel (eds.), *Governance Without Government: Order and Change in World Politics*. Cambridge: Cambridge University Press.

———. 1993. "Structural Issues of Global Governance: Implications for Europe." In Stephen Gill (ed.), *Gramsci's Historical Materialism and International Relations*, 259–289. Cambridge: Cambridge University Press.

Cumings, Bruce. 1984. "The Origins and Development of the Northeast Asian Political Economy: Industrial Sectors, Product Cycles, and Political Consequences." *International Organization* 38 (1): 1–40.

Daly, M. T. and R. Stimson. 1992. "Sydney: Australia's Gateway and Financial Capital." Chap. 18. in E. Blakely and T. J. Stimpson (eds.), *New Cities of the Pacific Rim*. Berkeley: University of California Institute for Urban and Regional Development.

Daniels, Peter W. 1985. *Service Industries: A Geographical Appraisal*. London and New York: Methuen.

———. 1991. "Producer Services and the Development of the Space Economy." In Peter W. Daniels and Frank Moulaert (eds.), *The Changing Geography of Advanced Producer Services*. London and New York: Belhaven Press.

Davis, Mike. 1990. *City of Quartz*. New York: Vintage Books.

Le Débat. 1994. *Le Nouveau Paris*, Special Issue (Summer). Paris: Gallimard.

De Klerk, Mike. 1984. "Seasons That Will Never Return: The Impact of Farm Mechanization on Employment, Incomes, and Population Distribution." African Studies Institute seminar paper, University of the Witwatersrand.

De Villar, Samuel I. 1991. "En defensa de la propiedad constitucional." *La Jornada*, 30 November.

Deblock, Christian and Michéle Rioux. 1993. "NAFTA: The Dangers of Regionalism." *Studies in Political Economy* 41 (Summer): 7–44.

Delauney, Jean Claude and Jean Gadrey. 1987. *Les Enjeux de la Societé de Service*. Paris: Presses de la Fondation des Sciences Politiques.

Delius, Peter. 1993. "Sebatakgomo and the Zoutpansberg Balemi Association: The ANC, the Communist Party, and Rural Organisation, 1939–55." *Journal of African History* 34: 293–313.

Deverre, Christine. 1978. "Transformations et crises agraires au Mexique: Le cas des Chiapas." Notes du GEREI. Groupe d'Etude des Relations Economiques Internaciones, INRA No. 4: 2–78.

Deyo, Frederic C. 1987a. "State and Labor: Modes of Political Exclusion in East Asian Development." In Frederic C. Deyo (ed.), *The Political Economy of the New Asian Industrialism*. Ithaca: Cornell University Press.

———. 1989. *Beneath the Miracle: Labor Subordination in the New Asian Industrialism*. Berkeley: University of California Press.

Deyo, Frederic C. (ed.). 1987b. *The Political Economy of the New Asian Industrialism*. Ithaca: Cornell University Press.

Dezalay, Yves and Bryant Garth. 1995. "Merchants of Law as Moral Entrepreneurs: Constructing International Justice from the Competition for Transnational Business Disputes." *Law and Society Review* 29 (1): 27–64.

Dicken, Peter. 1992. *Global Shift: The Internationalization of Economic Activity*, 2d ed. New York: Guilford Press.

"The Discreet Charm of the Multicultural Multinational." 1994. *The Economist* (London), 30 July.

Dodson, Michael. 1980. "Prophetic Politics and Political Theory in Latin America." *Polity* 12 (Spring): 388–408.

Doner, Richard F. 1991. *Driving a Bargain: Automobile Industrialization and Japanese Firms in Southeast Asia*. Berkeley: University of California Press.

Donnelly, Jack. 1982. "Human Rights and Human Dignity: An Analytic Critique of Non-Western Conceptions of Human Rights." *American Political Science Review* 76 (June): 303–316.

Drache, D. and M. Gertler (eds.). 1991. *The New Era of Global Competition: State Policy and Market Power*. Montreal: McGill-Queen's University Press.

Drainville, Andre. 1991. *Monetarism in the World Economy*. Ph.D. diss., York University.

———. 1994. "International Political Economy in an Age of Open Marxism." *Review of International Political Economy*. vol. 1, no. 1: 105–136.

Drennan, Mathew P. 1989. "Information Intensive Industries in Metropolitan Areas of the United States." *Environment and Planning A* 21: 1603–1618.

———. 1992. "Gateway Cities: The Metropolitan Sources of US Producer Service Exports." *Urban Studies* 29 (2):. 217–235.

Dunn, Seamus (ed.). 1994. *Managing Divided Cities*. Staffs, UK: Keele University Press.

During, Alan. 1989. *Action at the Grassroots: Fighting Poverty and Environmental Decline*. Washington, D.C: Worldwatch Institute.

Durkheim, Émile. 1930. *The Division of Labor in Society*. Glencoe, Ill.: Free Press.

Eber, Christine and Brenda Rosenbaum. 1993. "That We May Serve Beneath Your Hands and Feet": Women Weavers in Highland Chiapas, Mexico." In J. Nash (ed.), *Crafts in the World Market: The Impact of Global Exchange on Middle American Artisans*, 155–180. Albany: SUNY Press.

Eco, Umberto. 1986. *Travels in Hyper Reality*. New York: Harcourt Brace.

Economic Development Board. December 1992. "Communications Hub of Asia: MNCs Building Up Network Bases in Singapore." *Singapore Investment News*.

Economic Commission for Latin America and the Caribbean (ECLAC). 1994a. *Policies to Improve Linkages with the Global Economy*. Santiago, Chile: ECLAC.

———. 1994b. *Open Regionalism in Latin America and the Caribbean*. Santiago, Chile: ECLAC.

Economist Intelligence Unit (EIU). 1993/1994. *Dominican Republic, Haiti, Puerto Rico: Country Profile*. London: EIU.

Eidelberg, Phil. 1993. "The Unions and the African National Congress." *South African Historical Journal* 28.

Ekins, Paul. 1992. *A New World Order: Grassroots Movements for Global Change*. London: Routledge.

Ellison, Christopher and Gary Gereffi. 1990. "Explaining Strategies and Patterns of Industrial Development." In Gary Gereffi and Donald L. Wyman (eds.), *Manufacturing Miracles: Paths of Industrialization in Latin America and East Asia*, 368–403. Princeton: Princeton University Press.

Enderwick, Peter. 1985. *Multinational Business & Labour*. London: Croom Helm.

Erickson, Kenneth P. 1977. *The Brazilian Corporative State and Working Class Politics*. Berkeley: University of California Press.

Etkind, Roger and Suzanna Harvey. 1993. "Debating COSATU's Reconstruction Programme: The Workers Cease Fire." *South African Labour Bulletin* 17(4).

Evans, Peter et al. (eds.). 1985. *Bringing the State Back In*. Cambridge: Cambridge University Press.

Fainstein, Susan. 1993. *The City Builders*. Oxford: Blackwell.

Fainstein, S., I. Gordon, and M. Harloe. 1993. *Divided Cities: Economic Restructuring and Social Change in London and New York*. Oxford: Blackwell.

Faksh, Mahmud A. 1983. "Theories of State in Islamic Political Thought." *Journal of South Asian and Middle Eastern Studies* 6 (Spring): 62–79.

Falk, Richard. 1992a. "Democratising, Internationalising and Globalising: A Collage of Blurred Images." *Third World Quarterly* 13 (4): 627–640.

———. 1992b. "The Making of Global Citizenship." In Jeremy Brecher et al. (eds.), *Global Visions: Beyond the New World Order*. Boston: South End Press.

Fallows, James. 1994. *Looking at the Sun: The Rise of the New East Asian Economic and Political System*. New York: Pantheon.

"Farmers' Boycott." 1993. *Daily Nation*. Nairobi, 20 February.

Fazlur Rahman. 1982. *Islam and Modernity: Transformation of an Intellectual Tradition*. Chicago: University of Chicago Press.

Feldman, Shelley and Lourdes Beneria (eds.). 1992. *Unequal Burden*. Boulder: Westview.

Fine, Alan and Eddie Webster. 1989. "Transcending Traditions: Trade Unions and Political Unity." In Glenn Moss and Ingrid Obery (eds.), *South African Review 5*. Johannesburg: Ravan Press.

Finlayson, Jock A. and Mark W. Zacher. 1983. "The GATT and the Regulation of Trade Barriers: Regime Dynamics and Functions." In Stephen D. Krasner (ed.), *International Regimes*, 273–314. Ithaca: Cornell University Press.

Fischer, Michael M. J. 1982. "Islam and the Revolt of the Petit Bourgeoisie." *Daedalus* 111 (Winter): 101–125.

Fishlow, Albert. 1985. "The State of Latin American Economics." In Inter-American Development Bank (ed.), *Economic and Social Progress in Latin America— External Debt: Crisis and Adjustment*, 123–148. Washington, D.C.: Inter-American Development Bank.

Frank, Andre Gunder. 1991. "No Escape from the Laws of World Economics." *Review of African Political Economy* 50: 20–31.

Frederic, Howard. 1992. "Computer Networks and the Emergence of Global Civil

Society." In Linda M. Harasim (ed.), *Global Networks: Computers and International Communication*. Pacific Grove, Calif.: Cole.

"Free Market Intensifies Waste Problem." 1994. Washington Post, 23 March.

Friedman, Murray. 1980. "Religion and Politics in an Age of Pluralism, 1945–1976: An Ethnocultural View." *Publius* 10 (Summer): 45–75.

Friedman, Steven. 1987. *Building Tomorrow Today: African Workers in Trade Unions, 1970–1984*. Johannesburg: Ravan Press.

Friedmann, John. 1986. "The World City Hypothesis." *Development and Change* 17: 69–84.

— — —. 1995. "Where We Stand: A Decade of World City Research." In Paul Knox and Peter Taylor (eds.), *World Cities in a World-System*, 21–47. Cambridge: Cambridge University Press.

Fröbel, Folker, Jürgen Heinrichs, and Otto Kreye. 1980. *The New International Division of Labour: Structural Unemployment in Industrialised Countries and Industrialisation in Developing Countries*. Translated by Pete Burgess. Cambridge: Cambridge University Press.

Frost, Martin and Nigel Spence. 1992. "Global City Characteristics and Central London's Employment." *Urban Studies* 30 (3): 547–558.

Fukuyama, Francis. 1992. *The End of History and the Last Man*. New York: Free Press.

Gad, Gunter. 1991. "Toronto's Financial District." *Canadian Urban Landscapes* 1: 203–207.

Galbraith, John Kenneth. 1992. *The Culture of Contentment*. Boston: Houghton Mifflin.

Galtung, John et al. (eds.). 1980. *Self-Reliance: A New Development Strategy?* London: Bogle-L'Ouverture.

Gandy, Oscar H., Jr. 1993. *The Panoptic Sort: A Political Economy of Personal Information*. Boulder: Westview Press.

Gereffi, Gary. 1990a. "Paths of Industrialization: An Overview." In Gary Gereffi and Donald L. Wyman (eds.), *Manufacturing Miracles: Paths of Industrialization in Latin America and East Asia*, 3–31. Princeton: Princeton University Press.

— — —. 1990b. "International Economics and Domestic Policies." In Alberto Martinelli and Neil J. Smelser (eds.), *Economy and Society: Overviews in Economic Sociology*, 231–258. Newbury Park: Sage.

— — —. 1993. "Global Sourcing and Regional Divisions of Labor in the Pacific Rim." In Arif Dirlik (ed.), *What Is in a Rim? Critical Perspectives on the Pacific Region Idea*, 51–68. Boulder: Westview Press.

— — — —. 1994. "The Organization of Buyer-Driven Global Commodity Chains: How U.S. Retailers Shape Overseas Production Networks." In Gary Gereffi and Miguel Korzeniewicz (eds.), *Commodity Chains and Global Capitalism*, 95–122. Westport, Conn.: Praeger.

— — —. 1995. "Global Production Systems and Third World Development." In Barbara Stallings (ed.), *Global Change, Regional Response: The New International Context of Development*, 100–142. New York: Cambridge University Press.

— — —. 1996. "Mexico's 'Old' and 'New' Maquiladora Industries: Contrasting Approaches to North American Integration." In Gerardo Otero (ed.), *Mexico's Future(s): Economic Restructuring and Politics*, 83–105. Boulder: Westview.

Gereffi, Gary and Miguel Korzeniewicz. 1990. "Commodity Chains and Footwear Exports in the Semiperiphery." In William Martin (ed.), *Semiperipheral States in the World-Economy*, 45–68. Westport, Conn.: Greenwood Press.

Gereffi, Gary, and Miguel Korzeniewicz (eds.). 1994. *Commodity Chains and Global Capitalism*. Westport, Conn.: Praeger.

Gereffi, Gary and Mei-Lin Pan. 1994. "The Globalization of Taiwan's Garment Industry." In Edna Bonacich, Lucie Cheng, Norma Chinchilla, Nora Hamilton, and Paul Ong (eds.), *Global Production: The Apparel Industry in the Pacific Rim*, 126–146. Philadelphia: Temple University Press.

Gereffi, Gary and Donald L. Wyman (eds.). 1990. *Manufacturing Miracles: Paths of Industrialization in Latin America and East Asia*. Princeton: Princeton University Press.

Gerth, H. H. and C. Wright Mills. 1946. *From Max Weber: Essays in Sociology*. New York: Oxford University Press.

Ghai, Dharam and Cynthia Hewitt de Alcantara. 1994. "Globalization and Social Integration: Patterns and Processes." UNRISD Occasional Paper No. 2. World Summit for Social Development. Geneva: UNRISD.

Giddens, Anthony. 1990. *The Consequences of Modernity*. Cambridge: Polity.

Gill, Stephen. 1990. *American Hegemony and the Trilateral Commission*. Cambridge: Cambridge University Press.

———. 1991. "Reflections on Global Order and Sociohistorical Time." *Alternatives* 16: 275–314.

———. 1992a. "The Emerging World Order and European Change." In R. Miliband and L. Panitch (eds.), *New World Order? The Socialist Register 1992*, 157–196. London: Merlin.

———. 1992b. "Economic Globalization and the Internationalization of Authority: Limits and Contradictions." *Geoforum* 23: 269–283.

———. 1993a. "The Global Panopticon." Mimeo. Paper presented at the UN University symposium "The Global Political Economy and a New Multilateralism." Oslo, 15–17 August.

——— (ed.). 1993b. *Gramsci, Historical Materialism and International Relations*. Cambridge. Cambridge University Press.

———. 1993c. Personal correspondence with James H. Mittelman. 10 February.

———. 1994a. "Knowledge, Power and Neo-Liberal Political Economy." In R. Stubbs and G. Underhill (eds.), *Political Economy and the International System: Global Issues, Regional Dynamics and Political Conflict*, 75–88. Toronto: McLelland and Stewart.

———. 1994b. "The Global Political Economy and Structural Change: Globalizing Elites in the Emerging World Order." In Y. Sakamoto (ed.), *Global Transformation*, 169–199. Tokyo: UN University Press.

———. 1994c. "Global Institutions in a Changing World." Mimeo. Report to UN University Research Institute for Social Development. Geneva.

Gill, Stephen and David Law. 1988. *The Global Political Economy*. Baltimore: Johns Hopkins University Press.

———. 1989. "Global Hegemony and the Structural Power of Capital." *International Studies Quarterly* 33: 475–499.

Gindin, Sam and David Robertson. 1992. "Alternatives to Competitiveness." In D. Drache (ed.), *Getting on Track: Social Democratic Strategies for Ontario*. Montreal and Kingston: McGill-Queen's University Press.

Glickman, N. J. and A. K. Glasmeier. 1989. "The International Economy and the American South." In L. Rodwin and H. Sazanami (eds.), *Deindustrialization and Regional Economic Transformation: The Experience of the United States*. Winchester, Mass.: Unwin Hyman.

Gonzalez Esponda, Juan. 1989. "Movimiento campesino chiapaneco 1974-1984." Tesis para licenciado en economia, UNACH. San Cristobal de Las Casas.

Gordon, David. 1988. "The Global Economy: New Edifice or Crumbling Foundations?" *New Left Review* 168 (March/April): 24–65.

Gorz, Andre. 1989. *Critique of Economic Reason*. London: Verso.

Gramsci, Antonio. 1973. *Selections from the Prison Notebooks of Antonio Gramsci.* Edited and translated by Quentin Hoare and Geoffrey Nowell Smith. New York: International Publishers.

———. 1977. *Selections from the Political Writings 1910–1920.* With additional texts by Bordiga and Tasca. Selected and edited by Quentin Hoare. Translated by John Matthews. New York: International Publishers.

Gran, Guy. 1984. *Development by People.* New York: Praeger.

Gran, Peter. 1980. "Political Economy as a Paradigm for the Study of Islamic History." *International Journal of Middle East Studies* 11 (July): 511–526.

Griffin, Keith and Azizur Rahman Khan. 1992. *Globalization and the Developing World: An Essay on the International Dimensions of Development in the Post-Cold War Era.* Geneva: UN Research Institute for Social Development.

Grinspun, Ricardo and Robert Kreklewich. 1994. "Consolidating Neoliberal Reforms: 'Free Trade' as a Conditioning Framework." *Studies in Political Economy* 43 (Spring): 33–61.

Grosfoguel, Ramon. "Global Logics in the Caribbean City System: The Case of Miami." In Knox and Taylor (eds.), *World Cities*, 156–170. Cambridge: Cambridge University Press.

Guzman, Rodolfo. 1977. "Chiapas 76: Soldados en Vehiculos de UNICEF: Al Asalto de Pueblo Indigena." *Proceso* 13,29 de enero.

Haddad, Yvonne Y. 1982. "The Islamic Alternative." *Link* 15 (September–October): 1–14.

Haggard, Stephan. 1990. *Pathways from the Periphery: The Politics of Growth in the Newly Industrializing Countries.* Ithaca: Cornell University Press.

Hall, Peter. 1995. "Towards a General Urban Theory." In John Brotchie, Mike Batty, Ed Blakely, Peter Hall, and Peter Newton (eds.), *Cities in Competition,* 3–32. Melbourne: Longman Australia.

Halliday, Fred. 1990. "The Crisis of the Arab World: The False Answers of Saddam Hussein." *New Left Review* 184 (November/December): 69–74.

Hamilton, Gary G. and Cheng-shu Kao. 1987. "Max Weber and the Analysis of East Asian Industrialization." *International Sociology* 2 (September): 289–300.

Hancock, Graham. 1989. *The Lords of Poverty: The Power, Prestige and Corruption of the International Aid Business.* New York: Atlantic Monthly Press.

Harris, Nigel. 1987. *The End of the Third World.* New York: Penguin Books.

Harrod, Jeffrey. 1987. *Power, Production, and the Unprotected Worker.* New York: Columbia University Press.

Harsh, Ernest. 1992. "More African States are 'Least Developed.'" *Africa Recovery* 6 (April): 11.

Harvey, David. 1988. "The Geographical and Geopolitical Consequences of the Transition from Fordist to Flexible Accumulation." In G. Sternlieb and J. W. Hughes (eds.), *America's New Market Geography.* New Jersey: Rutgers.

———. 1989. *The Condition of Postmodernity.* Oxford: Basil Blackwell.

Harvey, L. P. 1992 *Islamic Spain, 1250 to 1500.* Chicago: University of Chicago Press.

Hawley, Ellis W. 1969. *The New Deal and the Problem of Monopoly: A Study in Economic Ambivalence.* Princeton: Princeton University Press.

Haworth, Nigel and Harvie Ramsey. 1984. "Grasping the Nettle: Problems with the Theory of International Trade Union Solidarity." In Peter Waterman (ed.), *For a New Labour Internationalism.* The Hague: International Labour Education Research and Information Foundation.

———. 1988. "Workers of the World Untied: International Capital and Some Dilemmas in Industrial Democracy." In Roger Southall (ed.), *Trade Unions and the New Industrialization of the Third World*. Pittsburgh: University of Pittsburgh Press.

Held, David. 1992. "Democracy: From City-States to a Cosmopolitan Order?" *Political Studies* 40 (Special Issue): 10–39.

Helleiner, Eric. 1990. "Fernand Braudel and International Political Economy." *International Studies Notes* 15 (3): 73–78.

— — —. 1994. *States and the Reemergence of Global Finance: From Bretton Woods to the 1990s*. Ithaca: Cornell University Press.

Henderson, Jeffrey. 1989. *The Globalisation of High Technology Production: Society, Space and Semiconductors in the Restructuring of the Modern World*. London: Routledge.

Henriquez, Elio. 1993. "150 PRI-istas detuvieron a 17 evangelicos en Teopisca." *El Tiempo* 1935.

Herzog, Lawrence A. 1990. *Where North Meets South: Cities, Space, and Politics on the U.S.-Mexico Border*. Austin: University of Texas Press.

Hicks, John. 1980. "Notions of Legitimacy in Islamic and Liberal-Democratic Political Thought." *Journal of South Asian and Middle East Studies* 3 (Summer): 9–22.

Hill, Christopher. 1980. *The Century of Revolution*. London: W. W. Norton.

Hirsch, Fred. 1976. *The Social Limits to Growth*. Cambridge: Harvard University Press.

Hitz, H., R. Keil, U. Lehrer, K. Ronneberger, C. Schmid, and R. Wolff (eds.). 1995. *Financial Metropoles in Restructuring: Zurich and Frankfurt en Route to Postfordism*. Zurich: Rotpunkt Publishers.

Hobsbawm, Eric. 1994. *The Age of Extremes: A History of the World, 1914–1991*. New York: Pantheon.

Hodgson, Marshall S. 1993. *Rethinking World History*. New York: Cambridge University Press.

Hoffman, Kurt (ed.). 1985. "Microelectronics, International Competition and Development Strategies: The Unavoidable Issues." *World Development* 13 (3): 263–463.

Hoffman, Kurt and Raphael Kaplinsky. 1988. *Driving Force: The Global Restructuring of Technology, Labor, and Investment in the Automobile and Components Industries*. Boulder: Westview Press.

Hofheinz, Roy, Jr. and Kent E. Calder. 1982. *The Eastasia Edge*. New York: Basic Books.

Hollnsteiner, Mary. 1979. "Mobilizing the Rural Poor Through Community Organization." *Philippine Studies* 27 (3): 387–411.

Holloway, S. R. and J. O. Wheeler. 1991. "Corporate Headquarters Relocation and Changes in Metropolitan Corporate Dominance, 1980–1987." *Economic Geography* 67: 54–74.

Hoodbuoy, Pervaiz. 1990. *Islam and Science*. London: Zed Press.

Hoogvelt, Ankie. 1987. "The New International Division of Labour." In Ray Bush (ed.), *The World Order: Socialist Perspectives*, 65–86. Cambridge: Polity.

Hopkins, Terence K. and Immanuel Wallerstein. 1986. "Commodity Chains in the World-Economy Prior to 1800." *Review* 10 (Summer): 157–170.

Hughes, Thomas L. 1990. "Pro Patria Per Orbis Concordiam." Remarks presented at the Carnegie Endowment for International Peace Trustees' Dinner. Washington, D.C., 18 November.

Humphrey, John. 1982. *Capitalist Control and Workers' Struggle in the Brazilian Auto Industry*. Princeton: Princeton University Press.

Huntington, Samuel P. 1993. "The Clash of Civilizations?" *Foreign Affairs* 72 (Summer): 22–47.

Hutchful, Eboe. 1991. "Eastern Europe: Consequences for Africa." *Review of African Political Economy* 50: 51–59.

Hyden, Goran. 1983. *No Shortcuts to Progress: African Development Management in Perspective*. London: Heinemann.

———. 1985. "The African Crisis and the Role of the Church." Paper prepared for a special workshop on Africa organized by the Lutheran World Federation at Ford Foundation. New York, 18 October.

Hymer, Stephen and Robert Rowthorn. 1970. "Multinational Corporations and International Oligopoly." In Charles P. Kindleberger (ed.), *The International Corporation*. Cambridge, Mass.: MIT Press.

Inglehart, Ronald. 1990. "Values, Ideology, and Cognitive Mobilization in New Social Movements." In Russell J. Dalton and Manfred Kuechler (eds.), *Challenging the Political Order: New Social and Political Movements in Western Democracies*. Cambridge: Polity.

Innes, Duncan. 1984. *Anglo American and the Rise of Modern South Africa*. Johannesburg: Ravan Press.

Isaacs, Harold. 1979. *Power and Identity: Tribalism in World Politics*. New York: Foreign Policy Association.

Jameson, Frederic. 1991. *Post-Modernism or the Cultural Logic of Late Capitalism*. Durham, N.C.: Duke University Press.

Jessop, Bob. 1989. *Thatcherism: The British Road to Postfordism?* Essex papers in politics and government. University of Essex.

Joffe, Avril and David Lewis. 1992. "A Strategy for South African Manufacturing." *South African Labour Bulletin* 16 (4).

Joffe, Avril, David Kaplan, Raphael Kaplinsky, and David Lewis. 1993. "Meeting the Global Challenge: A Framework for Industrial Revival in South Africa." In Pauline Baker, Alex Boraine, and Warren Krafchik (eds.), *South Africa and the World Economy in the 1990s*. Cape Town: David Philip.

———. 1995. *Improving Manufacturing Performance in South Africa: Report of the Industrial Strategy Project*. Cape Town: University of Cape Town Press.

Joffe, Avril, Judy Maller, and Eddie Webster. 1995. "South Africa's Industrialization: The Challenge Facing Labor." In Stephen Frenkel and Jeffrey Harrod (eds.), *Industrialization and Labor Relations: Contemporary Research in Seven Countries*. Ithaca: Industrial and Labor Relations Press, Cornell University.

Johnson, Chalmers. 1982. *MITI and the Japanese Miracle: The Growth of Industrial Policy, 1925–1975*. Stanford: Stanford University Press.

Jules-Rosette, Bennetta. 1981. *Symbols of Change: Urban Transition in a Zambian Community*. London: Alex Publishing.

Kaplinsky, Raphael. 1993. "Export Processing Zones in the Dominican Republic: Transforming Manufactures into Commodities." *World Development* 21 (11): 1851–1865.

Keck, Margaret E. 1992. *The Workers' Party and Democratization in Brazil*. New Haven: Yale University Press.

Keil, Roger and Klaus Ronneberger. "The City Turned Inside Out: Spatial Strategies and Local Politics." In Hansruedi Hitz et al. (eds.), *Financial Metropoles in Restructuring: Zurich and Frankfurt En Route to Postfordism*.

Kennedy, David. 1988. "A New Stream of International Law Scholarship. *Wisconsin International Law Journal* 7 (1): 1–49.

Keynes, John Maynard. 1936. *The General Theory of Employment, Interest and Money*. London: Macmillan.

Khaldun, Ibn. 1958. *The Muqaddimah: An Introduction to History.* New York: Pantheon.

Khor, Martin. 1992a. "Earth Summit: UN Restructuring Threatens Follow-up Capacity." *South-North Development Monitor* 2850 (2 June): 2–6.

———. 1992b. "Earth Summit: A Future of Hope or Race to Disaster?" *South-North Development Monitor* 2862 (19 June): 2.

Kimenyi, Mwangi S. 1993. "The Necessity for Economic Reform." *Finance.* Nairobi, 31 January.

King, A. D. (ed.). 1995. *Representing the City: Ethnicity, Capital and Culture in the 21st Century.* London: Macmillan.

Klandermans, Bert and Sidney Tarrow. 1988. "Mobilization into Social Movements: Synthesizing European and American Approaches." In Bert Klandermans, Hanspeter Kriesi, and Sidney Tarrow (eds.), *From Structure to Action: Comparing Social Movement Research Across Cultures.* Greenwich, Conn.: JAI Press.

Knox, Paul L. and Peter J. Taylor (eds.). 1995. *World Cities in a World-System.* Cambridge: Cambridge University Press.

Kooiman, Jan and Martin van Vliet. 1993. "Governance and Public Management." In K. A. Eliassen and J. Kooiman (eds.), *Managing Public Organizations: Lessons from Contemporary European Experience,* 58–72. London: Sage.

Korpi, W. 1983. *The Democratic Class Struggle.* London, Boston: Routledge & Kegan Paul.

Korten, David. 1990. *Getting to the 21st Century.* West Hartford, Conn.: Kumarian Press.

Kowarick, L. and M. Campanario. 1986. "Sao Paulo: The Price of World City Status." *Development and Change* 17 (1): 159–174.

Kunzmann, K. R. and M. Wegener. 1991. *The Pattern of Urbanisation in Western Europe 1960–1990.* Report for the Directorate General XVI of the Commission of the European Communities as part of the study "Urbanisation and the Function of Cities in the European Community." Dortmund: Institut fur Raumplanung.

Lambert, John. 1991. "Europe: The Nation-State Dies Hard." *Capital and Class* 43 (Spring): 9–24.

Lang, Tim and Colin Hines. 1993. *The New Protectionism.* New York: New Press.

Lardner, James. 1988. "Annals of Business: The Sweater Trade." Part 1. *The New Yorker* (11 January): 39–73.

Lee Suan Huang. 1991. Director, Industry Development Division and Marketing Support Division, Economic Development Board. Interview with the author, 10 December. Singapore.

Leftwich, A. 1994. "Governance, the State, and the Politics of Development." *Development and Change* 24 (4): 363–386.

Lewis, Bernhard. 1976. "The Return of Islam." *Commentary* 61 (January): 39–49.

———. 1988. "Islamic Revolution." *New York Review of Books* 34 (21 January): 46–50.

Lievano, Daniel Pensamiento. 1993. "¿Llegaran hasta Mexico las 'Arrieras Nocturnas'?" *El Tiempo* 1937.

Lipietz, Alain. 1985. *Mirages and Miracles: The Crisis of Global Fordism.* Translated by David Macey. London: Verso.

———. 1992. *Towards a New Economic Order.* Oxford: Oxford University Press.

Lively, Jack. 1977. *Democracy.* New York: G. P. Putnam's Sons.

Lloyd, John. 1994. "Polite Applause in Duma Greets Solzhenitsyn's Moral Outrage." *Financial Times* (29/30 October).

Locke, John. 1965. *Treatise of Civil Government and a Letter Concerning Toleration.* Edited by Charles L. Sherman. New York: Irvington Publishers.

Lomnitz, Claudio. 1992. *Exits from the Labyrinth: Culture and Ideology in Mexican National Space.* Berkeley: University of California Press.

Longcore, T. R. 1993. "Information Technology and World City Restructuring: The Case of New York City's Financial District." Unpublished thesis, Department of Geography, University of Delaware.

Lyons, Donald and Scott Salmon. 1995. "World Cities, Multinational Corporations and Urban Hierarchy: The Case of the United States." In Paul Knox and Peter Taylor (eds.), *World Cities in a World-System,* 98–114. Cambridge: Cambridge University Press.

Lyotard, J. 1984. *The Postmodern Condition.* Manchester: Manchester University Press.

Mabogunje, Akim L. 1991. *A New Paradigm for Urban Development Strategy in Developing Countries.* Washington, D.C.: World Bank.

MacEwan, Arthur and William K. Tabb (eds.). 1989. *Instability and Change in the World Economy.* New York: Monthly Review Press.

MacFarquhar, Roderick. 1989. "The End of the Chinese Revolution." *New York Review of Books* 36 (20 July): 8–10.

MacGaffee, Janet. 1983. "How to Survive and Become Rich Amidst Devastation: The Second Economy of Zaire." *African Affairs* 82: 828.

Machimura, Takashi. 1992. "The Urban Restructuring Process in the 1980s: Transforming Tokyo into a World City." *International Journal of Urban and Regional Research* 16–1: 114–128.

Macneill, John et al. 1991. *Beyond Interdependence: The Meshing of the World's Economy and the Earth's Ecology.* Oxford: Oxford University Press.

Macpherson, C. B. 1977. *The Life and Times of Liberal Democracy.* Oxford: Oxford University Press.

Macun, Ian. 1993. "South African Unions: Still Growing?" *South African Labour Bulletin* 17 (4).

———. 1995. "Growth, Structure, and Power in the South African Union Movement." Paper presented to the Second International Conference on Emerging Union Structures, 11–14 June. Stockholm: Swedish Institute of Work Life Research.

Madeuf, Bernadette and Charles-Albert Michalet. 1978. "A New Approach to International Economics." *International Social Science Journal* 30 (2): 253–283.

Magdoff, Harry. 1992. "Globalization—To What End?" In R. Miliband and L. Panitch (eds.), *New World Order? The Socialist Register 1992.* London: Merlin.

Malik, Hafeez. 1979. "Islamic Theory of International Relations." *Journal of South Asian and Middle Eastern Studies* 2 (Spring): 84–92.

Mandel, Ernest. 1992. *Power and Money.* London: Verso.

Markusen, A. and V. Gwiasda. 1993. "Multipolarity and the Layering of Functions in the World Cities: New York City's Struggle to Stay on Top." Presented in Tokyo at the Conference "New York, Tokyo and Paris" October 1991. Revised for publication.

Marshall, J. N. et al. 1986. *Uneven Development in the Service Economy: Understanding the Location and Role of Producer Services.* Report of the Producer Services Working Party, Institute of British Geographers and the ESRC, August.

Martin, William G. (ed.). 1990. *Semiperipheral States in the World-Economy.* Westport, Conn.: Greenwood Press.

Marx, Karl and Friedrich Engels. 1964. *The Communist Manifesto*. New York: Washington Square Press.

Massoud, Ibrahim. 1992. Speech delivered in Amman, Jordan.

Mather, Graham. 1993. "A Blueprint to Reshape Government." *Financial Times* (5 October).

Mazlish, Bruce and Ralph Buultjens (eds.). 1993. *Conceptualizing Global History*. Boulder: Westview Press.

Mazrui, Ali. 1990. "Islamic Revivalism and Expansion." *Africa Events* (February): 26–29.

McCormick, John. 1989. *Reclaiming Paradise: The Global Environmental Movement*. Bloomington: Indiana University Press.

Mericle, Kenneth. 1977. "Corporatist Control of the Working Class: Authoritarian Brazil Since 1964." In James Malloy (ed.), *Authoritarianism and Corporatism in Latin America*. Pittsburgh: University of Pittsburgh Press.

Merklinger, Philip M. 1993. *Philosophy, Theology, and Hegel's Berlin Philosophy of Religion, 1821–1827*. Albany: State University of New York Press.

Middlebrook, Kevin J. 1981. "The Political Economy of Mexican Organized Labor, 1940–1978." Ph.D. diss., Harvard University.

———. 1987. "Union Democratization in the Mexican Automobile Industry: A Reappraisal." *Latin American Research Review* 24 (2): 66–93.

Miliband, Ralph. 1968. *The State in Capitalist Society*. London: Weidenfeld and Nicolson.

———. 1977. *Marxism and Politics*. Oxford: Oxford University Press.

Miller, Roland E. 1979. "Renaissance of the Muslim Spirit." *Christianity Today* 23 (16 November): 16–21.

Minnesota Lawyers Advocate. 1993. *Civilians at Risk: Military and Police Abuses in the Mexican Countryside*. Minneapolis: Minnesota Lawyers Advocates.

Mittelman, James H. 1990. "The Dilemmas of Reform in Post-Revolutionary Societies." *International Studies Notes* 15 (2): 65–70.

———. 1991. "Marginalization and the International Division of Labor: Mozambique's Strategy of Opening the Market." *African Studies Review* 34 (3): 89–106.

———. 1994a. "Global Restructuring of Production and Migration." In Yoshikazu Sakamoto (ed.), *Global Transformation: Challenges to the State System*, 276–298. Tokyo: UN University Press.

———. 1994b. "The Globalization of Social Conflict." In Volker Bornschier and Peter Lengyel (eds.), *World Society Studies*, vol. 3: *Conflict and Its Solution in World Society*, 317–337. New Brunswick, N.J.: Transaction Publishers.

Moreira Alves, Maria Helena. 1988. "Democratization Versus Social Equality in Latin America: Notes for Discussion." Paper presented to the Conference on Comparative Politics: Research Perspectives for the Next 20 Years. City University of New York Graduate School.

Moss, Mitchell. 1991. "New Fibers of Urban Economic Development." *Portfolio: A Quarterly Review of Trade and Transportation*, 4 (1): 11–18.

———. 1986. "Telecommunications and the Future of Cities." *Land Development Studies* 3: 33–44.

Mozaffari, Mehdi. 1986–1987. "Authority in Islam: Muhammad to Khomeini." *International Journal of Politics* 16 (Winter).

Munck, Ronaldo. 1988. *The New International Labour Studies: An Introduction*. London: Zed Press.

Murray, Robin. 1971. "The Internationalization of Capital and the Nation State." *New Left Review* 67 (May–June): 84–108.

Naipaul, V. S. 1990. "Our Universal Civilization." *New York Times*, 5 November.

Nash, June. 1993. "Maya Household Production in the World Market: The Potters of Amatenango del Valle, Chiapas, Mexico." In *Crafts in the World Market: The Impact of Global Markets on Middle American Artisans*. Albany: SUNY Press.

— — —. 1994. "The Challenge of Trade Liberalization to Cultural Survival on the Southern Frontier of Mexico." *Indiana Global Legal Journal* 1 (1): 1–35.

Nash, June and Kathleen Sullivan. 1992. "The Return to Porfirismo." *Cultural Survival* (Spring): 13–16.

Nash, June and Maria Patricia Fernandez-Kelly (eds.). 1983. *Women, Men, and the International Division of Labor*. Albany: State University of New York Press.

National Public Radio. 1994. "Morning Edition," 21 November. Transcript p. 14.

Negri, Toni. 1995. "A quoi sert encore l'Etat." *Pouvoirs Pouvoir*, vol. 25–26 of *Futur Anterieur*, 135–152. Paris: L'Harmattan.

"New Fibers of Urban Economic Development." 1991. *Portfolio: A Quarterly Review of Trade and Transportation* 4 (1): 11–18.

Nordlinger, Eric A. 1981. *On the Autonomy of the Democratic State*. Cambridge: Harvard University Press.

Noyelle, T. and A. B. Dutka. 1988. *International Trade in Business Services: Accounting, Advertising, Law and Management Consulting*. Cambridge, Mass.: Ballinger Publishing.

Noyelle, T. J. and T. M. Stanback, Jr. 1984. *The Economic Transformation of American Cities*. Totowa, N.J.: Rowman and Allanheld.

Nueva Legislacion Agraria: Articulo 27 constitutional. 1992. Ley Agraria, Ley Organica de los Tribunales Agraria. Mexico: Gaceta de Solidaridad.

Nyang, Sulayman S. and Feraidoon Shams. 1990. "Fanon and Shari'ati on Alienation." *Journal of Asian and African Affairs* 89 (July): 125–134.

Nye, Joseph S. Jr. et al. 1991. *Global Cooperation After the Cold War: A Reassessment of Trilateralism*. New York: Trilateral Commission.

Nyong'o, Peter Anyang' (ed.). 1987. *Popular Struggle for Democracy in Africa*. London: Zed Press.

O'Connor, James. 1973. *The Fiscal Crisis of the State*. New York: St. Martin's Press.

O'Connor, Kevin. 1995. "Change in the Pattern of Airline Services and City Development." In John Brotchie, Mike Batty, Ed Blakely, Peter Hall, and Peter Newton (eds.), *Cities in Competition*, 88–104.

Offe, Claus. 1984. *Contradictions of the Welfare State*. London: Hutchinson.

Ohmae, Kenichi. 1990. *The Borderless World: Power and Strategy in the Interlinked Economy*. London: Harper Collins.

Olofsson, Gunnar. 1988. "After the Working-Class Movement? An Essay on What's 'New' and What's 'Social' in the New Social Movements." *Acta Sociologica* 31 (1): 15–34.

Onimode, Bade (ed.). 1988. *The IMF, The World Bank and the African Debt*. London: Zed Press.

Organization for Economic Cooperation and Development (OECD). 1988. *The Newly Industrializing Countries: Challenge and Opportunity for OECD Industries*. Paris: OECD.

— — —. 1989. *Programme of Research 1990–1992*. Paris: OECD.

Panitch, Leo. 1981. "Class and Dependency in Canadian Political Economy." *Studies in Political Economy* 6 (Autumn): 7–33.

— — —. 1986. *Working Class Politics in Crisis*. London: Verso.

Panitch, Leo and Donald Swartz. 1993. *The Assault on Trade Union Freedoms: From Wage Controls to Social Contract*. Toronto: Garamond.

Parikh, Bhiku. 1990. "The Rushdie Affair: Research Agenda for Political Philosophy." *Political Studies* 38 (December): 695–709.

Pausewang, Siegfried et al. (eds.). 1990. *Ethiopia: Options for Rural Development*. London: Zed Press.

Picciotto, Sol. 1991. "The Internationalisation of the State." *Capital and Class* 43 (Special Issue): 43–64.

Pijl, Kees van der. 1984. *The Making of an Atlantic Ruling Class*. London: Verso.

———. 1989. "Ruling Classes, Hegemony, and the State System." *International Journal of Political Economy* 19: 7–35.

Pipes, Daniel. 1990. "The Muslims Are Coming, the Muslims Are Coming." *National Review* 42 (19 November): 28–31.

Piscatori, James. 1990. "The Rushdie Affair and the Politics of Ambiguity." *International Affair* (London) 66 (October): 767–789.

Polanyi, Karl. 1957a. "The Economy as Instituted Process." In Karl Polanyi et al. (eds.), *Trade and Market in the Early Empires*. Chicago: Henry Regnery.

———. 1957b. *The Great Transformation: The Political and Economic Origins of Our Time*. Boston: Beacon Press.

Porter, Michael. 1990. *The Competitive Advantage of Nations*. New York: Free Press.

Portes, Alejandro and John Walton. 1981. *Labor, Class, and the International System*. New York: Academic Press.

Portes, Alejandro, José Itzigsohn, and Carlos Dore-Cabral. 1994. "Urbanization in the Caribbean Basin: Social Change During the Years of the Crisis." *Latin American Research Review* 29 (2): 3–37.

Poulantzas, Nicos. 1973. *Political Power and Social Classes*. London: New Left Books.

———. 1974. *Classes in Contemporary Capitalism*. London: New Left Books.

———. 1978. *State, Power, Socialism*. London: Verso.

Pradervand, Pierre. 1989. *Listening to Africa: Developing Africa from the Grassroots*. New York: Praeger.

Procuraduria Agraria. 1993. Primer Informe de Labores, Mmarch.

Pye, Lucien. 1985. *Asian Power and Politics*. Cambridge: Harvard University Press.

———. 1990. "Presidential Address." *American Political Science Review*.

Raghavan, Chakravarthi. 1991. *Recolonization: GATT and the Uruguay Round*. London: Zed Press.

Rahmato, Dessalegn. 1985. *Agrarian Reform in Ethiopia*. Trenton: Africa World Press.

Rapoport, David C. 1979. "Moses, Charisma, and Covenant." *Western Political Quarterly* 32 (June): 123–153.

Rau, Bill. 1991. *From Feast to Famine: Official Cures and Grassroots Remedies to Africa's Food Crisis*. London: Zed Press.

Renard, John. 1979. "Religion and Politics in Islamic History." *America* 141 (15 December): 383–387.

Roberts, Susan. Forthcoming. "Fictitious Capital, Fictitious Spaces?: The Geography of Off-shore Financial Flows." In S. Corbridge, R. Martin, and N. Thrift (eds.), *Money, Power and Space*.

Robertson, Roland. 1992. *Globalization: Social Theory and Global Culture*. Newbury Park: Sage.

Robinson, Ian. 1993. *North American Trade as If Democracy Mattered*. Ottawa: Canadian Centre for Policy Alternatives.

Rodriguez, Nestor P. and J. R. Feagin. 1986. "Urban Specialization in the World System." *Urban Affairs Quarterly* 22 (2): 187–220.

Rosenau, J. N. 1992. "Governance, Order, and Change in World Politics." In James Rosenau and E. O. Czempiel (eds.), *Governance Without Government: Order and Change in World Politics*, 1–29. Cambridge: Cambridge University Press.

Rosenblum, Mort and Doug Williamson. 1987. *Squandering Eden: Africa at the Edge*. New York: Harcourt Brace Jovanovich.

Roxborough, Ian. 1984. *Unions and Politics in Mexico: The Case of the Automobile Industry*. Cambridge: Cambridge University Press.

Rubin, Barry. 1990. "Religion and International Affairs." *Washington Quarterly* 13 (Spring): 51–63.

Rucht, Dieter. 1992. "The Strategies and Action Repertoires in New Movements." In Russell J. Dalton and Manfred Kuechler (eds.), *Challenging the Political Order: New Social and Political Movements in Western Democracies*. Cambridge: Polity.

Rueschemeyer, Dietrich, Evelyne Huber Stephens, and John D. Stephens. 1992. *Capitalist Development and Democracy*. Cambridge: Polity.

Ruggie, John Gerard. 1993. "Territoriality and Beyond: Problematizing Modernity in International Relations." *International Organization* 47 (1): 139–174.

Said, Edward W. 1978. *Orientalism*. New York: Pantheon Books.

Sakamoto, Yoshikazu (ed.). 1994. *Global Transformation: Challenges to the State System*. Tokyo: UN University Press.

Salacuse, Jeswald. 1991. *Making Global Deals: Negotiations in the Global Marketplace*. Boston: Houghton Mifflin.

Sandbrook, Richard. 1985. *The Politics of African Economic Stagnation*. Cambridge: Cambridge University Press.

Sassen, Saskia. 1996. *On Governing the Global Economy*. New York: Columbia University Press.

———. 1994. "The Informal Economy: Between New Developments and Old Regulations." *Yale Law Journal* 103 (8): 2289–2304.

———. 1994. *Cities in a World Economy*. Thousand Oaks, CA: Sage.

———. 1991. *The Global City: New York, London, and Tokyo*. Princeton: Princeton University Press.

———. 1988. *The Mobility of Labor and Capital*. Cambridge: Cambridge University Press.

Sassen, Saskia, and Bradley J. Orlow. 1995. "The Growing Service Intensity in Economic Organization: Evidence from the Input-Output Tables." New York: Department of Urban Planning, Columbia University.

Schlyster, Ann. 1993. "Social Movements for Democracy and Women's Rights: Community Organization in a Poor Urban Area During the Transition from One-Party to a Multi-Party Democracy in Zambia." Paper prepared for the Nordic Conference on Social Movements in the Third World, 18–21 August. Lund, Sweden.

Schneier, Steffen. 1983. "Occupational Mobility Among Blacks in South Africa." Working Paper no. 58, South African Labour and Development Research Unit, University of Cape Town.

Schreiner, Geoff. 1991. "Fossils from the Past: Resurrecting and Restructuring the National Manpower Commission." *South African Labour Bulletin* 16 (1).

Schumpeter, Joseph A. 1976. *Capitalism, Socialism and Democracy*. New York. Harper & Row.

Sclar, Elliott D. and Walter Hook. 1993. "The Importance of Cities to the National Economy." In Henry G. Cisneros (ed.), *Interwoven Destinies: Cities and the Nation*. New York: Norton.

Scott, James C. 1985. *Weapons of the Weak*. New Haven: Yale University Press.

———. 1993. *Everyday Forms of Resistance*. International Peace Research Institute Meigaku. Occasional Paper Series No. 15. Yokohama.

Seidman, Gay W. 1994. *Manufacturing Militance: Workers' Movements in Brazil and South Africa, 1970–1985*. Berkeley: University of California Press.

Shaalan, Mohammed. 1986. "Political-Psychological Influences in Islamic Revivalist Movements." *Political Psychology* 7 (December): 811–816.

Shank, G. (ed.). 1994. "Japan Enters the 21st Century." Special Issue, *Social Justice* 21 (2).

Shaw, Timothy. 1994. "The South in the New World (Dis)Order: Towards a Political Economy of Third World Foreign Policy in the 1990s." *Third World Quarterly* 15 (1): 17–30.

Shaw, Timothy and Julius Edo Nyang'oro. 1992. *Beyond Structural Adjustment in Africa*. New York: Praeger.

Shiva, Vandana. 1992. "GEF at Heart of North-South Dispute on UNCED Funding." *Third World Economics* 41 (16–31 May): 17–18.

Simkins, Charles. 1984. "African Population, Employment and Incomes on Farms Outside the Reserves, 1923–1969." Second Carnegie Commission Inquiry into Poverty and Development in Southern Africa, University of Cape Town, Paper no. 25.

Simon, David. 1995. "The World City Hypothesis: Reflections from the Periphery." In Paul Knox and Peter Taylor (eds.), *World Cities in a World-System*, 132–155. Cambridge: Cambridge University Press.

Sinclair, Timothy J. 1994. "Passing Judgement: Credit Rating Processes as Regulatory Mechanisms of Governance in the Emerging World Order." *Review of International Political Economy* 1 (Spring): 133–159.

Sitas, Ari. 1984. "African Worker Responses to Changes in the Metal Industry, 1960–1980." Ph.D. diss., University of the Witwatersrand.

———. 1985. "Moral Formations and Struggles Amongst Migrant Workers on the East Rand." *Labour, Capital and Society* 18(2).

Sklair, Leslie. 1991. *Sociology of the Global System: Social Change in Global Perspective*. Baltimore: Johns Hopkins University.

Skocpol, Theda. 1985. "Bringing the State Back In: Strategies of Analysis in Current Research." In P. R. Evans, D. Rueschemeyer, and T. Skocpol (eds.), *Bringing the State Back In*, 3–37. Cambridge: Cambridge University Press.

Smith, Adam. 1970. *An Inquiry into the Nature and Causes of the Wealth of Nations*. Middlesex: Penguin Books.

Smith, David A. and Michael Timberlake. 1995. "Cities in Global Matrices: Toward Mapping the World System's City System." In Paul Knox and Peter Taylor (eds.), *World Cities in a World-System*, 79–97. Cambridge: Cambridge University Press.

Social Justice. 1993. "Global Crisis, Local Struggles." Special Issue, *Social Justice* 20 (3–4).

Stanfield, Rochelle L. 1990. "Islam's Power." *National Journal* 22 (3 November): 2644–2648.

Stavenhagen, Rodolfo. 1992. "Challenging the Nation-State in Latin America." *Journal of International Affairs* 45 (2).

Stimson, Robert J. 1993. "Process of Globalisation and Economic Restructuring and the Emergence of a New Space Economy of Cities and Regions in Australia." Presented at the Fourth International Workshop on Technological Change and Urban Form: Productive and Sustainable Cities. Berkeley, California, 14–16 April.

Strange, Susan. 1986. *Casino Capitalism*. Oxford: Basil Blackwell.

———. 1990. "The Name of the Game." In N. X. Rizopoulos (ed.), *Sea Changes: American Foreign Policy in a World Transformed*. New York: Council on Foreign Relations.

Sullivan, Kathleen. 1992. "Protagonists of Change." *Cultural Survival* 16 (4).

Swyngedouw, E. 1986. "The Socio-Spatial Implications of Innovations in Industrial

Organization." Working Paper no. 22, Johns Hopkins European Center for Regional Planning and Research. Lille.

Tarrow, Sidney. 1991. "Struggle, Politics, and Reform: Collective Action, Social Movements, and Cycles of Protest." Western Societies Program, Center for International Studies, Cornell University, Occasional Paper no. 21 (2d ed.).

Taylor, Peter J. 1995. "World Cities and Territorial States: The Rise and Fall of Their Mutuality." In Paul Knox and Peter Taylor (eds.), *World Cities in a World-System,* 48–62. Cambridge: Cambridge University Press.

"Technology Without Borders Raises Big Questions for the U.S." 1992. *New York Times,* 1 January.

Thurow, Lester. 1993. "An American Common Market." *Guardian Weekly/ Washington Post* (21 November).

Tickell, Oliver. 1991. "Indigenous Expulsions in the Highlands of Chiapas." IWGIA Newsletter. Vol. 2.

Timberlake, Lloyd. 1986. *Africa in Crisis.* London: Earthscan.

Todd, Graham. 1995. "Going 'Global' in the Semi-Periphery: World Cities as Political Projects. The Case of Toronto." In Paul Knox and Peter Taylor (eds.), *World Cities in a World-System,* 192–214. Cambridge: Cambridge University Press.

Toleda Tello, Sonia. 1985. "El papel de la cultura en el proceso de subordinación de las mujeres indígenas de Chiapas." *Anuario Chiapaneca* 1:73–87.

Touraine, Alaine. 1982. *The Voice and the Eye.* Cambridge: Cambridge University Press.

Trachtman, Joel. 1993. "International Regulatory Competition, Externalization, and Jurisdiction." *Harvard International Law Journal* 34: 47.

Trubek, David M., Yves Dezalay, Ruth Buchanan, and John R. Davis. 1993. "Global Restructuring and the Law: The Internationalization of Legal Fields and Creation of Transnational Arenas." Working Paper Series on the Political Economy of Legal Change. No. 1. Madison, Wis.: Global Studies Research Program, University of Wisconsin.

UN. 1991a. *Economic Crisis in Africa.* Final Review and Appraisal of the Implementation of the UN Program of Action for African Economic Recovery and Development (UNPAAERD). Report of the UN Secretary-General, 3–13 September.

———. 1991b. *World Investment Report 1991.* New York: UN Centre on TNCs.

UN Conference on Trade and Development (UNCTAD). 1993. *World Investment Report 1993: Transnational Corporations and Integrated International Production.* New York: UN.

———. 1992. *World Investment Report 1992: Transnational Corporations as Engines of Growth.* New York: United Nations.

UN Economic Commission for Africa. 1990. *African Charter for Popular Participation in Development and Transformation.* Addis Ababa.

———. 1991. *Foreign Direct Investment as Source of Development Finance for Africa.* Addis Ababa.

UN Population Fund. 1993. *The State of World Population.* New York: UN Population Fund.

UN Research Institute for Social Development (UNRISD). 1995. *States of Disarray. The Social Effects of Globalization.* Report for the World Summit for Social Development.

U.S. Department of Commerce, Office of the U.S. Trade Representative. 1983. *U.S. National Study on Trade in Services.* Washington, D.C.: Government Printing Office.

U.S. International Trade Commission (USITC). 1989. *Production Sharing: U.S. Imports Under Harmonized Tariff Schedule Subheadings 9802.00.60 and 9802.00.80, 1985–1988.* USITC Publication 2243. Washington, D.C.: USITC.

Vico, Giambattista. 1744 [1984]. *The New Science of Giambattista Vico.* Unabridged translation of the 3d ed. with the addition of "Practice of the New Science." Translated by Thomas Goddard Bergin and Max Harold Fisch. Cornell University Press.

Vieille, Paul. 1988. "The World's Chaos and the New Paradigms of the Social Movement." In Lelio Basso Foundation (eds.), *Theory and Practice of Liberation at the End of the Twentieth Century.* Bruxelles: Bruylant.

Von Holdt, Karl. 1991. "Towards Transforming South African Industry: A Reconstruction Accord Between Unions and the ANC?" *South African Labour Bulletin* 15 (6).

Wade, Robert. 1990. *Governing the Market: Economic Theory and the Role of Government in East Asian Industrialization.* Princeton: Princeton University Press.

Wallace, Tina and Candida March (eds.). 1991. *Changing Perceptions: Writings on Gender and Development.* London: Oxfam Books.

Wallerstein, Immanuel. 1974. *The Modern World-System.* New York: Academic Press.

———. 1984. *The Politics of the World-Economy.* Cambridge: Cambridge University Press.

Walzer, Michael. 1979. "The Islamic Explosion." *New Republic* 181 (8 December): 18–21.

Ward, Sally K. 1994. "Trends in the Location of Corporate Headquarters, 1969–1989." *Urban Affairs Quarterly* 29 (March): 468–478.

Waterman, Peter. 1991. "Social-Movement Unionism: A New Model for a New World." Working Paper Series no. 110. The Hague: Institute of Social Studies.

Waterman, Peter (ed.). 1984. *For a New Labour Internationalism.* The Hague: International Labour Education, Research and Information Foundation.

Waters, Malcolm. 1995. *Globalization.* New York: Routledge.

Watt, W. Montgomery. 1972. *The Influence of Islam on Medieval Europe.* Edinburgh: University Press.

Weber, Max. 1930. *The Protestant Ethic and the Spirit of Capitalism.* London: George Allen and Unwin.

Webster, Eddie. 1988. "The Rise of Social-Movement Unionism: The Two Faces of the Black Trade Union Movement in South Africa." In William Cobbett and Robin Cohen (eds.), *Popular Struggles in South Africa.* Trenton: Africa World Press.

———. 1991. "Taking Labour Seriously: Sociology and Labour in South Africa." *South African Sociological Review* 4 (1): 50–72.

———. 1995. "It's Time for Left Social Democrats to Come Out of the Closet." *Weekly Mail and Guardian* (18 August).

Webster, Eddie (ed.). 1983. *Essays in Southern African Labour History.* Johannesburg: Ravan Press.

Wheeler, J.O. 1986. "Corporate Spatial Links with Fiscal Institutions: The Role of the Metropolitan Hierarchy." *Annals of the Association of American Geographers* 76: 262–274.

Whitehead, Lawrence. 1993. "Democratic Transitions." In *Oxford Companion to World Politics,* 224–227. New York: Oxford University Press.

Willoughby, K. W. 1990. *Technology Choice*. Boulder: Westview Press.

Wills, Gary. 1978. "What Religious Revival?" *Psychology Today* 11 (April): 74–75, 77–78, 80–81.

Winn, Peter. 1986. *Weavers of Revolution: The Yarur Workers and Chile's Road to Socialism*. New York: Oxford University Press.

Winters, Jeffrey A. 1994. "Power and the Control of Capital." *World Politics* 46 (April): 419–452.

Wolfe, Alan. 1977. *The Limits of Legitimacy*. New York: Free Press.

Womack, James P., Daniel T. Jones, and Daniel Ross. 1991. *The Machine That Changed the World*. New York: Macmillan.

Wong Chin Yeow. 1991. Director, Training, Research and Public Relations Division, Singapore Manufacturers Association. Interview with the author, 18 December. Singapore.

Wood, Christopher. 1993. "Mexico: Respect Restored." *The Economist* 326 (7798): 6–22.

World Bank. 1989a. *Sub-Saharan Africa: From Crisis to Sustainable Growth*. Washington, D.C.: World Bank.

———. 1989b. *World Development Report 1989*. New York: Oxford University Press.

———. 1990. *World Development Report 1990*. New York: Oxford University Press.

———. 1992. *World Development Report 1992*. New York: Oxford University Press.

———. 1993. *World Bank News*. Washington, D.C.: World Bank.

———. 1994. *Adjustment in Africa: Results, Reforms and Performance*. Washington, D.C.: World Bank.

Wriston, Walter. 1992. *The Twilight of Sovereignty: How the Information Revolution Is Transforming Our World*. New York: Scribner's.

Xianming Chen. 1993. "China's Growing Integration with the Asia-Pacific Economy." In Arif Dirlik (ed.), *What Is in a Rim? Critical Perspectives on the Pacific Region Idea*, 89–119. Boulder: Westview Press.

Yoffie, David B. 1983. *Power and Protectionism: Strategies of the Newly Industrializing Countries*. New York: Columbia University Press.

Young, O. R. 1989. *International Cooperation: Building Regimes for Natural Resources and the Environment*. Ithaca: Cornell University Press.

"Zimbabwe's Flower Exports Take to the Sky." 1994. *Financial Times* (London) (21 December).

Index

About the Book

This book analyzes the empirical trends constituting the globalization process in the late twentieth century and explains its underlying causes and consequences.

The authors explore the globalization of production, challenges to the state system represented by the contradictory pressures of sub- and supranationalism, and linkages between regionalism and globalizing tendencies. They also consider the new social movements—among them, prodemocracy groups in Africa, peasant organizations in Latin America (including a case study of the Zapatistas in Mexico), and Islamic groups—attempting to assert popular control.

In light of the contradictions inherent in the contemporary phase of global restructuring, the chapters on future directions do not fail to consider the potential for the downfall of globalization.